Education in Britain

WITHDRAWN

In memory of my parents
Frances Richards, Capel Hendre
Jack Jones, Pontardawe

Education in Britain

1944 to the Present

Ken Jones

polity

First published in 2003 by Polity Press in association with Blackwell Publishing Ltd.

Editorial office:
Polity Press
65 Bridge Street
Cambridge CB2 1UR, UK

Marketing and production:
Blackwell Publishing Ltd
108 Cowley Road
Oxford OX4 1JF, UK

Distributed in the USA by
Blackwell Publishing Inc.
350 Main Street
Malden, MA 02148, USA

A catalogue record for this book is available from the British Library.

Library of Congress Cataloging-in-Publication Data

Jones, Ken, 1950–
    Education in Britain : 1944 to present / Ken Jones.
        p. cm.
    Includes bibliographical references (p.) and index.
    ISBN 0-7456-2574-6 (h/b)—ISBN 0-7456-2575-4 (p/b)
        1. Education—Great Britain. I. Title

LA632 .J59 2003
370′.941′09045—dc21

Typeset in 10.5 on 12pt Sabon
by Kolam Information Services Pvt Ltd, Pondicherry
Printed and bound in Great Britain by TJ International, Padstow, Cornwall

For further information on Polity, visit our website:
http://www.polity.co.uk

Contents

Introduction

This book is first of all an attempt to describe and account for schooling policy in Britain over the last sixty years. By schooling, I mean the institutions – private and public – which organize the period of compulsory, formal education. By 'policy', I mean the designs for schooling developed by such social actors as political parties, government ministers, civil servants, local politicians and administrators and professional associations. But the book is not limited to an account of the obvious manifestations of policy – legal frameworks, party manifestos, policy documents, mission statements and so on. It tries to establish the wider contexts – social and cultural, economic and political – of schooling. It aims to connect exploration of policy shifts to changes and continuities at other levels of schooling: those of classroom, school culture, administrative practice. It also takes policy to be one outcome of wider developments on a site that some have called the 'educational space', an arena stretching beyond the policy community, in which questions of schooling's meaning, value and purpose have been debated and contested. The educational space is not just a parallel world to that of policy or the everyday activity of schooling, one of commentary rather than practice. It is better understood as an area, inhabited by groups that vary greatly in their communicative power and material resources, in which the implications of practice are elaborated, in which purposes and possibilities are suggested and vetoed, criticisms made and answered. What happens in the educational space establishes conditions for policy and for practice, helping to enable some options and constrain others. In the chapters that follow I aim to locate policy in the shifting educational space of the post-war period, conscious that others before me have followed a similar track, but hoping that the perspective of this book is sufficiently different to justify another attempt.

The book differs from other accounts of the post-war period. It owes a factual and interpretative debt, as any writer in this area must, to Brian Simon's *Education and the Social Order* (1991), to Richard Johnson and his colleagues at the Centre for Contemporary Cultural Studies (1981; Johnson 1989), to McPherson and Raab's *Governing Education* (1988), and to the work of Gareth Elwyn Jones on Wales (1990, 1997) and of several writers, including Sean Farren and Penny McKeown, on Northern Ireland. In other respects it has benefited from the consciously gendered history presented by Arnot et al. (1999), and from Iain Grosvenor's treatment of race, identity and nation (1997). In these writings it is possible to find descriptions and analyses of national or 'sectoral' histories of schooling whose detail this book does not intend to match. What it rather does, I hope, is to present a broader perspective on educational change than is usually managed, with a more consistently maintained cultural dimension, a greater attention to political conflict, a fuller sense of the range of social actors involved in policy, practice and the educational space, within a framework which conveys something of the varying national experiences of schooling in Britain. If it is successful in these respects then much is owed to the educational activists with whom I have worked in the past, and to my present colleagues on the journal *Education and Social Justice*, whose pages are much referenced in my final chapter.

England and Britain

When most writers about education use the terms 'Britain' or 'UK', they would do better to say 'England'. Their data are English, their narratives and analyses are structured by an English experience. There is some sense in this – England has by far the largest population and education system, and perspectives developed at Westminster level have informed policy-making throughout Britain. Nevertheless much is lost in this narrowing of focus and one of the things this book tries to do, in beginning to rediscover Britain as an object of study, is not just to expand the space of analysis, but to identify complexities, alternative viewpoints and possibilities that usually get written out of the picture.

There are many difficulties involved in this process; the previous paragraph has already got me into one. What name do I settle on for this entity or set of entities – England, Northern Ireland, Scotland, Wales – which I have announced as important to my study? How do I conceptualize the kinds of entity they are? In response to the first question, I have rejected, largely I must say for personal reasons, 'United Kingdom' – I prefer to think about where I live in terms of geographical space rather than as the Queen's domain. I use 'Britain' instead. It is also a problematic term – does it include Northern Ireland? – but it has been used inclusively by other writers something of whose outlook I share, and it has the advantage of brevity (Nairn 1977). In response to the second question, I considered using 'nation' – along the lines of Hugh Kearney's book *The British Isles: a history of four nations* (1989) – but 'nation' seems not to fit Northern Ireland, and though it affirms identity it overstates the autonomy of Wales and even of Scotland. Hence I use mostly the weaker, simpler and more capacious term 'country'.

Four countries, then, that share in many aspects a common educational history. As David Raffe and his co-authors point out, the differences in education systems across Britain 'map on to social relations and contexts of education that are in many respects similar': similar levels of social mobility and class inequality; a similar pattern of certification; a labour market that has helped sustain a distinctive British pattern of participation in education and training, centred on a relatively low take-up of full-time education post-16 (Raffe et al. 1999: 16). But they are four countries whose educational patterns have never been identical and whose trajectories seem now to be divergent. Britain, in educational terms, is not a single policy space. Relations between educational actors in the four countries – teachers, parents, national and local government and so on – vary greatly, and on such key themes of current policy as selection and social inclusion there are strong differences of inflection, in which much is at stake. These differences have recently become sharper, but they are not of recent origin. Rather, they are tied to longstanding institutional patterns and value systems, whose development in the post-war period this book tries to trace.

There is a wider and ultimately political point to this focus. The social and political experience of Wales and Scotland, pre-war, provided a powerful impetus to the creation of the British welfare state. But the central dynamic of educational change in post-war Britain, especially since 1979, has been English. England has been at once the most radical and the most elitist of the four systems, as well as the country in which the pattern of educational change has been least settled: there has still been no conclusive outcome in England to the arguments which surrounded the establishment of the tripartite system in the 1940s, and the comprehensive reform of the 1960s. Out of these unfinished arguments, much (conflicting) policy has come, and England's particularities have become Britain's problems. Since the 1970s, England has been the homeland of a Conservatism which has remade Britain, economically, politically, socially and culturally; and of a New Labour party whose preoccupations with target-setting, strong management and auditing are shaping schooling policy across Britain, even if they look odder from Cardiff and Edinburgh than they do from Westminster. For these reasons, English experiences, events and processes are placed at the centre of the book's focus. But in privileging an English experience I have also tried to problematize it. In the most influential discourses about education politics, even when they imply a more general applicability, it is a story about England that is being told. New Labour's current educational philosophy is haunted by a history that it sees as a catalogue of public-sector failure, and it is the perceived depth of this failure that helps drive its policy towards the embrace of selection and the private sector. But all the reference points in Labour's historiography lie in an *English* past. It does not look across its northern border to consider the experience of a system which has claims to being more inclusive, more successful – and less privatized; nor does it look across the Irish Sea to a polity where secondary selection is increasingly seen as a legacy to be rejected rather than a future to be welcomed.

There is a usefulness, in this context, in expanding the range of educational possibility, and escaping from English accounts of desperate failure and longed-for regeneration which have become as claustrophobic as they are familiar. England, after all, is in educational terms a peculiar place, more differentiated than the European or the British norm, and with an educational memory and imagination to match. To draw attention to these peculiarities and their limitations, and to stress what can be learned from other experiences within Britain, can have a useful contemporary purpose. It can disturb not only the dominant versions of educational history, but also – perhaps – the practices they serve to justify.

Schooling and Culture

If the book is relatively unusual in placing England in a British context, it is also distinct in the stress it places on the cultural dimension of schooling. By 'cultural dimension' here I point towards a number of interrelated processes, the first of which was eloquently identified a century ago by Emile Durkheim. Dated of course in their detail, his 1925 writings on 'moral education' are still remarkable in their theoretical and normative insistence that micro-processes connect to macro-purposes, and that schools should try to shape the intimate subjectivities of their students, by rendering the meanings and values of society 'alive and powerful' (Durkheim 1961). I'm interested in the various ways in which schooling in Britain has taken up the Durkheimian project – from the efforts of Ellen Wilkinson in 1947 to revalue manual labour, to those of educationalists who have tried to embody, in the Curriculum Cymreig, an ethos which is distinctively Welsh. I differ, though, from these engineers of the national soul, in seeing culture as more than a one-way street. The school isn't a place where the designs of the policy-makers are imprinted on the student population. On the contrary, it has been a site where those designs have been much contested, both consciously and unconsciously. In terms of meanings and values the school is a complex space. Teachers have not been united around a single project of schooling, and students and parents have responded to grand educational projects in ways which have made their outcomes very different from those their initiators intended.

Such workings out of conflicts and difference do not often lie on the surface of history. They have been pursued obscurely and locally, in particular cities and classrooms, or they have involved groupings – such as black parents – whose presence in the public sphere has mostly gone unnoticed. But although dispersed and barely acknowledged they helped give educational practice for much of the post-war period a strikingly dialogic and argumentative character, and even in defeat they preoccupied the victors, for the passion of Conservative curriculum policy after 1974 is incomprehensible without an understanding of the Other – the classroom supposed chaotic and subversive – which instilled it with fear. Exploring this cultural dimension, I make loose but I hope productive use of the term 'discourse' and the practice of discursive analysis. Discursive analysis as employed here takes as its objects texts and groups of texts and attempts to identify between them a coherence of language and thought which it takes to be related to particular, shared, social interests and positions; additionally it seeks to identify terms in which discursive positions mark themselves out from each other. It is a way of understanding what have been called the 'assumptive worlds' of social actors (McPherson and Raab 1988), or in other usages their mentalities or their structures of feeling.

The chapters that follow stage encounters with a variety of such worlds, from the patrician nostalgia of Richard Law to the dogmatic pragmatism of New Labour. I try to show the ways in which these discursive entities and speaking positions are constructed and how they are motivated – how they relate to the social and cultural interests of the speakers. Education writing in Britain is a political business, even in its quieter recesses, and I have not, in researching the book, come across any accounts of educational process and purposes which are not connected to a strong social motivation. Nor have I come across many which are not in some sense historicized. Each significant policy actor in education seems compelled to go over past ground, and to justify their current preferences in terms of a history which they will continue, or recover, or redeem. New Labour, here, is only the latest in the post-war line. When the authors of *The New Secondary Education* (1947) or *Primary Education in Wales* (1967) or *Schools Building on Success* (2001) write of educational experience and aspiration they do so in terms which not only outline the directions of policy, but evoke a history, imagine a community and go on to construct its future. Exploring such discourses – the ways in which they identify themselves, and seek connections with or distinctions from predecessors and opponents – is a way of recognizing thus the richness of educational arguments and their links to a more general social imagination.

'Equality'

If the book's focus is novel in some respects, in others it is unavoidably traditional. Harold Silver wrote in 1973 that for most of his century 'equality' and 'equal opportunity' had been the terms around which educational policy discussion had centred. Attention had therefore been directed towards 'the structure of the education system and access by children from different social groups to its different component parts' (Silver 1973: xi). My book, like Silver's anthology, tracks these issues of structure, access and social class, and the arguments that have surrounded them, through the phases of twentieth-century history.

Many others, most notably Halsey and his various co-authors (Halsey 1972, 1988; Halsey et al. 1980; 1997) have worked within this field. In the 1950s, a great body of sociological research established that there persisted, even after the supposedly decisive reforms of 1944–7, class-based patterns of uneven access to higher levels of education. In the same period, and even more strongly in the 1960s, such studies were complemented by policy modelling which distinguished between different versions of 'equality', and in its strongest form envisaged an education system which discriminated positively in favour of working-class students so as to secure their access to higher education to an extent proportionate to their number in the population (Halsey 1972). The policy shifts of the late 1970s and '80s did much to discourage further large-scale research, and the redress of class-based inequalities in education receded as an objective of government; in the last fifteen years of the twentieth century, the kinds of research favoured by policy-makers placed an emphasis not on general social determinants of educational achievement, but on the difference that effective schooling could make to overcoming disadvantage, via 'the creation of a technology of educational policy and practice ... so strong that it outweighs the effects of outside school influence and helps bring all schools to high standards of achievement, independent of their different backgrounds and starting points' (Reynolds 1997: 23, cited in Whitty 2001b: 288). But, if these recent currents in educational research have sought to forget or cancel out the effects of class, this hardly means that the relationships identified in the past as central to inequalities in access and achievement have gone away. It is true that comprehensive schools, where their populations are socially mixed, have had a disproportionately beneficial effect on the achievement of working-class students (McPherson and Willms 1987); it is also the case that the absolute number of working-class students taking public examinations and securing access to post-16 and post-18 education has increased enormously in the post-war period. But this has not greatly altered relative patterns of access and achievement. Heath, writing in 1989, wrote of two tendencies in post-war education in England: on the one hand, rising levels of educational attainment; on the other 'a resilience in class inequality' (Heath 1989: 186–7). A more general study of the British class structure concluded in the same period that 'the association between an individual's class of origin and his or her eventual destination has proved remarkably stable, despite economic expansion, egalitarian social policies and educational reform' (Marshall et al. 1988: 272). Reid, writing ten years later, and utilizing data from the 1990s, reached a similar conclusion (Reid 1998: 157–87).

In these respects, class remains central. In others, it appears less salient. It may remain structurally important to education's role in allocating opportunities, but, in terms of policy and educational practice, social class has been decentred. There is a much greater awareness of inequality's other dimensions. Disability, gender and race have become essential to thinking about reform. At the same time the extent to which class-based identities provide reference-points for educational practice has diminished: in the 1960s, it seemed important to policy-makers and educationalists to make sense of working-class culture and consider the implications for learning of its distance from the official cultures of the school; there is no such interest now.

Moreover, if questions of social class are now addressed it is through the medium of measures to promote 'social inclusion'. This is a project which – as chapter 5 discusses – may envisage 'widening participation' at higher levels of the education system, but is very different in its political and social implications from earlier programmes. The aspiration to remake education, so as to create a 'common school' in which students from all social classes can be educated, is not a strong component of the contemporary educational space; its absence has consequences across all dimensions of inequality.

Organization of Chapters

The book is organized chronologically, and in a conventional fashion, with the periodization of its chapters corresponding to the electoral fortunes of the major parties: 1944–51 – secondary education for all and post-war reconstruction; 1951–64 – Conservative rule, expansion and the unravelling of post-war arrangements; 1964–79 – Labour and the deepening and then the crisis of reform; 1979–97 – Thatcherism, and the remaking of schooling; and then a final chapter on the complex phenomenon that is New Labour. In some senses, it is a Westminster chronology – from the perspective of Belfast, for instance, 1947, 1969 and 1998 would make more sense as markers of change – but it is nevertheless a useful one, which I hope corresponds to a deeper logic of change.

Each chapter begins by presenting the wider context of schooling, and continues by setting out the general features of education in its period. In doing so, it discusses the ways in which cultural, social, economic and political factors have helped configure education. Sandra Taylor and her colleagues write that educational purposes have always been diverse. At any moment, there are likely to be several different sorts of purpose in circulation, that variously prioritize nation building, the preparation of students for an economic role, meeting individual needs for personal development and so on. Taylor et al. (1997) suggest that the ways in which 'these at times conflicting demands have been reconciled, and which purposes have received policy priority at any given time, are reflected in *policy settlements* reflecting prevailing economic, political and social circumstances.' The concept of 'policy settlement' is of course fairly well established, especially in theoretical traditions which recognize a debt to Gramsci, and it has been effectively utilized in accounts of post-war social policy (Centre for Contemporary Cultural Studies 1981; Clarke and Newman 1997; Ainley 1999). Settlements, according to Clarke

and Newman (1997: 8) are not just reflections of prevailing circumstances but 'limited and conditional reconciliations of different interests'. Settlements are fairly lasting sets of arrangements, but they
are never static. They have inbuilt tensions and limits. They are
shaped by conflict as well as agreement. They do not finally endure.
Not every period has a settlement of its own, and the parties to one
settlement are not necessarily those who come together for the next.

It is the making and remaking of settlement which organizes the
book. The period 1944–7 – providing secondary education, strong
forms of selection and decentralized professional space – responded
to the pressures of reformers, the programme of civil servants and
the interests of teachers and established clear institutional forms for
the elaboration of their projects. The making of this settlement is the
focus of chapter 1. The unravelling of 1944–7 in the 1950s, under the
pressure of occupational change, parental demand, labour movement
discontent and professional activism, is the substance of the second
chapter. The third covers the period in which the post-war settlement
was both substantially revised, by Labour reforms in the 1960s, and
eventually undone, by economic pressures, social and cultural unrest
and Conservative discontent, in the 1970s. Chapter 4 addresses the
long period of Conservative rule from 1979, the increasing differences
between the systems of the four countries, and the eviction of previously central interests from the framework of settlement as Conservatism tried to rule, as it were, alone. It treats the settlement embodied
in the Education Reform Act of 1988 as a remaking of education, in
which the role of some actors was weakened and a new institutional
logic based on competition and centralization established. The final
chapter considers New Labour, its attempts to ground its rule on a
managerial cadre and the promise of a rapid rise in standards. Like
Conservatism, New Labour seeks no political or professional allies in
its reshaping of the system, and derives its strategy mainly from an
English experience. It offers a settlement – a definitive resolution of
longstanding problems in education's economic, social and cultural
functions – without social partners. Whether this amounts to a plausible politics of education is discussed in the book's final pages.

Schooling and its Futures

Finally, something about the book's wider focus – and perhaps about
the impending disintegration of its object of study, to the point where
it will be difficult unproblematically to write either of an institution
called 'the school' or of a place called 'Britain'.

It is about 'schooling', which I have interpreted as the compulsory, mass phase of education. The society in which British schooling is located has changed enormously in the period that the book covers. The decline of agriculture and manufacturing, and the rise and diversification of service industries, have reshaped the occupational structure, and placed new demands on the school system – mediated always by social and political interests. The increase in managerial, professional and technical jobs, the formation of a white-collar semi-skilled proletariat, and the overall upgrading in skills and certification of the higher levels of the workforce have had similar effects. The outcome of this constant change, whose essential tendencies have been visible since the 1950s, is that in terms of its certification processes, its relation with other social agencies – the family, business, other sectors of the apparatus of governance – schooling has been transformed. At the same time, the rapid proliferation of information technology raises new possibilities of connecting the school and other centres of knowledge production. In the process, it has been suggested, the boundaries between the school and other forms of learning institution will become porous (Bentley and Selzer 1999).

This isn't a prognosis I share, at least in its stronger forms. The connectedness of the school – its relationship to other agencies and centres of knowledge production – has undoubtedly increased. Information technology has enabled much of this connectivity and has, moreover, done something to convert the middle-class home into a place of more intense learning activity, in the form of computer-based learning and edutainment (Buckingham and Scanlon 2002). But what is striking about the last sixty years – the period of the book – is less the dissolution of the school than its strengthening. In the demands it makes of students, parents and teachers the school is a much more intense institution than at any previous time. Its assessment processes are wider-reaching, and given enormous public significance. What is expected of it as a socializing agency has increased, and its place as the first stage in a process of lifelong learning is enshrined in government policy. There are tensions, of course, between the school and other centres of learning activity and cultural practice – the home, commercialized youth culture and so on – but these are perhaps best seen as the contemporary continuation of old relationships, rather than new phenomena that herald the dissolution of the school.

Similar arguments circle around globalization. Sometimes the term is used to imply the creation of a 'shapeless planetary space' (Laïdi 1998, cited in Lawn 2002) in which national reference-points and purposes will be lost, and in which education will be subject more to the borderless forces of 'international consortia and private corporations' than to governance at either national or European level (Lawn 2002). This isn't a view I share, partly because I am not convinced of the novelty of internationalization as a constraint upon national polities and partly because – as the rest of this book will show – I think that education's location within national cultural formations has a decisive influence on its character and limits. The resources, ethos and purpose of education in Britain have always been shaped by Britain's international position. The elitism and nostalgia embodied in aspects of the English system, for instance, are inseparable from the once-imperial role of its ruling class. Periodic crises of funding – in the 1940s, early 1950s, mid-1960s, mid-1970s and early 1990s – are likewise connected to Britain's international financial role and its famed industrial decline, which have been cause rather than conse-quence of educational failings. It is plain that since the 1980s the British system has become more internationalized: its policy elite is connected to global organizations and shares in their strategic think-ing; its sense of its own success and failure is shaped by an intense process of comparison with other systems. The book aims to trace this recent process, and the 'travelling policy' – the international models of systemic change – which accompany it, in their interaction with the local educational cultures of Britain. The outcome of the process is not at all settled, but one thing is clear. The fate of the British systems is not inscribed in global policy dictates, and different local perspec-tives on – for instance – inclusion, differentiation and educational purpose will result in the pressures of globalization being inflected in varying ways across Britain. Far more likely in this scenario is the further separation of British schooling into its national components, than the incorporation of the whole ensemble into a global commu-nity of policy and practice, or an educational space determined by the priorities of European policy networks. For these reasons, I think this book will not be the last of its line.

1

Post-War Settlements

Contexts of Reform

Between 1943 and 1947, the coalition government led by Churchill and the Labour government of Attlee committed themselves to full employment, instituted a more effective system of social security, and – in Labour's case – constructed a National Health Service, freely available. Central among the motives for these reforms was a political recognition of the strength of the demand for change, a strength expressed by Labour's overwhelming victory in the general election of 1945. The effects of reform were many and enduring. The lifting of the threat of unemployment and dire poverty greatly strengthened trade-unionism. The creation of new and massive institutions of health and welfare brought into existence a large professional or semi-professional class, which developed policies and interests of its own. At the same time, the fact that reform was the result of decisive action at the political centre served to cement the support of the majority of the Welsh and Scottish populations for the British state. The depression of the 1930s had devastated the Welsh and Scottish economies – Wales had lost one-fifth of its population. The creation of the welfare state, 'the most important reform for raising the quality of working-class life in the twentieth century', was manifestly the work of national government, which possessed a 'capacity for regeneration' which no individual polity could match (Morgan and Mungham 2000).

But this capacity was limited, first of all, by economic circumstance. Impoverished by war, Britain was able to fund the welfare state only with financial aid in late 1945 from the American government. Resolving a further financial crisis in 1947 likewise required US assistance, in the process of which Britain ran up political as well as economic debts. Problems at this level were increasingly bound up with global shifts in the military and political balance. As the USA, supported by Britain, worked to create a world order based on the rebuilding of war-torn capitalist economies, hostility grew between the Western supporters of this project and the non-capitalist powers of the Soviet Union and China. The resulting Cold War, which reached an early peak with the Korean conflict of 1950–3, had a substantial impact on economic and social life: in its early stages, it demanded levels of spending which further limited welfare provision, and at the same time served to stimulate an intense domestic politics of anti-communism, which muted the radical ideologies that had accompanied earlier demands for social change.

Ultimately, as Andrew Gamble points out, many British companies – multinationals – benefited from British commitment to an American-sponsored world order, based on more open trading arrangements than had existed in the protectionist 1930s (Gamble 1981). Important sections of the British economy, however, did not. Manufacturing and extractive industries – including steel, coal, shipbuilding and engineering – experienced some limited post-war growth, as other still more damaged national rivals took time to renew their economies. But the overall failure of industry to invest in new capacity was striking, as was the inability of the Attlee government to direct them. The historian Eric Hobsbawm, comparing the 'enthusiastic planned modernization' undertaken by French governments in the post-war period with the British record, suggests that the Labour government, despite its nationalization of several large and inefficient sectors, 'showed a lack of interest in planning that was quite startling' (Hobsbawm 1994: 272).

In central economic respects, then, post-war society was not remade to anything like the depth that the more heroic accounts of 1945–51 would suggest. The radicalism that accompanied demands for extended welfare provision was to this extent defensive. To use Aneurin Bevan's phrase, it had established 'in place of fear' a set of institutions that provided a safeguard against ill-health and poverty; but it had not gone on to achieve a more substantial economic redesign. The same story can be told of other, social and cultural, spheres. In many cases, not least in education, the reforms of 1943–7 had been supported – outside government circles – in terms which were explicitly egalitarian as well as modernizing. They thus posed a challenge to institutions, administrative systems and ideologies which had been created by old elites, in the interests of dominant classes. But in practice these radical impulses did not prevail. The economic stringencies of the period, combined with the resistance of elites, worked to nullify or deflect their impact, so that in social and cultural terms the immediate post-war years had a relatively conservative character.

But this does not mean that demands for more substantial change than that engineered by a cautious government had disappeared. 'I dreamed that life was over,' said Churchill to his doctor on the eve of the 1945 election, and in the immediate panic of defeat many Conservatives imagined that the hour of radical change had come (Schwarz 1991: 148). It had not, but 1945 nevertheless marked a phase in the cultural defeat of the traditionalist right. The very fact that new institutions had emerged, charged with the welfare of the mass of population, and staffed by professional groups committed at least to some extent to ideas of the public good, meant that the ground had been prepared for a slow shift of cultural power, in which the meanings and values treasured by conservatives were placed under siege. Right-wing thinkers were more alert to this development than those on the left, and predicted the most awful consequences for a society in which social hierarchies and cultural and moral authority were no longer taken for granted. 'What we are witnessing now', wrote the politician Richard Law in 1950, 'is something more terrible than the collapse of a civilisation. . . . It is the collapse of all absolute and social values, the end of man as a moral being' (1950: 29). This was hyperbolic, to be sure, but not untypical. Like the novels of Evelyn Waugh or the cultural commentary of T. S. Eliot, it represented a perception that something important had changed, and that the dynamic of post-war society centred on a relationship between the new, enlarged institutions of the welfare state and the interests, needs and cultures of the mass of the population.

Reshaping Schooling

Between 1944 and 1947 the education systems of England, Wales, Scotland and Northern Ireland were substantially changed, via a series of Education Acts – in England and Wales in 1944, Scotland in 1945 and Northern Ireland in 1947. The initiative for legislative change was taken in England and Wales. It was there that conflicts between different interest groups were at their sharpest and most multi-faceted, and there that the negotiating capacities of the governing class were most called for. In Scotland, politicians and civil servants were convinced both that there was a broad national consensus in favour of change, and that policies were already in place to effect it. In Northern Ireland, there was a similar commitment to change, though an awareness that its patterning would be determined as much by religious factors as by the classic themes of educational reform (Akenside 1973: 163).

The Acts, and the debates that led up to them, were complex and fundamentally contradictory events. On the one hand, they provided the focus for pressure, especially from labour movement organizations, for fundamental change. In Northern Ireland there were calls, across religious and political divides, for social reform (Bew et al. 1995). In England and Wales, campaigners claimed there was 'real evidence of a popular demand for a democratic system of education', a demand expressed through alliances between the main teachers' union, the National Union of Teachers (NUT), and the Trades Union Congress (TUC) (Giles 1946). In Scotland, the widespread desire for a system more democratic and more egalitarian than its predecessors, which would 'suit the many as well as the old fitted the few', was given voice at the centre of educational discussion, through the work of the advisory committee appointed by the Secretary of State (Scottish Education Department 1947: 4). On the other hand, however, the ways in which the Acts were interpreted by administrative elites, endorsed by the Labour leadership, worked to support existing patterns of privilege and class advantage, and selective mechanisms remained at the heart of the system. Despite the radical clamour which accompanied the passing of the legislation, notes Gareth Elwyn Jones, the 1944 Education Act as it was applied in Wales was faithful in essence to the blueprint drawn up by civil servants in 1941 (G. E. Jones 1990: 45). Likewise in Scotland the 1945 Act did no more than codify changes that had been agreed on in the years before the war, and attempts to extend policy in ways that would achieve more fundamental change were defeated (Lloyd 1983).

'What does the Act promise?' asked the communist and teachers' leader G. C. T. Giles of legislation for England and Wales. 'Does it wipe out . . . class discrimination? Does it promise for the average child something better than the disgracefully low standards of the ordinary elementary school? Does it contain any advance towards equality of opportunity?' (Giles 1946: 20). He turned for his answers to the text of the legislation, and found there a 'drastic recasting of our educational system' (1946: 21). In place of the divide between mass elementary education and a secondary system resting on selection and fee-paying, he identified a commitment to organizing public education in three stages – 'primary education', 'secondary education' and 'further education', with the school-leaving age raised to 15 by 1947, and to 16 as soon as practicable thereafter. It mandated local authorities to provide nursery education, to expand provision 'for pupils who suffer from any disability of mind of body', and it envisaged compulsory part-time education for 16–18-year-olds. 'Not less important', wrote Giles, 'is the extension of provision for the physical welfare of the children' (1946: 22). Local authorities were now obliged to provide free medical treatment, as well as milk and meals for all who wanted them .

Thus far, the concerns of Giles, and of thousands of reformers like him, were satisfied: the Acts seemed to promise a free and universal system of education that involved students of all ages up to 18 in a common system, based on the idea that the 'nature of a child's education should be based on his capacity and promise, not by the circumstances of his parents' (White Paper 1943: 20). But, as Giles acknowledged, this picture was more an ideal than a working model. Responding to the economic climate of the late 1940s, the Labour government made short-term choices that turned out to have longer-term consequences. The provisions of the 1944–7 Acts for compulsory part-time education after the age of 15 were never implemented. Restrictions on capital spending helped ensure that technical schools were left unbuilt. Nursery education declined from its wartime peak, as financial arguments combined with a belief in the necessity of domestic maternal care to stop its growth (David 1980). The integration of students deemed to have special needs into the mainstream of the system was not pursued even to the limited extent envisaged by the designers of legislation. At the time, these failings were explained in terms of the constraints of a 'war-crippled economy': 'the facts of the nation's situation did not allow it,' wrote one commentator of the non-emergence of the post-15 county colleges planned for the late 1940s (Dent 1954: 148). But it is difficult to see finance as the only factor involved. In practice, the Act was blurred, contradicted and compromised not only by the effects of economic crisis but also by its encounter with a variety of vested interests.

Private schooling

First among these was private education, which included schools of both lowly and elevated status. It is the fate of the high-status schools – the public schools – which concerns us here. During the war, public schools considered themselves a threatened species: teacher unions and the TUC had called for their abolition and headteachers had feared for their survival. But in fact the Acts of 1944–7 left the public schools untouched, and the notion of a universal system of state schooling was thus compromised from the first. R. A. Butler, the Conservative politician whose skill in reconciling different educational interests was celebrated and revered on all sides of the House of Commons, manoeuvred to keep the public-school question out of parliamentary debate, and neither the Education Acts nor any other subsequent post-war legislation addressed them. As a result, there remained alongside the state system an elite, private, fee-paying form of education that continued to dominate university entrance and access to positions of social and political power. Under Attlee's government, its position was secure. George Tomlinson, Attlee's Minister of Education from 1947 to 1951, urged upon public-school headteachers a batch of explanations as to why the government would not move against them:

> My party has issued a statement of policy in which it looks forward to the day when the schools in the state system will be so good that nobody will want their children to go to independent schools. It is obviously going to be a great many years before such consummation is achieved. At present our hands are full enough coping with the increase in the birth-rate and the movement of population to new housing estates. . . . Personally I do not see the sense in getting rid of something that is doing a useful job of work, or making everything conform to a common pattern. (Blackburn 1954: 193)

Postponing, thus, any reform of private education to the distant future – and compromising even this position with the suggestion that creating a 'common pattern' of education was undesirable, Labour's Education Ministers also endorsed, throughout Britain, the continued existence, under various names, of 'direct grant' secondary schools. These were self-governing institutions partly supported by the state in return for offering a percentage of their places free to holders of local authority scholarships. Academically very successful for more than three decades after the war, the schools served as a kind of top layer of the state secondary sector, and provided another element in the diversity so much appreciated by Tomlinson.

Religion

The second set of interests with which the makers of the Education Acts had to deal were religious ones. In Wales, Anglicanism was not the established church, nor a powerful force in education. Scotland had already seen a religious settlement in 1918, in which Catholic schools, particularly, gained state funding while retaining control over the appointment of teachers and institutional ethos. But in England and Northern Ireland religious questions expressed themselves with particular force. In England, since the 1870 Education Act, the Anglican Church had controlled the great majority of rural elementary schools, as well as many in urban areas. They were in many cases the epitome of low-level mass education. As Butler pointed out to the Archbishop of Canterbury, 90 per cent of them were housed in pre-1900 buildings, and were 'appallingly old and out of date' (Butler 1971: 98) – 'pigsty schools', as Giles called them (Giles 1946: 35). The church could not afford their upkeep, and, if government attempted simply to subsidize the church in its running of the schools, the political costs would be unsustainable – there was already a long history of nonconformist and secular opposition to the financial links between public funds and the church sector.

Butler's solution was to trade influence for cash – public funding of church schools in return for majority local authority representation on governing bodies. At the same time, he pledged that religious education and religious worship, organized on non-denominational lines, would be at the centre of state schooling. (Even so, there remained many Church of England schools that chose to be funded less generously, so as to retain greater control over appointments and curriculum.) Catholicism, in England and Northern Ireland, presented a different set of issues, ideological as well as financial. The Catholic Church demanded the right to control children's education, and sought theological justification for doing so. As the Catholic bishops in Northern Ireland put it, 'it is necessary that all the teaching and the whole organisation of the school and its textbooks in every branch be regulated by the Christian spirit under the direction and material supervision of the Church' (Akenside 1973: 170). From this position, there were no grounds on which the state could legitimately claim educational influence over Catholic schooling, and the Catholic hierarchy in England rejected Butler's compromise. Catholic schools therefore received a lower level of state funding, with the difference being made up by intensive money-raising campaigns that served among other things to strengthen the bond between Catholic communities and the church.

In Northern Ireland, the religious question was more closely tied to the very existence of the state. The Catholic hierarchy regarded the Unionist regime at Stormont as, in its own words, an 'oppressor state'. It had opposed wartime conscription, because Catholics had no interest in 'fighting for our oppressor' (Akenside 1973: 170). It was hence little inclined to compromise with state authorities offering extra funding in return for greater state influence. At the same time, Protestant churches and the Orange Order pressed the Unionist government not to resource Catholic education. 'Institutions are being set up', warned the working-class Protestant politician Harry Midgley, 'which will be seats of power in the future, and now they are increasingly looking to public funds for the support of these institutions' (Farren 1992). Organized grassroots Unionism welcomed educational reform as an extension of opportunity, but at the same time it was determined to limit the operation of that opportunity so as largely to exclude Catholic-run schooling. State-provided schools remained *de facto* Protestant schools. Catholic schools 'were firmly outside the system', enjoying only modest support from state funds (Cormack and Osborne 1995), and educational expansion was organized in ways that favoured Protestant/Unionist interests: there was an underprovision of grammar schools in Catholic areas; new secondary modern schools were located, overwhelmingly, in Protestant rather than Catholic areas; and the travel and boarding costs of children at Catholic grammar schools were not subsidized (Farren 1992).

Diversity

Writers on social policy often emphasize that the post-war settlement involved a much greater role for the state, at the expense of the private and voluntary agencies which before the war had organized a great deal of health, welfare and education (Glennerster 1995: 7); the result of this shift is said to be a greater uniformity of provision. But this generalization is only partly true of education. The Acts of 1944–7 did envisage a strong role of local state agencies – the elected local education authorities – in planning and managing provision. But what was established, between 1944 and 1947 over a large part of Britain, was less a system characterized by uniformity than one which was institutionally diverse and divided, with the lines of division corresponding especially to class and religion, and with the further complication that secondary education in both public and private sectors was liable to institutional separation on grounds of gender. The settlement of the post-war years was not a replacement of an earlier hierarchical system but rather something grafted on it. And, as Richard Johnson has pointed out, the 'multiplication of institutional differences' which resulted from this mode of development offered 'maximum opportunities for social division and exclusiveness', especially in England (Johnson 1989).

The post-1944 system was diverse, then – but not all aspects of diversity related to inequality. In terms of governance, education was a national service, locally provided. Local authorities had the duty to produce plans for the local development of education, which the Ministry of Education could and sometimes did veto in the light of what it took to be national policy: advocates of the non-selective school were to have bitter experience of the use of these powers. Some historians have seen in the 1944 Act a strengthening of the centre against the locality, and in some respects, especially perhaps in Wales, this was true. But to stress centralization too strongly is to miss something about the dynamic that 1944 in effect encouraged. Local authorities had some power to organize and reorganize schooling. In addition, because the Act made no stipulations about curriculum and pedagogy, teachers had considerable capacities to initiate school-level change. As future chapters will suggest, these capacities were often under-used, but none the less the elements of decentralization built into the Act were later the basis for significant initiatives of local curricular reform.

Secondary Education for All

The main reason that the legislative provisions for inequality survived political scrutiny so easily – Butler noted the absence of any sharpness in parliamentary debate about the 1944 Act – was that the new laws delivered that for which reformers had long been pressing, secondary education for all. This had been the Labour Party's objective since the 1920s, and had increasingly been advocated by official reports. In 1926, the Hadow Report had called for the raising of the school-leaving age to 15, and the general establishment of post-primary education. At the end of the 1930s, repeating the call, the Spens Report had argued that 'the existing arrangements ... for ... education above the age of 11+ ... have ceased to correspond with the actual structure of modern society and with ... economic facts' (Spens Report 1938: 353). The legislation of 1944–7 was a belated response to these long-held positions. It claimed to shift British schooling from a nineteenth-century system in which secondary education was available only to a minority, to one in which it would be the birthright of all children, the means for securing economic advance and a way of building an inclusive national community. This was its central promise, and the basis of its mass appeal. It was also the locus of its ambiguities and the source of the conflicts which later came to surround it. Understanding the 1944–7 settlement, therefore, requires analysing what was involved in 'secondary education for all', both organizationally and in terms of the kinds of learning it sought to promote.

In establishing secondary education for all, neither the 1944 Act nor its Scottish and Northern Irish counterparts specified the institutional forms that secondary schooling should take. It was the duty of every local education authority, according to the Act, to ensure that schools existed in their area 'sufficient in number, character and equipment to afford all pupils opportunities offering such variety of instruction and training as may be desirable in view of their different ages, abilities and aptitudes'. Beyond this, it was silent. However, there already existed policy resources, ideological positions and administrative preferences strong enough to stipulate with great clarity the institutional character of the new system. The Spens Report had sketched a system based on a tripartite division into modern schools, grammar schools and technical high schools. The Norwood Committee in 1943 had decided that these distinctions corresponded to the facts of social existence. Individuals had 'enough in common as regards capacities and interests' to justify the separation of individuals into 'certain rough groupings' (Norwood Report 1943: 1). In first place, here, there was the type of student 'who can grasp an argument or follow a piece of connected reasoning', who was 'interested in causes', 'sensitive to language as expression of thought' and perceived 'the relatedness of related things, in development, in structure, in a coherent body of knowledge'. This was the kind of student suited to, and developed by, the grammar school. Second came the pupil 'whose interests and abilities lie markedly in the field of applied science or applied art', and destined therefore for the technical school. Then came a third grouping, composed of students who 'deal more easily with concrete things' rather than with ideas. Into this group fell those who were 'interested in things as they are'. The report imagined such a student in these terms:

> His mind must turn its knowledge or its curiosity to immediate test; and his test is essentially practical. He may see clearly along one line of study or interest . . . but he often fails to relate his knowledge or skill to other branches of activity. Because he is interested only in the moment he may be incapable of a long series of connected steps; relevance to present concerns is the only way of awakening interest; abstractions mean little to him. (Norwood Report 1943: 2–15)

Norwood thus imagined an entire mental and emotional universe for its groupings, each of which as it were lived on different worlds, inhabiting different subjectivities. Plainly, then, far more was involved in the reconstructions of 1944–7 than the setting up of an institutional system: what was also at stake was the role of education in forming particular types of individual, imbued with particular intellectual and affective capacities. The civil servants who shaped the thinking of the Ministry of Education had a similar tripartite view of the child population, but their vision was a harsher one than Norwood's. Deriving their authority from classical philosophy – in particular, from Plato – they referred habitually (Ozga and Gewirtz 1994) to the divisions of humanity established by Socrates, in Plato's *Republic* (*c*. 380 BC). 'You are all of you in this land brothers,' he wants to tell the citizens of his imagined society, using terms perfectly compatible with wartime rhetorics of community. 'But when God fashioned you, he added gold in the composition of those who are qualified to be Rulers; he put silver in the Auxiliaries, and iron and bronze in the farmers and the rest' (Plato 1955: 160).

Plato's myth, of course, involves not just the identification of particular almost-fixed types of human being. It also attempts, by naturalizing difference, and suggesting that it is an intrinsic feature of the social order, to strengthen social unity. From this angle, there was no contradiction between appealing to social unity and identifying fixed differences. Harold Dent, editor of the *Times Educational Supplement*, who demanded 'radical changes in the social order', based around 'a planned society infused with a democratic spirit', managed to reconcile his democratic impulses with support for Norwood, in which he found a 'reasoned philosophy of education' (Simon 1991: 54).

In this perspective, reform appeared not as a matter of fundamentals. It became – as Sir Maurice Holmes, Permanent Secretary to the Board of Education put it in 1943 – a matter of 'tempering and blurring' class distinctions which had otherwise lost none of their force or authority (Thom 1986: 101). Yet, clear-headed though it was as an account of policy-making intentions, Holmes's approach contained little that was in popular terms persuasive, either to educationalists or to parents. Norwood, from this point of view, provides a much better sense of the justifications which surrounded and dignified selective arrangements. For, during and after the war, measures of differentiated expansion were combined with a heavy ideological investment in justifying the appropriateness of the separate types of education in terms of the ways in which they corresponded to the interests and capacities of different groups of students. In this context, two types of discourse became important. The first was that of 'intelligence'. Selection for the tripartite system took the form of tests in reading, writing and 'aptitude', the last of which trivium owed its place to the pre-war development of techniques of testing for IQ. By the end of the 1940s most local authorities used IQ tests, on the grounds that they provided a fair means of selection for secondary school and an accurate identification of those children who would benefit from a grammar school education (Thom 1986). Accompanying this scientifically underpinned but empirically unvalidated discourse of fairness was another kind of justification, which took on a passionately child-centred tone. It is this second discourse which is key to understanding how Labour politicians were able to reconcile themselves to the limitations, from the point of view of equal opportunity, of a tripartite system.

Tensions

Lecturing at Cambridge in 1949, the sociologist T. H. Marshall contrasted education in the early part of the century with the system envisaged by the Act of 1944. Before the war: 'The state decided what it could afford to spend on free secondary and higher education, and the children competed for the limited number of places provided. There was no pretence that all who could benefit from more advanced education would get it, and there was no recognition of any absolute right to be educated according to one's capacities' (Marshall 1963: 112). Turning to the 1944 legislation, Marshall observed the emergence of a different principle – the passage (quoted above) 'which says that the supply of secondary schools will not be considered adequate unless they "afford for all pupils opportunities for education offering such variety of instruction and training as may be desirable in view of their different ages, abilities and aptitudes"'(1963: 112).

Respect for individual rights, he noted, could hardly be more strongly expressed; 'yet I wonder whether it will work out like that in practice.' For Marshall, there was an irresolvable tension between the language of rights and individual development on the one hand, and the occupational order on the other: he saw 'no relaxation of the bonds that tie education to occupation', and observed on the contrary 'the great and increasing respect' which was paid to 'certificates, matriculations, degrees and diplomas as qualifications for employment' (1963: 113). These bonds demanded a balance between occupational demand and educational supply, and would therefore set limits to the number of places at grammar and technical schools. The future of schooling would not be one in which 'the pupil would be treated entirely as an end in himself'; the school was an instrument of social stratification in a necessarily unequal society, and the educational right it conferred on the citizen was not absolute – the fullest possible development of the individual – but qualified, 'the equal right to be regarded as unequal' (1963: 114).

Marshall's clarity was apparently at odds with the purposes ascribed to education from other positions. The reforms of 1944–7 were attended by a discourse of hope, in which education came to stand for the development of a different kind of human being, embedded in a national community organized around values of democracy and citizenship. Ellen Wilkinson, Minister of Education, wrote of the new kind of schooling that would be created, with 'laughter in the classroom, self-confidence growing every day, eager interest instead of bored uniformity' (Wilkinson 1947: 5). The *Times Educational Supplement* imagined children as 'wards of the state', each of whom would be given by benign authority 'the fullest opportunity to develop every innate power' (Thom 1986: 102). The London County Council (LCC), probably the most innovative of local authorities, envisaged education as 'a matter of all-round growth and development' and thought it 'indefensible to categorise schools on the basis of intellect only' (Giles 1946: 77). Texts used in the education of primary teachers imagined how this principle could be realized by the close aligning of children's school lives with their presumed interests outside the school, so that their 'vigour and delight in activity, natural curiosity and desire for experience' could be harnessed to educational goals (Daniels, quoted in Cunningham 1988: 40). Documentary films of the period present a similar investment of hope: the government-sponsored *The Children's Charter* of 1945 depicts children running free in fields, embodiments of a future from which war, poverty and illness have been eradicated. These free individuals were to become what Wilkinson called 'the citizens of the future', the 'Britons' who will 'stride high' into the 'new scientific age'. A burgeoning individuality was in this way linked to a national community in which social bonds were stronger and class divisions weaker: R. A. Butler imagined that it had created one nation, not two (Butler 1971: 96). The LCC wanted schools to promote 'a feeling of social unity among adolescents of all kinds and degrees of ability'. Tom Johnston, Secretary of State for Scotland, concerned for the 'future generation of the race', considered it 'most urgent' to promote in schools a sense of common citizenship (Lloyd 1983: 108–11). Finally, if we believe Harold Dent's account of the 'tremendous spiritual uplift' that teachers experienced with the abolition of the elementary school in 1945, and the establishment of a common pay scale for teachers in all types of school, then they too had solid grounds for sharing in the jubilation of the epoch (Dent 1954: 69).

Within such a context, there was a concerted attempt by politicians to mediate between the irreducibly selective and segregated nature of institutional arrangements noted by Marshall, and the hopes that accompanied the extension of mass education. Marshall's interest lay in the possibilities of citizenship – shared social rights, such as those embodied in the welfare state – as a means of offsetting the inequalities of market society. Less explicitly than him, some political voices talked about the same tensions, and saw in the new school system a way of reconciling them. Much here turned upon the ways in which the possibilities of mass secondary modern education were interpreted. Formally speaking, secondary modern education was introduced in 1945, and the school-leaving age everywhere except in Northern Ireland was raised to 15 in 1947. This did not mean, of course, that 'all-age' schools immediately disappeared – in fact, they lingered on, especially in rural areas until the early 1960s. Nor was the new type of mass school suddenly made free from the physical constraints of the old. Rather, they inherited a legacy of poor building and unprepared teaching staff, such that in all material terms their status was evidently an inferior one. Yet the expectations placed upon them were, at first, immense, and widespread – even R. H. Tawney, one of the main instigators of Labour's commitment to secondary education for all, thought that the secondary moderns 'if wisely planned' were 'likely to provide the education best calculated to give the majority of boys and girls a hopeful start in life' (Barker 1972: 80).

Labour's first Education Minister was Ellen Wilkinson, who had in her own words 'fought her way through to university from a working-class home' (Barker 1972: 89) and in the process developed strong loyalties to the selective secondary education which had helped her to do so. Wilkinson's political background was in the socialist education movements of the 1920s and the hunger marches of the 1930s, and she brought from this experience a passionate if not always convincing belief that the road to educational improvement lay through a revaluing of the dignity of labour, via the work of the secondary modern. With her Parliamentary Secretary, David Hardman, she sought to convince public opinion, against the grain of popular perception, that all secondary schools, of whatever kind, now enjoyed parity of esteem. Parents must be convinced, she reminded her civil servants in 1946, 'that the grammar school is now a specialised type of secondary school and not the real thing, any others being substitutes' (McCulloch 1998: 62). This was not a view that was universally shared. It was challenged in Parliament by the Labour left, and by evidence to the government's Central Advisory Council on Education, which suggested that the new system was not based so much on parity as on 'three social grades, arranged in . . . order of prestige and preference' (McCulloch 1998: 70). One of Wilkinson's last acts before her death in 1947 was to compose an eloquent foreword to the Ministry's pamphlet on *The New Secondary Education* in which she attempted a socialist defence of the tripartite system, based on an attempt to value all forms of education, like all forms of labour, as contributions to the social good. She linked the existence of different types of school to an argument about the uniqueness of the individual child, and the necessity of developing forms of education that could relate to individual needs and interests. 'These plans', she wrote, 'put the child first.... Their variety is designed to suit different children, not different income groups' (Wilkinson 1947: 3). Wilkinson contrasted this approach with the demand put forward by her critics in the National Association of Labour Teachers, who were demanding at the time a 'grammar school education for all' (Hansard 1946c). 'No child', she argued, 'must be forced into an academic education which bores it to rebellion, merely because that type of grammar school education is considered more socially desirable by parents' (Wilkinson 1947: 4). She went further, to call not just for a revaluation of types of education, but also for a revaluation of the hierarchies of the labour process – the hierarchies which underpinned differentation in schooling. Manual work, in this perspective, took on a new meaning: in the war and amid the difficulties of post-war reconstruction, the 'British people are learning the hard way how dependent is a civilised community on its farmers, transporters and miners, its manual and technical workers' (1947: 4).

The rest of the pamphlet, composed by civil servants, reiterates Wilkinson's personal concerns at greater length, basing itself on the one hand on a commitment to differentiation, and on the other to the kind of child-centredness long associated with the progressive movement in education. The first involves a Norwood-like belief that, while 'some are attracted by the abstract approach to learning', others, the majority, 'learn most easily by dealing with concrete things' (Ministry of Education 1947: 23). The second reveals something of the complex dynamic of post-war mass education, in which differentiation is combined with claims about the needs of the individual, the full development of the student's personality and the freedom of the teacher. The focus of the secondary modern, the pamphlet asserts, should be 'the development of the whole child', and 'everyone knows' 'that no two children are alike' (1947: 31, 22). Consequently, 'the curriculum must be made to fit the child, not the child the curriculum.' The pamphlet thus announces a break with a past that is imagined as being dominated by desk-bound, rote learning. Secondary moderns must not be pale shadows of the grammar school, and must break from academic models of learning: 'lacking', as the Ministry of Education put it, 'the traditions and privileged position of the ... grammar school their future is their own to make' (White Paper 1943: 29). From now on, experimentation, guided by teachers enjoying an autonomy in curriculum development, and encouraged to approach learning through activity rather than through books, will be the norm. As the modern schools develop, promises the pamphlet, 'parents will see that they are good' (Ministry of Education 1947: 47).

Thus the mass school began its development as an institution both segregated and experimental, second-grade and 'free'. It was not a type of education aiming to communicate universal or high-status forms of knowledge – nor even to encourage the acquisition of formal qualifications, since until the early 1950s its students were not allowed to enter public examinations – but rather one in which teachers were encouraged to stay close to the local, the experiential and the practical. In proceeding thus, the Ministry was launching a complex dialectic. On the one hand, it was linking a movement – progressivism – that had radical credentials, to a process – segregated education – which many felt, *pace* Plato and Marshall, was socially retrograde. On the other, it was encouraging an approach to education, based on dialogue between teachers and students, outside established curriculum frameworks, that would ultimately, in some patchy sort, result in a challenge to the curricular norms which were installed at the apex of the state system, in the grammar schools.

The Ministry, in keeping with the doctrine of local autonomy in curricular matters, did not seek to lay down any definite guidelines. But its pamphlets did try to establish a broad set of purposes for mass education, based on a particular interpretation of social change. 'The rapid industrialisation of the last century', it noted, 'has brought with it many material benefits' (Ministry of Education 1947: 31). But at the same time it was a process that provoked trepidation. 'For the town-dweller' it entailed a loss: of standards of craftsmanship, of 'directness and simplicity' in social relationships and of a 'sense of community'. The 'closeness of nature' enjoyed by those brought up in traditional communities had been lost. It was education's job to 'give back' to the student some of these 'good things that had been lost' (1947: 31). It could do this by concentrating its attention on a 'balanced and harmonious development' in children, in which intellectual growth was seen as just 'one facet' of the whole child. Equally important here was the role of the school in creating community, in a world that was dominated by those disintegrative processes that were understood as 'industrialism'. To this end, Dean notes, the Ministry of Education encouraged schools to create within their walls an image of the idealized home, as a haven from the pressures of society (Dean 1991). Education was assigned a role in relation to industrialization and economic development – the 'deadening routine of much industrial work' is how one Ministry pamphlet described it

(Central Advisory Committee – England 1947:58) – that was both critical and compensatory. The antipathy noted by Hobsbawm, towards any deep involvement with questions of modernization, applied not just to the reluctance to invest in the forms of industrial training that compulsory education after 15 would have generated, but also to the deepest and most extensive levels of ethos and motivation in the new system. Behind the new secondary school stood the lost village. Or, to put it another way, the school was encouraged to turn its back on the industrial world and the forms of occupational preparation it required.

Discontents

Tripartism brought together an institutional form and a variety of justifications for educational division. In England and Wales it was pervasive, but not completely dominant. The Labour Party had been committed to 'multilateralism', a form of comprehensive secondary organization, since 1939. After the war, some local authorities, including Swansea, Middlesex and the London County Council, drew up educational development plans based on this principle. Their progress was fraught. The Swansea plan, for instance, was opposed by the Welsh Department of the Ministry of Education and by the Welsh Inspectorate. To this latter body, as to many other educationalists and politicians in Labour-dominated Wales, comprehensive education seemed an unnecessary and damaging experiment. Wales, during the 1930s, had built up a grammar school system which admitted a greater percentage of the age-group than that of England. Its generous provision of non-fee-paying places had been tenaciously defended by Labour councils against central government attempts to reduce it. In the process, the grammar school had become a focus of deep and popular loyalty. In a society marked by poverty, emigration and industrial decline, it seemed to offer a means of advance and, literally, escape, for the most talented sections of the Welsh population. HMI J. E. Daniel's criticism of the new proposals in the name of tradition and established loyalty, therefore, had a wide resonance: 'What is gained by substituting for the sound traditions of those well-run and successful schools which have established themselves in the lives and affections of their localities a new and untried system whose losses are manifest and whose gains are problematical?' (G. E. Jones 1990: 83).

Thus there were many local interests favouring the grammar school, often in the name of equal opportunity. From this Welsh perspective, the grammar school was a people's school. It was not so much the creation and the preference of a Civil Service elite, but the result of a process whereby localities had tried to open up secondary education to the widest number. The grammar school had therefore to be defended – against both 'multilateral' and technical alternatives. This was the pattern, too, of Scottish attitudes from the 1940s to the 1960s, and helped ensure that in both countries the building of technical schools was still more of a rarity than it was in England. Even the position of a multilateralist reformer like W. G. Cove, an MP and long-time Rhondda-based teacher union activist, paid homage to this tradition when he declared that he wanted the benefits of grammar school education to be available to all, distrusting all forms of schooling, including technical education, which – neglecting a 'liberal education' – led only to 'menial jobs' (Cove, in Hansard 1946c: col. 2233).

Nevertheless, Cove, like a few other Labour MPs, was a powerful critic of tripartite education. The official attitude of the Ministry of Education, he told the House of Commons, was 'that the vast mass of children have not the capacity to benefit from the development of their talents' (Hansard 1946b: col.2232). He was joined by the feminist Leah Manning, who attacked the Civil Service assumption that children had fixed and natural capacities. The result of such a belief, she pointed out, could be found 'in the prospectuses of some technical schools, [where] one sees offered to . . . girls cookery, laundry, millinery and embroidery – all those arts in which women are supposed to surpass men but which really are intended to give women the components with which to make men happy and comfortable' (Hansard 1946a: cols 2196–7).

Criticisms like these were tenacious but had no immediate effect on government policy. Local antipathies to multilateral reform were reinforced by the rigorously enforced preferences of civil servants at the centre of the system for selective education. Although in curriculum matters the English ideology of education stressed autonomy and teacher discretion, at the level of structure there was no such latitude. Swansea's reorganization scheme was delayed and eventually rejected, as was that of Middlesex, with considerations of cost being less important than the Civil Service's principled hostility to more radical kinds of reform. Denied advance through the normal channels of due process, reformers took their protests to the Labour Party conference. Repeatedly, in the late 1940s, the conference – against the arguments of Wilkinson and Tomlinson – reiterated its commitment to multilateral reform. Thus, in 1947, it warned against the perpetuation via tripartism of 'the undemocratic tradition of English secondary education, which results in all normal children born into well-to-do homes being educated together in the same type of school, while the abler children in working-class families are separated at the age of 11 from their less gifted brothers and sisters' (Craig 1982: 184). Ministers responded to these complaints with statements couched in the language of priorities. The vital tasks were to build new schools and to train teachers to work in them. Questions of organization came second, and, in any case, the secondary modern was, as Wilkinson said, an achievement to be defended, not a liability to be attacked (Hardman, in Hansard 1950: col. 1871–2). These arguments, especially the first, were respected by Labour activists, but were not finally persuasive. They not only ran counter to a powerful current of Labour opinion, but also were contradicted by an emergent mass experience of secondary modern education. The reality of secondary modern schooling – without curricular pattern, without hope of qualification – created a permanent substratum of student discontent. The North London students of the late 1940s about whom Edward Blishen wrote in *Roaring Boys* felt that the raising of the school-leaving age 'amounted to a year's malicious and probably illegal detention' (Blishen 1955: 6). Their parents were likewise discontented: as Giles commented, it was difficult 'to sell the secondary modern school to parents because it does not appear to them to lead anywhere' (Giles 1946: 71).

Discontents were well founded. Sociological research carried out in the early 1950s demonstrated a continuing pattern of class-based advantage and disadvantage that 'secondary education for all' had not very much disturbed. In 1953, Floud et al., investigating grammar school admissions in two parts of England, found that the son of a 'skilled manual' father had a 14–18 per cent chance of entering grammar school, compared with the 59–68 per cent chance enjoyed by the son of a professional/managerial father (1956: 42–3). Himmelweit, researching London schools in 1951, reached similar conclusions: the proportion of working-class students in grammar schools had risen, but in absolute terms their numbers were small; the middle-class 'continues to be over-represented' (Himmelweit 1954). Whereas Marshall, like many others, had assumed that the new secondary system would break down old inequalities of class by rigorous selection on grounds of merit, the post-1944 experience suggested otherwise; class continued to influence the allocation of educational opportunity, and the supply of places was by far exceeded by the scale of demand.

Discontents and criticisms like these eventually found political expression, and were increasingly, in the 1950s, the subject of media coverage. Other grievances and inequalities were more hidden. There existed a further dimension to education provision, related to special educational needs, that in effect rendered it a quadripartite system. Tawney, in his original call for universal secondary education in 1922, had imagined that it would include 75 per cent of the age-group, 'all normal children' (Tawney 1973a). Reform, seen in this light, was hardly based on an aspiration of total inclusion. The 1944 Act was an advance on Tawney. According to Warnock, 'modest attention' was given to special education in the consultation which preceded the 1944 Act, and the view that 'provision for handicapped children' should be regarded as an aspect of ordinary education 'exactly accorded with the spirit of post-war reconstruction' (Warnock Report 1978: 19). The Act, and its 1945 Scottish counterpart, thus extended the categories of children for whom special provision was made, beyond the former designations of 'blind, deaf, defective and epileptic'. The proportion of children thought likely to have special educational needs was estimated to be between 14 and 17 per cent of the school-age population; most of these, it was thought, would be educated in ordinary schools. But it was here that inclusion began to meet its limits. The secondary moderns were ill prepared to meet the needs of any section of the school population: large classes and under-trained teachers presented extra problems for children deemed to be educationally subnormal (Dent 1954). Facilities outside the 'ordinary' school system were slow to be built, and, at the same time, the rigid categories introduced by the Act – 'defective of speech, blind, partially sighted, deaf, partially deaf, delicate, diabetic, educationally subnormal, maladjusted and physically handicapped' – tended to locate the source of problems firmly and permanently in the nature of the child, rather than in factors pertaining to the relationship between the child and the world. Children were to be diagnosed, principally by medical authorities, and then assigned to particular disability groups with which particular institutions and curriculum forms were associated. One group of children, those with a measured IQ of below 50, were placed entirely outside the scope of local authority institutions, in training centres under the control of health authorities. Intelligence testing and medical examination were thus crucial to the workings of special education, and – just as in the tripartite system – inclusion was a heavily qualified principle, while exclusion was justified on quasi-scientific grounds (Daniels 1990; Wedell 1990).

Scotland

In Scotland, the overall situation was in some important respects different. The (Scottish) Education Act of 1918 had been based on the principle of free secondary education for all, in schools of a common type (Paterson 1996). Practice did not match principle: the Scottish Education Department organized its schools on a largely bipartite basis, providing a full course of secondary education for the academically able and lower-level vocational work for the majority. Even so, despite this rigid segregation, Paterson points out, the very assertion of inclusiveness was important. It provided a starting point and a rhetoric for further reform, and contributed to what has often been called the myth of Scottish education (McPherson and Raab 1988) – a myth which among other things served to distinguish in the minds of Scottish educationalists the features of Scottish education from those of England. 'Myth' does not indicate here a purely fabricated or fictional account. It is selective, of course, in ways that tend to omit from its repertoire of stories any elements that contradict its central motifs. But it has nevertheless a strong basis in historical experience, and constitutes the way in which that experience is imagined or relived by present generations. The material basis of the myth of inclusive Scottish education lay in a history that involved greater public access and a greater uniformity of practice than in England (McPherson and Raab 1988: 29). The centre of the system, the Scottish Education Department, was created in 1872, and its powerful centralizing influence allowed subsequent development to occur along distinctively Scottish lines. There was less diversity and institutional separation than in England, with a smaller private sector, and a large number of rural secondary schools – omnibus schools – that already, before 1945, admitted students of all abilities and aptitudes.

The Scottish myth was non-Platonic: it imagined a system that was open to students from all classes, and that organized teaching and learning on the basis of liberal academic values of open debate, classical tradition and intellectual rigour. The figure of the 'lad o'pairts' – the talented boy from a humble background – was its chief protagonist, a character very different from the students conjured up by Norwood. In reality, the system was less democratic, less egalitarian than those who ran it imagined. It rested, just like the English system, on strong boundaries of academic / vocational difference. But in the postwar years it experienced for a time a far more radical challenge to this division than anything that occurred in England. Tom Johnston, Secretary of State for Scotland in the wartime government, had been permitted by Churchill to create a Scottish Council of State, which Johnston used as a vehicle to investigate aspects of economic and social policy and to make planning proposals for post-war reconstruction (Harvie 1999: 135). Johnston was determined that Scotland should have an educational system in keeping with what he saw as its radical tradition, and inclusive in ways that responded to the experience of national unity in wartime (Lloyd 1983: 198). In pursuing these objectives he attempted to circumvent the influence of the Scottish educational bureaucracy, which was strongly committed to bipartism, by setting up an advisory committee, drawn to some extent from among teachers, which would as a 'parliament' on education freely debate questions both of organization and of curriculum. One of the first results of the committee's work was its 1947 report on secondary education, a document that in the view of McPherson and Raab was key to the post-war renewal of the myth of Scottish education.

The Scottish Education Department had established over the previous fifty years a system based on clear differentiation between different types of secondary course. 'Senior' secondary students followed a predominantly academic line of study and took examinations at 17–18 that enabled access to higher education. The rest – the 70–80 per cent who were designated 'junior' secondary students – took no national examinations (McPherson and Raab 1988: 248). The advisory committee challenged this time-honoured division, just as it took its distance from the English view that children 'sorted themselves out neatly into three categories'. It argued for omnibus (comprehensive) schools and for a common, non-vocational curriculum for all students. National certification should be open to all, at 16+, and would no longer be linked solely to the requirements of university entrance. This was its 'education for the many', and in devising it the committee was inspired by 'the complex of feelings and ideas born of the war itself' – unity, community, democracy. In England, of course, a similar set of values was appealed to. The difference in this Scottish document was that the disparity between rhetorics of hope and institutional forms was very much less. In Wilkinson's efforts to reshape perceptions of the value of manual labour and of the kinds of schooling that were linked to it, there was a certain desperation, born of a tacit recognition that real distinctions in status and material reward could not so easily be wished away. The advisory committee was much clearer about the ways in which selection for secondary school created 'roots of bitterness' (Scottish Education Department 1947: 33). It doubted whether 'the best type of working-class parents, earnest, provident, and properly ambitious, would readily acquiesce in what they regard as a slamming of the door of opportunity at the very outset' (p. 33). Much more fitting was the generalization of the omnibus school, 'the natural way for a democracy to order the post-primary schooling of a given area' (p. 36).

The committee was more willing than its English counterparts to specify the curriculum of such a school, and did so in explicitly Scottish terms. It listed, in an appendix, 'moral and intellectual characteristics which have been identified as typically Scottish: pride; national liberty; integrity of thought and character; personal and intellectual independence; generosity and kindness; adventurousness; freedom from class-consciousness' (Scottish Education Department 1947: 179). These qualities, it declared, 'must be in the air of a school', so that schools would no longer be places where 'uninterested, restless boys and girls, drifting or muddling through years of schooling, carrying away at the last little more than gobbets of ill-digested knowledge and a distaste for what was yielded so little' (p. 25). The curriculum must relate to emotional and aesthetic life, as well as to academic knowledge; it must be 'realistic and relevant', base itself securely on the distinctive features of Scottish culture, and aim always to further the 'progress of the young towards social selfhood (p. 12).

The committee's vision was not a revolutionary one: it did not envisage overturning existing social hierarchies, or reordering the division of labour or the collective sharing of society's wealth. It expressed itself, rather, in explicit 'Christian Democratic' terms. It sought to create a more inclusive society, in which the education available to the mass of the population was better than before, in which education tried to develop new, more rounded types of individual, and in which it served as a means of promoting social concord rather than bitter division. To these extents, the committee's work, just as much as that of its English counterparts, was preoccupied with the role of mass education in a society damaged by industrialization, by the 'vast incoherent complex' (Scottish Education Department 1947:11) of urbanization and the new kinds of culture it promoted. If the social preferences of English educationalists were for the country village, then those of the advisory committee were for settlements which preserved something of the 'simple and stable community life of earlier times' (p. 11). It celebrated the 'natural and pithy speech of country and small town folk in Aberdeenshire and adjacent counties' and in other parts 'outside the great industrial areas'. It deplored the cultural life and linguistic habits of these areas where language had 'degenerated' into a 'worthless jumble of slipshod ungrammatical and vulgar tones, still further debased by the less desirable Americanisms of Hollywood' (p. 181). And just as sternly as the reports of the early part of the century (Newbolt Report 1921) it demanded that schools 'war unceasingly against' the mass of 'debased and incorrect speech', in a 'campaign against the speech of the street, the cinema and the illiterate home' (Scottish Education Department 1947: 63). As McPherson and Raab suggest, Scottish reformers were motivated by a vision of a particular imagined community, located far from Clydeside or the coalfield of West Fife: they sought to reshape Scottish education in the image of the Scottish small town, with its 'homely' culture, and its common institution – the omnibus school. Arguably, this sort of social vision was almost as limited as its English counterpart: neither provided a strong basis for addressing the specific issues of mass education in urban contexts.

Nevertheless, the advisory committee's report represented the most coherent and articulate alternative to the tripartism, or bipartism, that lay at the heart of post-war educational policy. In the short-term, its effect was limited. Johnston had ceased to be Secretary of State at the end of the war, and had no comparable successor. The report's ideas for comprehensive restructuring appeared unnecessary to those who believed that Scottish senior secondary education was already inclusive enough, especially in comparison to England. In the absence of effective political pressure, the Scottish Education Department was able to wait for five years before responding and then to ensure that none of its major recommendations, whether concerning organization or curriculum, was implemented. But in the longer term, its effects were more strongly felt. Because it had paid as much attention to curricular as organizational aspects of reform, and because it considered questions of educational purpose as well as institutional form, it helped render Scottish reflections about educational restructuring a great deal more detailed and far-reaching than anything that occurred at official level in England. It became an authoritative source for curriculum rethinking, and a justification for linking questions of educational organization to those of social good. The result, according to McPherson and Raab, who perhaps share something with the myth they deconstruct, was that the emergent shape of Scottish education in the final decades of the twentieth century 'bore some comparison with the model proposed in 1947' (1988: 48).

Conservatism and Tradition

There were thus attempts of several kinds, from within the system and from political organizations operating outside it, to modify the 1944–7 settlements in what were seen as more egalitarian directions. But arguments about the problems of the settlements were not confined to the left, and were not fuelled only by progressive educational thinking. Consistently in this period the settlements were subjected to both economic and cultural critique from the right. Many Conservatives thought the welfare state was ruinously expensive. Angus Maude and Roy Lewis thought that 'wartime planners' had completely miscalculated both the 'future economic situation' and 'the costs of individual services' (Maude and Lewis 1952: 202). Others launched attacks on the cultural decline that they thought integral to educational expansion. The most influential of these was the poet and literary critic T. S. Eliot, whose *Notes Towards the Definition of Culture* shaped the thinking of many who staffed the grammar schools of the next two decades. 'In our headlong rush to educate everybody,' wrote Eliot, 'we are lowering our standards, and more and more abandoning the study of those subjects by which the essentials of our culture... are transmitted; destroying our ancient edifices to make ready the ground upon which the barbarian nomads of the future will encamp in the mechanised caravans' (1949: 111). Likewise the headmaster of Manchester Grammar School criticized the 'over-optimistic belief in the educability of the majority' and the 'willingness to surrender the highest standards of taste and judgment to the incessant demands of mediocrity' (James, cited in Young 1958: 40). Others thought that the welfare state was complicit in 'the increasing mechanisation of life' and the 'impersonality of human relationships' (Bantock 1947: 171): the political philosopher, Michael Oakeshott, wrote in *The Cambridge Review* of the dangers of a 'rationalism' which uprooted tradition and dissolved communities of knowledge in the name of abstract programmes unrelated to the organic life of society, and in the process created institutions that were unworkable, politically driven monstrosities, that lacked all contact with the deeper levels of social experience.

This note of disillusionment is one that is regularly struck in the writings of post-war conservatism, nowhere more strongly than in the work of Richard Law, who was briefly a Minister of Education in the wartime government, later 'one of the most influential back-bench MPs of the forties and fifties' (H. Jones 1996: 6) and later still a figurehead of the right-wing revival of the 1970s. It is in his work that economic and cultural themes are most strongly related. Leaning on the work of the economist Friedrich von Hayek, Law argued that market arrangements were both efficient and inherently non-despotic. Interference with them necessarily involved both the suppression of freedom and the importation of inefficiency. The welfare state combined both evils. It 'subordinated economic policy to a social revolution' and as economic difficulties increased 'the revolution was fulfilling itself in frustration and disillusionment' (Law 1950: 42). It embodied 'the right of the majority to impose its will, as interpreted by a ruling caste' of politicians and administrators (p. 29). It corrupted, as any large-scale system of state provision would, 'the sense of personal responsibility and personal initiative which is the mainspring of social and economic activity' (p. 37). Hence the apocalyptic judgement that 'what we are witnessing today is something more terrible than the collapse of a civilisation. . . . It is the collapse of all absolute moral values, the end of man as a moral being' (p. 29). As an evaluation of the Attlee government, this lacked persuasiveness, but as evidence of a Conservative frame of mind it is more significant. For what impelled sections of Conservatism throughout the post-war period, as a kind of stream of opinion that went underground in the face of the popularity of the 1944–7 settlement, and resurfaced later at the welfare state's moment of crisis, was this conviction that there were worms – of tyranny, inefficiency and cultural degradation – in the bud of post-war reform.

Law and his co-thinkers produced no plans for change. Present decadence, in his perspective, was most clearly grasped not in relation to the possibility of a better future but rather in contrast to a past that rested securely on different values. Hence, for Law as far so many other Conservatives, the importance of nostalgic comparison, between the 'amplitude and power of the early years of the century' and the 'shadows of evening' that were now setting in. A key reference point in this structure of juxtaposition is provided by Law's own (public) school days, which stand for a lost ease and certainty, juxtaposed with contemporary anxiety

> Much that has happened in the forty years that have passed since I used to lie on my stomach in the lee of the pavilion, reading Scott and listening to the click of bat and ball in the distance, has been for the good. . . . The improvement in what used to be known as the condition of the people has been remarkable. . . . But for the first time for 300 years a popular movement in England has produced an impulse to suppress personal liberty rather than to assert it. . . . If we have traded our freedom for the material advantages of democracy we have made a bad bargain [for] there is plenty of evidence that democracy is incompatible with freedom. (Law 1950: 180–4)

Law, later Lord Coleraine, had Northern Irish as well as English connections, but his summoning up of public school days to connote a vanished ease develops a motif that is central to a specifically English myth of education. Whereas in Scotland the dominant myths had to do with opportunity and a certain egalitarianism, in England they centred on nostalgia for the experience of an elite education – its sights, sounds and melancholia – against which the present, the era of the masses, is judged and found wanting. Particularly galling, from this point of view, is the intrusion of 'government' ever more widely into 'the daily life of the people' and the consequent narrowing of political and personal freedoms. This connection of social democracy with attacks on freedom, presented often in ways that were linked to yearnings for past glory and polemics against present-day mediocrity, provided the dominant tone for a popular conservative critique of the welfare state. It also provided a rationale for rejecting any modification of the 1944 settlement in a more radical direction, and in this sense offered a perspective from which to denounce threats against public schools, comprehensive reorganization and professionally driven curriculum change. The existence of such a privileged-libertarian mindset did not mean that Conservatives tried to unravel the settlement, but consistently expressed at party conferences (Gamble 1974) and voiced by Conservative intellectuals such as Angus Maude, it meant that attitudes towards the welfare state were never entirely consensual. Leaders like Macmillan may have supported post-war reform, but in the commitments of the Conservative Party rank and file and of part of its intellectual cadre a different passion was at work. Here there remained a deep residuum of scepticism, and a conviction that expansion and a decline in standards were closely linked. Certainly, the Conservative hope, expressed in a 1945 party conference resolution, that secondary modern schools would become places of experiment, did not survive the 1940s.

To one aspect of the 1944–7 settlement, however, Conservatives were swiftly and *en masse* converted: the grammar school. The establishment of free, local-authority-supported selective secondary education benefited middle-class children. As McKibbin puts it, 'denied the right to buy places at grammar school by the 1944 Act, the middle class won them instead by examination', so that the proportion of 'free places' won by working-class children was no higher in 1950 than in 1914 (McKibbin 1998: 260–2). In relation to both primary and secondary education, middle-class parents swiftly proved adept at working the post-settlement system to their children's advantage. Jackson and Marsden describe a Yorkshire middle-class community secure 'in their command of all ranges of state education', able to make informed and accurate judgements about which state schools would best advantage its children, and in the process abandoning the private schools of which an earlier generation had made use (Jackson and Marsden 1962). Grammar schools had become the jewel in the middle-class educational crown. They came to represent not just avenues of educational opportunity but ideal, well-ordered communities and were by the early 1950s being fiercely defended against reform. By 1951, by which time the Labour Party had shifted to a position in favour of the multilateral schools, Conservatives were 'deploring any attempt to replace the tripartite system' (Craig 1982: 184).

2

The Golden Age?

Eric Hobsbawm calls the 1950s the start of capitalism's golden age, 'when even weak economies like the British flourished and grew' (1994: 274). United against communism, the societies of the West lived at peace with each other, and new international organizations emerged to harmonize the economic and social policies of capitalist states. Production increased rapidly. Rising wage levels allowed higher levels of mass consumption, thus sustaining the long boom. State spending – military and social – was likewise both an effect of economic expansion and throughout the period a perceived means of supporting it. Governments throughout the 'developed' world worked in the belief that 'more and better education was both desirable in itself and at the same time one of the most important factors in economic growth' (Papadopoulos 1994: 38). Accordingly, education spending increased at an unprecedented speed – between 1951 and 1975, roughly the period marked out by Hobsbawm, spending on education rose from 6.5 per cent to 12.5 per cent of public expenditure, from 3.0 per cent to 6.2 per cent of GDP (Lowe 1993; Simon 1991). In the process, despite the scepticism of some on the right, education became from the mid-1950s onwards a policy area of relative consensus, where those concerned with economic growth and those committed to increasing levels of educational opportunity could find themselves in agreement. Latent tensions between these positions could be suppressed, 'because expansion seemed to offer an explanation of how several purposes might simultaneously be achieved' (Gray, McPherson and Raafe 1983: 300). In this context, a socialist academic like A. H. Halsey could comfortably work as policy adviser to the Organization for Economic Co-operation and Development (OECD), educationally the most important of the new international policy centres funded by governments, and to widespread agreement formulate the proposition that 'in the modern world economic growth creates popular ability and also supplies the resources to pay for the deserved opportunities of working-class children' (Halsey 1996: 121).

Economic expansion was accompanied by occupational change, with a shift from mining, manufacture and agriculture to service occupations and a decline in the availability of unskilled jobs; the proportion of professional and semi-professional occupations among the workforce was growing – a development whose implications for education were frequently recognized (Crowther Report 1959: 123). Though nursery provision was not expanded (Plowden Report 1967: 116) and though male dominance of the occupational hierarchy was not disturbed (David 1980: 170), women re-entered the workforce in greater numbers, after a period in which they had been encouraged to stay in the home. Black and Irish migrants arrived in Britain to fill vacancies left open by the drift to service sector employment. But none of these developments was evenly spread throughout Britain, nor was employment opportunity equally available to all. Almost all parts of Britain became more prosperous, but some rapidly became more prosperous than others, while the old industries of Northern Ireland, South Wales and the west of Scotland entered a decline that ultimately no policies of regional assistance could avert. In 1965, midway through the golden age, Scotland's growth rate was running at half the British level (Harvie 1993). Northern Ireland – more particularly, its eastern part – entered the last stage of its transformation from a core industrial area to a peripheral region (O'Dowd 1995). Wales, though it benefited greatly from government support for industrial start-up and relocation in the 1950s and 1960s, was by the end of the period once again under economic pressure, especially in the valleys of a southern coalfield that each year became more derelict (Morgan 1981). Even in its strongest regions, however, British economic development did not compare well with the rates of growth of what Sanderson calls the 'competitor nations' of Japan, the USA, France and Germany (1999: 75), a failure which was often tentatively assigned to problems in the education system. 'All these countries', suggested a government White Paper in 1956, 'are making an immense effort to train more scientific and technical manpower and . . . we are in danger of being left behind' (1956: 4). Thus, underlying the commitment to educational expansion were anxieties about competitiveness, and a perception that education was an area that was both a key to improved performance and a seriously underdeveloped sector of national life.

Class, Race, Generation

The pace and unevenness of economic change raised problems for education. Changes in the occupational structure created a greater demand for higher levels of education and certification. Lowe (1993) argues that it was this demand, as much as government planning, which drove the expansion of higher education in the 1960s; other evidence suggests that it fuelled parental discontent with restricted access to a grammar school education, and to public examination (Rubinstein and Simon 1973: ch. 4). But the rising demand for 'opportunity' among newly mobile social groups was not the only feature of the 1950s. Occupational shifts mixed with new patterns of settlement to create a geography of polarization. As Cohen has noted in a London-focused account of 'subcultural conflict and working-class community', the 1950s saw a growth in 'highly specialised skilled jobs' in the new industries of the suburbs. The inner city did not lose the 'dead-end, low-paid and unskilled jobs' which had always accounted for a large section of its workforce. But what was now missing from the inner city was 'the labour aristocracy, the traditional source of leadership' which had 'virtually disappeared' along with the 'artisan mode of production' which had sustained skill, diversity, self-organization and relative wealth. As jobs and industry migrated from the city, so a split occurred that separated blighted urban areas from suburban sites of growth (Cohen 1997). Sociologists like Michael Carter in Sheffield and John Barron Mays in Liverpool charted the cultural and educational effects of these changes, and in doing so reidentified some old phenomena, which it turned out that the welfare state had not dispelled – the slum school, and the deprived area. Carter contrasted the new, airy, well-resourced secondary moderns of the Sheffield suburbs, which dispatched their cohorts of students to public examinations, with the much older, crowded, academically unsuccessful schools of the inner city, where the traditions of elementary education were still alive (Carter 1962). Mays identified in central Liverpool, in the midst of national affluence, a 'more or less stabilised minority pattern of living which is . . . in conflict with the norms of the community as a whole' (Mays 1962: 89). Post-war change had done nothing to undermine such 'closely knit pockets of resistance' to the dominant culture, and, just as much as in pre-war years, there remained 'between the ordinary teacher and the child in the down-town school a cultural gap' (1962: 92). Observations like these fed a constant substratum of post-war policy. Underneath the perception of beneficial social and educational change – of measurably substantial improvements in the health of children, for instance (Plowden Report 1967: 76), and rising standards of literacy (Newsom Report 1963) – lay an unyielding, urban-located worry about continuing social and cultural division. 'Some schools have everything', noted the Newsom Report, 'and some virtually nothing' (1963: 250).

To these polarities, related to class and location, should be added others, with sources equally rooted in economic history. The British Nationality Act of 1948 recognized citizens of the Commonwealth as British subjects, entitled to enter, work and settle in the country. The lower-paid regions of the service sector, and older industries like textiles, drew in many such workers, as well as many from Ireland. During the 1950s and early 1960s there developed a concern about the challenges posed by migrants from South Asia and the Caribbean to the cultural integrity of Britain. Official strategies stressed the requirement upon migrants to assimilate to a 'British way of life'. For some groups, this was a possibility. Mary Hickman has suggested that the Catholic Church played an important part in achieving such an assimilation among migrants from Ireland: its schools recreated their students as Catholics rather than as Irish people, and laid no special emphasis on Irish culture and history (Hickman 1995). But no such form of controlled assimilation was available to non-white migrants: urged to assimilate, they found within the educational system a depth of discrimination that denied them the possibility of doing so. They remained, thus, a troubling and excluded presence, on the margins of a system that viewed them as a problem.

Theirs was not the only form taken by cultural difference. In 1954 the novelist Anthony Burgess left England for Malaya. Returning in 1959 he found that England had become 'affluent, telly-haunted, burgeoning with a cult of youth'. Burgess claimed that his novel A Clockwork Orange arose from this perception of a sudden break between generations (Burgess 1983). His concerns were elaborated, less apocalyptically, by other writers. Generational difference was viewed as an effect, perhaps the most spectacular effect, of changes in the patterns of work and consumption. The cultural critic Richard Hoggart had depicted in The Uses of Literacy (1958) the impact of occupational change and new forms of popular culture on settled working-class communities. By the end of the decade he was much in demand as a contributor to official policy documents that sought to understand the patterns of the new. In the 1960 Albemarle Report on the Youth Service his influence is clear, and the distinctive note of post-war social interpretation is struck:

> The society which adolescents now enter is in some respects unusually fluid. Old industries change their nature as new processes are adopted;

new industries appear and help shift the location of industry itself.... A series of Education Acts are causing some movement across class and occupational boundaries....British society is beginning to acquire greater mobility and openness.... As the changes develop so old habits, old customs, old sanctions, old freedoms and responsibilities will be called into question....In such a world young people are between conflicting voices. They can sense a contradiction between what they are assured at school are this society's assumptions, and much they are invited...to admire once they leave [this] sheltered environment. (Albemarle Report 1960. 260–1)

In this perspective, there was an emerging generational conflict over cultural and moral meanings and values, which had strong implications for schooling. Central to the conflict, according to Albemarle, was the new economic status of young people: young workers had more money, and were targeted as consumers by a growing commercial popular culture, which reached out also to those still at school. Others agreed: there were new patterns of culture and consumption among youth; the social researcher Mark Abrams described them as 'proletarianization' – the spread of popular culture across social classes – and 'Americanization' (Abrams 1959), tendencies which were drastically different from those of the pre-war period. Likewise, among children, there was a break from the paternalism of officially directed children's culture. The most convincing evidence here comes from the experience of television. When independent, commercial television began broadcasting in 1955, children deserted the BBC in hundreds of thousands. They preferred ITV's mix of Anglo-American adventure stories and American cartoons to what one market researcher called the BBC's 'atmosphere of a kindly middle-class nursery' with its output of adaptations of 'classic' novels and educative magazine shows (Buckingham et al. 1999). These preferences were indicative of a wider shift. The Scottish 6th Advisory Committee in 1947 had criticized the youth culture of the inner cities for its barbarous language and Americanized cultural preferences; by the 1950s such criticism was widespread. Many educationalists believed that children had rejected Britain for America, tradition for novelty, established values based on careful adult evaluations of children's needs for the instant gratification of children's wants. The sense of a cultural decline, in which childhood was implicated, and the focus on youth culture as a battleground of opposing forces, were commonplaces of the period, and formed a striking counterpoint to the optimistic discourses that attended educational expansion. Far from the ideals of a Wilkinson – or a Law – the popular film *The Blackboard Jungle* presented the school as a battleground of antagonistic values and cultures; and when in the Manchester of the late 1950s the DJ Jimmy Saville began his lunchtime sessions at the Plaza, and the neighbouring schools and colleges began to empty, he prepared a standard answer for complaining headteachers that went to the heart of the battle: 'If you make your school more attractive than my dancehall, you can keep them' (Haslam 1999). Faced with this explicit conflict, educationalists developed a troubling sense of generational apartness, as if the distance between school and the cultures of youth could not be bridged.

Other kinds of diversity were older in their origin. For the most part, the Welsh language depended for its survival on rural society. Gareth Elwyn Jones notes the post-war difficulties of the Welsh countryside, in the form of the decline of small farming, and outward migration (1990: ch. 9). But, however much the economic and social policies of governments brought on the crisis of rural Wales, in education they were willing to sponsor the Welsh language, which was its most distinctive cultural feature. The 1951 census had revealed a dramatic decline in the number of Welsh-speakers since the previous census in 1931 (G. E. Jones 1997: 182). Partly in response, the Welsh Department of the Ministry of Education published a booklet on *The Curriculum and the Community in Wales* which suggested that the 'prime inheritance' of Wales lay in its language; and a Welsh Office circular of 1953 urged 'Welsh education authorities and schools to visualise Wales as a bilingual country' (G. E. Jones 1990: 194). In response to parental pressure, the first bilingual secondary school was opened in 1956, and three more in 1962 (1990: 195). As Jones remarks, there was 'no conscious policy of repression of the Welsh language in education in the twentieth century' (G. E. Jones 1997: 144). On the contrary, policy-makers demonstrated an increasing, practical sympathy for it; the comprehensive school was problematic for civil servants and politicians, the language much less so – 'Wales is allowed to be different' (G. E. Jones 1990: 195).

In Northern Ireland the relationship of government to national culture(s) was of course more difficult, and there issues of nationality and statehood continued to be fought out on the grounds of education. Schooling was divided into two separate spheres, with very different systems of funding, and entirely different attitudes to the Northern Irish state. State – that is to say, Protestant – schooling was better funded and strongly policed by Loyalist politicians (Farren 1992). Catholic education was firmly under the control of the church, which resisted any attempt by state inspectors to influence its procedures, while also ensuring that its schools were not subject to the influence of Catholic laity (O'Connor 1993: 312). Refusing the

Stormont government's offers of financial assistance in return for a stronger government role in the running of the school, the church tried to solve its problems through what the Republican activist Bernadette Devlin called a 'mass movement' of fund-raising within the Catholic community. In this way, the loyalties of Catholic populations to a separate education system were secured. Under the authority of the church, the schools defended a particular version of Irishness, 'militantly Republican' in the midst of a government system which, though it sought occasionally to suppress manifestations of Irish identity, was on the whole forced into a kind of unwilling tolerance (Devlin 1969: 63).

The start of the 'golden age,' then, was a time not only of economic and educational expansion but also of difficulties both continuing and emerging around social polarization, cultural and generational difference and nationality. These were sites whose conflicts ran deep, and flowed towards further turbulence, rather than calm resolution. What is more – to pursue the metaphor further – they flowed through the public sector, whose growing workforce was charged with controlling them, and was thus placed at what became in the 1960s and 1970s some central points of social and cultural disturbance.

Conservatism and equal opportunity

For the first part of the golden years, between 1951 and 1964, Britain was ruled by Conservative governments. From 1954 onwards, these governments, accepting the prevailing wisdom about the necessity of education spending, greatly increased the resources available. In the process, early Conservative doubts about the excessive costs of education ebbed away, as spending ministries, including education, fought and won a battle with the Treasury (Glennerster 1995: 78). When it came to office in 1951, Churchill's government had immediately cut spending on education, with serious effects on the programme of replacing old school buildings and relieving overcrowding (1995: 76). In 1953, when funding the war in Korea had drained government reserves, Butler, by then Chancellor of the Exchequer, had worried that 'the size of our educational apparatus is in excess of our resources' and that 'we are attempting to do much more than we can in the long run really afford' (Dean 1992: 15). As the reality of economic growth dawned upon government, concerns like these diminished. Conservatives no longer entertained the possibility – floated by Churchill in the early 1950s – of rolling back the 1944 Act, to the point of reducing the school-leaving age once again to 14 (Dean 1992: 18).

On the contrary, driven by a rising school population and by a demand for education expressed in a higher staying-on rate post-16, resources were increased. Some of the unfinished business of 1944–7 was completed. In Northern Ireland, the school-leaving age was at last raised to 15, and the secondary modern sector was expanded at the expense of all-age schooling to the point at which by the late 1950s the numbers of students in secondary modern schools exceeded those in grammar schools (Cowan Report 1976: 92). In England and Wales likewise there was by the late 1950s a building programme aimed at eliminating the all-age village schools that still, in 1954, educated more than 600,000 children. According to Simon's figures, in 1953–4, public expenditure on education across Britain was 3 per cent of GDP; by 1964–5, when the Conservatives left office, it had risen to 4.3 per cent (Simon 1991: 599).

The Conservative commitment to expansion was underpinned by the collective wisdom of the policy elites in other Western countries that investment in education was causally connected to economic growth. It was also based firmly on strong principles of differentiation, between various types of elite education and those available to the mass of students. In this respect, Britain resembled most other advanced capitalist societies, which were likewise committed simultaneously to expansion and differentiation. Britain was exceptional, however, in the extremes of educational achievement to which its policies led – in 1961, for instance, 73 per cent of students in England and Wales left without having ever attempted a public examination, and over 90 per cent of Scottish school-leavers left at 15, without qualifications (Aldcroft 1992: 36; Harvie 1993: 79). In such a situation, where educational and occupational destinies were decided at an early point, the fairness and efficiency of mechanisms of educational selection came to assume an enormous significance. As Halsey and his colleagues argued, 'the selective stakes became higher' after 1944; fee-paying in local authority grammar schools had ended, and middle-class and working-class children now competed for the same restricted supply of places (Halsey et al. 1980: 202). In this competitive process, there was little evidence of increasing opportunity for working-class students. Although the 'graduate output' of each social class was rising, in relative terms inequalities remained 'remarkably stable' (1980: 205). 'The likelihood of a working-class boy receiving a selective education in the middle fifties and sixties was very little different from that of his parents' generation thirty years earlier' (1980: 203); and, in a situation where grammar school education was unevenly available across regions, and more amply provided for boys than for girls, inequalities accumulated to a drastic point. In Simon's summary, 'the opportunity to reach full-time university education for a middle-class boy living in Cardiganshire was roughly 160 times as great as that for a working-class girl living in West Ham' (Simon 1991: 215).

These features of division were identified to policy-makers and to a more general audience both by well-publicized sociological research, and by a series of reports from government advisory committees (e.g. Himmelweit 1954; Floud et al. 1956; Central Advisory Council for Education (England) 1954; Crowther Report 1959). The relationship between class, schooling and opportunity, the inability of the 1944 settlement to make inroads into established patterns of success and failure and the consequent continuing existence of a large pool of untapped educational ability, much of it located in the working class (Robbins Report 1963), dominated public discussion of the school system. Discontent also focused on the methods by which students were assigned to one or another category of school. From the early 1950s onwards, the testing system that was employed for this purpose – in England, the 11+– was criticized as inefficient and unfair (Simon 1953). Selection mechanisms had presupposed that children possessed a fixed quantity of intelligence and that testing accurately measured this quality. Educational psychologists came increasingly to doubt these propositions, and in the process to undermine the Platonically underpinned belief that there existed three distinct types of mind, to which the tripartite system exactly corresponded (Vernon 1957). Yet, to their great political cost, the essential character of educational division and the means by which children were assigned at 11 to its separate parts, were defended by Conservatives. The bedrock of Conservative policy, fervently supported at the base of the party, was the maintenance of the grammar school, the means by which the middle class secured educational opportunity, and the model for many Conservatives of an ordered, purposeful, traditional educational world, which concentrated – as one Conservative minister put it – 'on what was classic and avoided what was fashionable' (Kenneth Pickthorn, quoted in Dean 1992: 25). The government intended to do nothing that would threaten the grammar school – a position which of course also involved it in acting also as apologist for the secondary modern system, and as defender of selective mechanisms.

These commitments led Conservatism into major difficulties, from which its education programme did not recover until the 1970s. On the whole, secondary modern schools were low-status institutions, which did not enjoy the parity of esteem imagined by the makers of the 1944–7 settlement. Conservative policy in the later 1950s hoped to find tactical responses to this problem that would preserve the essential institutions of the selective system. 'There are still too many areas', acknowledged a White Paper of 1958, 'in which it has not yet been possible to give...the secondary modern schools the resources they need.' If the secondary modern could be revitalized, thought ministers – if it could be better funded, if its students could be encouraged to stay on to take public examinations – then perceptions of the school would change, so that parents would come to believe that their children would have a fair start in life (Ministry of Education 1958: 11). Hence the attempt by ministers to present the secondary modern as 'an alternative route to high qualifications and well-paid jobs' (Eccles, quoted in Simon 1991: 185). For this reason, the government endorsed the arguments of the Crowther Report that new forms of examination should be introduced, aimed at the middle 40 per cent of the age group; likewise it accepted the Scottish move towards the introduction in 1962 of a 'Standard' grade exam, and thus broke with the Scottish tradition of linking examinations only to university entrance. In supporting these moves, and in accepting the Scottish and Welsh tendency to maximize the number of students entering grammar school / senior secondary education, the government was committing itself to funding a substantial rise in the proportion of students staying on beyond the age of 15. It was responding to a rising level of demand for certification – but without significantly reshaping the existing pattern of institutions.

Change was not entirely ruled out. Conservatives were willing to tolerate experiments in multilateral, or comprehensive, education provided they did little to disturb the grammar school. In rural and under-populated Anglesey it was happy for there to exist a single, all-purpose secondary school, and on new council estates in Swansea it allowed the opening of multilateral schools, provided they did not try to recruit students from those middle-class catchment areas which were the suppliers of students to the grammar schools (G. E. Jones 1990). This latter policy effectively prevented the local development of comprehensive schools. On a larger scale, the devotion to the grammar school wrecked the Conservatives' capacity to construct a modernized, substantial system of technical education. Secondary technical schools were always the weakest element in the tripartite system, never more than 4 per cent of its number. The facilities they provided were relatively expensive, and the implicit challenge they offered to the mode of education that dominated the grammar school was distrusted by Conservatives (Sanderson 1999: 80–1). In both Scotland and Wales, dominated by the tradition of academic secondary education, they were a rarity. In 1955, the Minister of Education, David Eccles, decided that no new technical schools would be approved in England and Wales, 'unless there was a very strong case' (Simon 1991:

184). Those students who did demonstrate marked technical ability could develop it in the academic context of the grammar school. Those whose technical aptitude was of a more immediately practical kind would be better off in the craft classes of the secondary modern.

Conservative leaders often made attempts to dignify or idealize the educational experience they offered, but in doing so they found themselves returning to precisely the distinctions between mental and manual labour, academic and vocational study, which were the source of their problems. Thus Quintin Hogg, Secretary of State in 1964, portrayed the modern school as one in which each girl and boy would have an education 'tailor-made to their desires'; but at the same time he evoked the physical experience of this education in terms which were firmly vocational and very much in line of descent from the rhetoric of Ellen Wilkinson. The visitor to the school would encounter, he said, 'the pleasant noise of banging metal and sawing wood', 'a smell of cooking with rather expensive cooking equipment', and 'girls and boys getting an education tailor-made to their desires' (McCulloch 1998: 137). But others saw the schools differently. The historian A. J. P. Taylor advised students to 'run away to sea rather than go to secondary modern' (Carter 1962: 5). The judgement of John Brunton, Chief Inspector of Schools in Scotland, was just as harsh. The courses that junior secondary schools provided were 'little more than watered-down versions of the somewhat academic courses which had been found inappropriate for many pupils in senior secondary schools'. Buildings were drab, teachers minimally prepared and less well paid; and pupils bored and uninterested (McPherson and Raab 1988: 358). Levels of student certification were low. As a result, there developed among parents, particularly in new occupational categories, a sense of anxiety about what the secondary modern school offered their children. Media treatment of education often focused on these fears. 'Is your child doomed at secondary modern school?' asked one women's magazine of its readers. 'Is it failure to send John to a new-type Modern School?' asked another (W. Taylor 1963: 164). Looking back from the vantage-point of the late 1960s on this whole experience of low status, examination failure, under-resourcing and parental discontent, the Conservative educationalist Kathleen Ollerenshaw concluded that it had all been a 'disaster' (McCulloch 1998: 139).

Labour

While Conservative policy moved towards unsustainability, the Labour Party developed a 'modernized' argument against selection.

Throughout this period, the Labour Party shared the international conviction that quantitative educational growth offered a simultaneous route to social justice and economic efficiency. In doing so, it was taking a step away from the policies of the 1940s. In the immediate post-war years, Labour had aimed to shape Britain's economic future via a programme of nationalization aimed at least at some of the commanding heights of the economy – transport, heavy industry and the utilities. The National Health Service and education reform were seen in this context as providing safety nets and opportunities, but not as agencies for the fundamental reshaping of society; this was partly why the controversies over selection did not cause a deeper crisis in the party. In the 1950s, policy and the motivation for policy changed. Anthony Crosland's influential book *The Future of Socialism* rejected the idea that the road to social justice passed through the further measures of nationalization prioritized by the left wing of the Labour Party. Crosland sketched a different vision, to which education was more central. In contemporary Britain, economic life was no longer in the direct control of monopolies run by small numbers of the wealthy. Control of the economy had been diffused; economic life was shaped by a mix of public and private interests, and those who managed the activity of firms were more influential, in practical terms, than the shareholders who exercised formal control. In such a society, where powerful inequalities existed still but ownership and inheritance were less important, the most effective forms of socialist politics would be those – such as equal opportunity in education – that increased the social capacities of working-class people, freed them from dependence, and prioritized opportunity to the point where people's occupations and destinies no longer corresponded to their social origins. Such a social order, characterized both by mobility and by the equal sharing of goods like education and health, was Crosland's 'alternative to nationalization as a means of creating a socialist society' (Crosland 1956; Halsey 1996 121). It would also be a more efficient society: higher levels of universal education would provide a skilled workforce, and a better-trained scientific and managerial elite (Centre for Contemporary Cultural Studies 1981: 97).

From positions like these, the Labour Party called for a revision of the 1944 settlement. 'The 1944 Education Act', Crosland wrote, 'set out to make secondary education universal. Yet opportunities for advancement are still not equal' (Crosland 1956: 188). Deploying the findings of sociological research, Crosland argued that 'the class distribution of the grammar-school population is still markedly askew' (p. 188); many working-class children of above-average ability were denied opportunity by the exclusive character of the grammar school; many children of average ability suffered from the 'appallingly low quality of some parts of the state system' (p. 190). Considering the 'divisive and stratifying effect' of this situation, as well as the need to raise the 'average technical ability' of the population, there was no longer a case for selection, and every reason to move to a non-segregated, comprehensive system of schools' (pp. 197–204). Positions like these provided Labour with a new rationale for its policies on comprehensive reorganization, as well as a clear line of divide from Conservatism. Educational reform could be linked to a wider vision of social and economic regeneration than anything that Conservatism possessed, and at the same time could respond to popular frustration. But this did not mean that Labour's policy was entirely coherent. For one thing, as Crosland himself noted, it combined a commitment to reform of the state sector with an inability to agree on any concrete measures relating to the top levels of elite education, the public schools. For another, it combined a rhetoric of urgency with a timescale that was very relaxed: Crosland thought that the creation of a comprehensive system would be a slow business, limited by the supply of teachers and the resources available to build schools. Thirdly, as Michael Young pointed out in his satire *The Rise of the Meritocracy* (1958) reformers took division by 'ability' as a given, and thought about the detail of change in terms which centred on the needs of 'bright' children. Roy Jenkins, in his 1959 election pamphlet *The Labour Case*, insisted that students 'must [still] be divided according to intelligence and aptitude, but the divisions will be less sharp and less final' (Jenkins 1959: 96). Crosland himself wrote of the 'alpha' and 'beta' material with which schools had to deal, and believed that divisions into streams according to ability remained essential (Crosland 1956: 147, 202). This central belief in ability and differentiation helps explain why Labour's presentation of the need for change took a traditional form. In Young's words, 'they made a grammar school first and added the other bits after' (Young 1958: 41). In Ellison's, Labour devised a policy format which advocated the extension not of grammar schools but of the grammar school tradition; via the creation of the comprehensive school and the abolition of the 11+ its benefits would now be made available to many more children (Ellison 1996). Thus Labour's 1964 election promise that it would provide 'a grammar school education for all' was not just a deft piece of rhetoric, but an expression of the intentions and confusions of its leaders (Labour Party 1964). It was a weak basis on which to develop a new school system and it was strangely out of touch with developments under way in schools.

Teachers, Curriculum, Reform

Official policy – expressed by government reports and embodied in the actions of policy-makers – was committed to expansion and modernization. 'Education is a vital part of the nation's capital investment,' stated the Crowther Report (1959: 108). The Newsom Report likewise believed that the 'economic argument' for investment was compelling (1963: 7). On this basis, the reports then proceeded, as policy-makers did throughout the OECD countries, to address quantitative questions of educational input: greater numbers of teachers, whose period of training would be extended; higher overall levels of spending, with extra funds available for particularly deprived areas; a raised school-leaving age; new types of examination. These were crucial decisions, which shaped the education system and the distribution of resources within it. But other, equally important questions – the nature of curriculum, the ways in which teaching and learning should be organized, the ways in which the motivation, attitudes and identities of school students should be shaped – were treated at an official level only in a general and impressionistic way. This was in part a collective intellectual failure of the national policy-making elite. But it was also a systemic failure. The educational systems of Britain were all – to a greater (England) or a lesser (Scotland) extent – based on the principle of indirect control. Governments could set financial limits, could shape by legislation or veto the overall character of institutional provision, and could seek to frame the dominant educational discourses. But they could not secure a grip on the detail of process: the *laissez-faire* policies under which the grammar and public schools had operated had been extended to schooling as a whole; and particular interest groups – local authorities, educationalists advancing progressive ideas, some teacher unions – had established positions entrenched enough to make impossible nationally directed change on matters which had become the traditional preserve of local policy. So when in 1962 the Ministry of Education set up a 'Curriculum Study Group', intended to ponder and influence questions of curriculum and pedagogy, the initiative was defeated by opposition both from teachers' organizations and from local authorities. The development of detailed and practical solutions to problems of schooling had thus to be worked out at a non-governmental level, where not policy-makers but teachers had greater influence. The Schools Council, set up by government in 1964 to disseminate ideas about curricular reform in England and Wales, was dominated by representatives of teachers and it was teachers – through their organizations and as individuals – who had a leading influence on curriculum change.

Autonomy

The position of teachers, throughout Britain, was ambivalent. Classroom autonomy was everywhere at least a rhetorical norm, though in Scotland a system depending on a greater degree of monitoring and control by an active national inspectorate qualified this emphasis. The Scottish Consultative Committee on the Curriculum, established in 1965, was, like the Schools Council, based on an advisory rather than a stipulative approach; but it was much more closely connected to the Scottish Education Department, and much less likely to promote the 'process of experimental trial' that characterized its English counterpart (Ross 1999: 187). In Northern Ireland, the active educational involvement of Catholic priests and Protestant clergy had a similar, but more conservatizing, effect. In England and Wales, autonomy was probably more strongly established. Teachers' leaders there celebrated the values of a school system in which 'a quarter of a million teachers ...are free to decide what should be taught and how it should be taught' (Gould, cited in Grace 1987: 212). 'By the 1950s,' writes Martin Lawn of the educational discourse of the post-war period, 'teachers were praised as the bedrock of the new welfare society, as the foundation of the reconstruction of the education system and as the guardian of the citizenry of the future. Teachers were professionals, fostered by the state, partners in the deliberation of policy' (Lawn 2001: 175). These claims had some basis in institutional and professional change. In England there was a general rise in teachers' levels of qualification towards Scottish norms (Lowe 1997); from 1955, new kinds of teacher education provided a cadre of teachers to work in special education (Warnock Report 1978); from 1960, the length of initial courses of teacher education was expanded to three years. Between 1955 and 1961, equal pay was introduced for women teachers. But, on the other hand, as Grace points out, teachers were poorly paid, and though they worked in conditions of some autonomy they were not in any strategic sense contenders for the label of 'partnership' which the rhetorics of settlement in 1944–7 had conferred upon them (Grace 1988). Nor were they a strong collective force for change: their unions were divided and notably unsuccessful on matters of pay and conditions; in the classroom, most made use of their autonomy to reproduce rather than break from established forms of teaching and learning. This rather self-imposed conservatism was perhaps more prevalent in Wales than England (Gittins Report 1967: 17); certainly, most of the evidence about classroom-based innovative change in the 1950s is English rather than Welsh in origin.

Progressivism

Nevertheless, members of this expanding, somewhat better-qualified teaching force began to rediscover aspects of a pre-war sense of educational possibility which the initial hard labour of educational reform in the 1945–50 period had tended to cover over. Most evident here was the growth among a section of primary teachers of progressive ideas about curriculum and pedagogy. Progressivism was a diverse and complex movement, but it centred fundamentally on three assertions: children were unique individuals; learning was the product of the active relationship between individuals and their environment; learning was best organized through collaboration between students, and between students and their teachers (Cunningham 1988: 20). These beliefs were fervently held. Since the start of the century progressives had contrasted the dull routines of mass education with the possibilities that might be activated if only children could be released from a regime based on harsh discipline, a narrow curriculum – didactically communicated – and a denial of the capacities of the child for creativity, emotional involvement in learning and participation in a community of learners. This was a language far removed from that of economic calculation – it rejected ways of thinking about education that saw it as the preparation of the future labour force. The communication of particular forms of knowledge was less important to it than the development of individual capacities defined in broader terms than those allowed for by the traditions of mass elementary education.

Progressivism, despite these deep criticisms of schooling as it actually existed, had taken root in important sections of the education system. It had supporters in colleges of teacher education, among inspectors at local authority and at national level, and among some local authority administrators. These people formed a loose and persistent pressure group for change, who in a decentralized system found many places in which their ideas could be promoted. Christian Schiller, an HMI (Her Majesty's Inspector) who was also an influential teacher educator, thought as many did in terms of an organized but dispersed and network-like movement, made up of the 'patient and persistent pulling of pioneers, scattered far and wide, each at work in his or her own school, determined to find a way in which their children shall live and learn more abundantly' (Cunningham 1988: 60). Thus in particular areas – Oxfordshire, the West Riding of Yorkshire, Leicestershire – inspectors would work with schools, promoting some ideas, disparaging others (in Leicestershire, the necessity of religious assemblies), creating local networks that seemed both immediately practical, in terms of what they offered teachers as resources for classroom work, and visionary in the sense of the deeper principles they embodied and the example they set.

In this way there had developed among some teachers and among those who framed the strategic discourses of primary schooling, and had some responsibility for its daily operation, a position which was not immediately compatible with economically motivated definitions of educational purpose. Government focus on educational expansion, and on the provision of inputs of a general or quantitative kind, could not repair this disparity. Inasmuch as the education / economy relation was present at all in the progressive discourse, it was in terms of the supposed congruity between the economic requirement for flexible labour, the social and political requirement for the development of 'free', inquiring citizens, and the principles of progressive education. 'We can afford free men and we need them,' wrote one educationalist of the 1960s (James 1968: 35). This was a bold attempt to square a circle of difficulty, but it was not a plausible one, and there remained throughout the golden age an unresolved difference between the purposes ascribed to education by politicians, and those worked for by influential sections of educational opinion.

Constraints

The development of progressivism, and its ability to gain something more than a foothold in primary schools, linked to changes in salary regulations and training arrangements, might suggest that teachers were becoming a more autonomous and self-confident professional group. This was partly true: both primary and secondary schools were slowly and patchily becoming places of greater competence and experiment. But this tendency was heavily qualified by other influences: the claims to a professional identity that was based on classroom autonomy and expertise were contradicted by the everyday pressures of teachers' working lives: official ideologies of primary education stressed the freedom of the teacher and the importance of child-centred and activity-based learning; but in most schools what happened for much of the period this chapter covers was governed by the necessity of preparing children for selective examinations at 11

or 12. Since the exams consisted in most places of 'objective' tests in
the 3 Rs alongside a paper designed to measure 'intelligence', the
curriculum to which they connected was a narrow one, resembling
more that of the old elementary school than of any progressive-
inspired modernized alternative. As Galton and Simon put it, 'the
fate of the junior school and its educational role depended on developments at the upper levels' of the system, and these developments
worked to limit change in primary schools' (Galton et al. 1980: 42).
Thus, the modernization programme discussed at the level of Central
Advisory Committee reports – with its vision of the flexible worker
and the committed citizen – had little chance of being concretely
implemented in a system so starkly geared to segregation at an early
age. Progressivism meant that discourses of educational change
tended to be inflected towards the question of the realization of
individual potential in ways that had a critical edge, and it is this
disparity which has often caught the eye of critical historians (Barnett
1986; Wiener 1981). But in reality it was the pervasive effects of
tripartism which constituted the biggest barriers to change: as
McPherson and Raab note of secondary education in Scotland,
whereas there existed for senior secondary students a clear, if narrowly academic, pathway, for the great majority of (junior) secondary
students, 'there was in effect no national policy' and schools 'had to
do the best they could in the difficult circumstances' (1988: 248). Any
programme of expansion which neglected the depth of these problems
of institutional segregation was unlikely to produce substantial
results.

Nor did the upper levels of the school system – which generally
possessed higher status than primary education – provide resources
for the secure development of teachers' professional identity. Teachers
in grammar and senior secondary schools were separated from their
colleagues in secondary moderns and junior secondaries by a gulf
created by a carefully guarded set of distinctions. Grammar school
teachers possessed claims to high-status knowledge, embodied in
degrees rather than teaching certificates. They tended to belong to
teacher unions (or 'associations') that insisted on their special status,
related to a belief that those who taught in grammar schools had
unique claims to subject expertise and exam-related responsibility.
Secondary modern schools, whatever the hopes of their founders, in
practice swiftly reverted to a curriculum based on the 3 Rs for most
students, and on General Certificate of Education (GCE) exams for
the minority who stayed on at school beyond the school-leaving age
(Dent 1954). Lacking in academic status, they contained a strong
nucleus of teachers who were both relatively militant in trade union

terms, and also determinedly 'masculinist' in their educational orientation. A union for men teachers, the National Association of Schoolmasters, grew in strength, at the expense of the NUT, in the secondary moderns of the late 1950s by contrasting its determination to secure an adequate salary for the male breadwinner with the passivity of the main union, the NUT, which was numerically dominated by women primary teachers. It considered equal pay for women to be 'calculated to injure vitally the interests of schoolmasters and schoolboys' (Seifert 1987: 62) and, as a further part of its appeal to male teachers, distinguished itself rigorously from progressive ideologies of education. It accepted the teacher's role in the terms in which it was given by a divided system, devoted to preparing the majority of students for immediate participation in the workforce. It made few claims to pedagogic expertise, other than those which related to teachers' ability to control and rudimentarily educate these masses. It was exactly such an attitude which Hargreaves (1967) discovered at 'Lumley School' in the north of England and Mays encountered in Liverpool, where the idea 'that children should be encouraged to develop their innate abilities to the utmost extent was neither generally understood nor widely accepted' (Mays 1962: 57).

Culture and Class: the Grammar School

Educational expansion was not then a coherent or a pervasive project. Schooling was a complex space in which varying and contending currents were active. But if it was held together discursively in this period, and if there was a strong connection between different elements of policy and practice, then 'social class' provided some of the cement. A central theme, which ran through official reports, educational research, media commentary and teachers' practice, was the relationship between class and academic success and failure, and this relationship was treated almost as much in cultural terms as in economic. Tawney had addressed in the 1930s questions of the 'soul', 'spirit' and 'temper' of schooling. In 1931 he had written of the 'hereditary curse' of social class that had been visited upon education, and the ways in which this had helped perpetuate 'the division of the nation into classes of which one is almost unintelligible to the other' (Tawney 1973b). Pearl Jephcott in the 1940s had noted the ways in which these perceptions of fine-grained and pervasive cultural difference had been expressed in popular culture: 'when you sit the exam', girls had told her of the grammar school entrance test, 'if you don't go in good clothes they fail you' (Jephcott 1942: 51). For Tawney and

Jephcott, as for many other reformers, the 1944–7 settlements offered some hope that the curse would be lifted. But of course nothing of the sort happened. Working-class disadvantage continued, and inequality, as before, took in some respects a cultural form. A summary of research cited by Silver refers to 'cultural as well as crude material factors: class differences in educational aspirations, occupational orientations, language, intellectual climate and so on' (Little and Westergaard 1964). These factors did not only affect performance in the 11+. They continued, and intensified, after working-class children attained grammar school places. At grammar school, the Central Advisory Council's 1954 report on *Early Leaving* in England discovered, those children of 'semi-skilled' and 'unskilled' workers who were academically successful at 11 were likely to be much less successful than their peers at 16 (Maclure 1979: 238). Similar concerns were expressed in Scotland: at the start of the 1950s two-thirds of students admitted to selective secondary schools had left, uncertificated, by the beginning of their fifth year (Gray et al. 1983: 47). The grammar school, noted Crosland (1956: 189), worked not simply to reflect social inequality but to intensify it; and Himmelweit (1954), seeking to explain the phenomenon, identified a strong teacher bias towards middle-class students. The confidence expressed by thinkers like Marshall that the 1944 system was the embodiment of equal opportunity came to seem misplaced.

This is not to say that the grammar school was of no use to working-class students. For some groups, it had a transformative effect. Many writers on Northern Ireland have underlined how the post-1947 expansion of grammar school education produced from the Catholic community a new middle class. 'Several generations of working-class catholics', writes Fionnula O'Connor about Belfast, 'saw the 11+ . . . as their best chance for progress in an unequal society. Catholic folk wisdom knew that poor protestants had the pick of unskilled labour and could hope for apprenticeships in the shipyard: if poor catholics had the brains for it, education should instead be their salvation: it became a doctrine' (1993: 24). In this case, educational opportunity did not only help create a new middle class. For the Cameron Committee, which investigated the Northern Irish troubles of 1968–9, it also contributed to political conflict, by producing a generation 'much less ready to acquiesce in the acceptance of a situation of assumed or established inferiority than was the case in the past' (Cameron Report 1969: 15). More sympathetic analysts saw the Catholic grammar school of the 1950s and '60s as the matrix of a new intelligentsia and political leadership. According to Mulhern, among the most significant leaders of the civil rights movement of 1968–70, which was both more militant and more orientated towards social issues than the forms of nationalism which had dominated Northern Ireland since partition, were teachers, graduates of the post-1947 system who acted as the 'organic intellectuals' of the working class from which they came (Mulhern 1998). The novelist Angela Carter makes a similar point about England, and attributes the social and political upsurges of the later 1960s to the legislation of 1944, which

> extended the benefits of further education to a select group of kids from working-class backgrounds, picked out on account of how they were extra bright.... And were they grateful? Were they hell! Did they say to themselves, 'God, if it hadn't been for the 1944 Education Act I'd have gone the way of Jude the Obscure'? Never. We simply took what was due to us, whilst reserving the right to ask questions. (Carter 1988: 209)

In these analyses and perceptions, elite institutions are the seedbeds of radical change, or at least of a social fraction which saw its role as to promote social and political transformation. Yet this was never the whole story. The grammar school's overall function had more to do with supplying new and conservative-minded recruits to an expanding middle class than with providing social struggles with radical human resources, and most surveys make this clear (Jackson and Marsden 1962; Greenslade 1976). O'Connor's interviewees insist with special vehemence that Catholic grammar schooling was devoid of any commitment to equality and social justice (1993: 315); its students were exhorted to see themselves as a race apart. In many parts of Northern Ireland in the 1950s, there was no alternative secondary school and the 11+ failures 'ended up weeding the parish priest's garden...or whatever'. Grammar school offered an escape from such a fate, but the few who took it were discouraged from identifying with the many who did not.

Increasingly through the 1950s, these perceptions of a process of social division in which schools were actively implicated were elaborated into a fuller account of how the culture of secondary education served to consolidate and reproduce class differences. The most influential of these accounts came at the end of the period, when Brian Jackson and Dennis Marsden, using data from the 1940s and early 1950s, published their exploration of grammar schooling in West Yorkshire, *Education and the Working Class*. Selection, they argued, was not a once and for all event. It was better understood as a process 'that is at work all the time from the moment the child enters the school to his final leaving' (Jackson and Marsden 1962: 210). In this process, the ways in which the grammar school sought to distance itself culturally from the world of working-class students was immensely important. Jackson and Marsden list them: the uniform which marked out the grammar school student from her neighbours; the insistence in the boys' grammar school on Rugby Union – rather than football or Rugby League – as the centre of the school's sporting life; the objection that grammar schools raised to their students' attending local youth clubs; the honours board that listed entrants to university; the school cadet corps; morning assembly; the public decorum which did not include the eating of the chips or, for girls, the casting off of gloves. These cultural processes, in which the values, activities and meanings associated with middle-class life were placed above those familiar to working-class students, formed part of a process of attrition whereby such students were 'sieved out' of grammar school education: the 'wastage' of working-class talent was not in this view so much a result of deficiencies in parenting or community life as a low-level form of class warfare, and those students who retained a loyalty to family and neighbourhood life against the demands of the school were its casualties.

Alternatives

Jackson and Marsden, like many other educationalists, concluded that the major problem facing education was how it could be opened to the working class. But the ways in which they framed their answers were significantly different from those of a Crosland or a Jenkins, and indicative of a strengthening current of more radical opinion. For them, the problem was not only one of securing greater access, nor of finding more effective ways of compensating for working-class deficiency. What was necessary, rather, was a rethinking of what constituted education itself, in ways which were much more appreciative of the already existing achievements of working-class culture. On this basis, Jackson and Marsden criticized the uses of 'intelligence': it was a term 'immensely useful' to the processes of bureaucratic sorting. But it 'vastly simplified' human situations, and provided no means of responding to the linguistic and cultural complexities which were already present in 'working-class living' (1962: 213). 'The educational system we need' was one that was more sensitive to these meanings, and that understood them as forms of understanding and expression providing resources for education, not obstacles to it. Education in this sense had to be recast as a process of cultural dialogue, and central to it was the work of the teacher, as

someone who was capable of understanding, appreciating, and responding to the cultures of working-class students.

Education and the Working Class synthesized and brought to
public attention issues which were already animating some teachers.
Since the late 1940s they had been attempting to develop a form
of education in secondary modern schools that, like the option
favoured by Jackson and Marsden, was based on dialogue rather
than on cultural imposition. The best known of them was Edward
Blishen, novelist, author of *Roaring Boys* and supporter of the pro-
comprehensive journal *Forum*. In the 1950s, Blishen had begun to
link his pedagogical ideas to a more general thinking about educational reform in which questions of cultural difference and its negotiation were at the centre. For Blishen, the basic relational framework
of the school world, even that of the secondary modern, was one in
which opposites collided:

> The staff in their neat suits, even in their old sports jackets and flannels,
> looked like visitors from another world. And in fact, in Stonehill Street,
> the two worlds clashed. You couldn't help seeing it that way. The
> masters and the boys had very different backgrounds. And even though
> a teacher managed in the end to master the manners of his charges, it
> was always an act of mastery and never one of intimacy. Even the most
> experienced members of staff would dismiss the boys as barbarous
> Celts might have been discussed by a Roman garrison....I was para-
> lysingly aware that most of the boys hated school with a coarse, sullen
> hatred. (Blishen 1955: 42)

In short, the attitude of the secondary modern teachers seemed to
endorse the judgement of one of Blishen's old colleagues from a prep
school where he once taught. 'This Education Act' was 'rather like
these big classical concerts in sports arenas. Trying to fetch along the
wrong people' (p. 182). Elite educators, like the neat-suited teachers,
thus agreed that education post-1944 was doomed to repeat a cycle of
conflict and failure. Blishen himself offered no large-scale alternative
to such a grim prognosis, but throughout the book he focused on
moments – art classes, drama periods, school trips – in which there
occurred some kind of hard-won connection between the cultures of
students and the broader knowledge and experience that the school
could offer. Out of these encounters he improvised a pedagogy, based
at least to some extent on a learned habit of dialogue:

> You had to be simple, down-to-earth. You hadn't to surrender to their
> own coarse scepticism, but you had to respect it, to go delicately and
> tactfully about developing new attitudes. And you couldn't develop a

single new attitude without giving some practical proof that it was also valid, not a mere pious, verbal figment. (p. 256)

Martin Lawn, writing about the secondary modern school in the 1950s, suggests that Blishen's problems, and his ways of resolving them, were not unique. The old elementary school lived on – not just in unreconstructed buildings, but in the work habits of senior staff, and in a system of discipline that relied heavily on the beating of children. Even, as David Hargreaves noted, where harshness was replaced by a degree of informality in the relations between teachers and pupils, there remained in secondary modern schools 'a non-academic, custodial atmosphere' in which life at school was seen by both parties as 'a necessary evil' and potential conflict resolved by a 'minimal imposition of demands upon one another' (Hargreaves 1967: 85–7). No national injunctions to experiment and reform could transform these patterns. But, all the same, the working relations of the secondary modern school did, Lawn suggests, open up at least a small space in which a more liberal and child-centred curriculum could develop, attentive and to some extent sympathetic to students' experience (Lawn 1996). If we accept Lawn's account, then what was embodied in Blishen's style of teaching – not commonplace, but not completely idiosyncratic either – was one of the more dialogic and pedagogically productive ways in which cultural difference was recognized in the 1950s.

These questions were not explored only in individual classrooms, nor among teachers alone. J. B. Mays, like many reformers, had called, Tawney-like, for a general educational programme to close 'those gaps of habit across which our two nations have gazed at each other in fundamental incomprehension of each other's way of life' (Mays 1962: 93); and a realization that educational change needed to involve cultural revaluation as well as wider forms of access to secondary education was also, sometimes, part of labour movement politics. When, in 1955, Labour members of the Swansea Education Committee met the Minister of Education to press their long-delayed proposals for comprehensive reform, they argued not just that comprehensivization would make available a 'grammar school education for all', but that it would also involve a recasting of culture. Rose Cross, chair of the committee, argued that, out of school, students did 'not ordinarily divide themselves into secondary modern and grammar groups'. Schools should learn from this. 'If there was to be a common culture', she said, and a 'common means of communication', then there needed to be a school 'system which did not strengthen and deepen social divisions'. To which David Eccles, the Minister, replied that her arguments were not educational but social (G. E. Jones 1990: 73). Eccles rejected the Swansea proposals, but, as his criticism suggests, there were circulating within the movement for reform arguments which went beyond questions of access to embrace a broader set of positions about social and cultural change. For working-class students to be successfully educated, what counted as culture – the central set of meanings and values which the school tried to inculcate – required alteration. This claim was never a commonplace of the Labour Party's programme – if it had been, later events would have turned out differently. But it did become the argument of an important minority on the British left, and a preoccupation of teachers associated with the New Left which, critical of both the Labour Party and orthodox communism, developed after 1956 (Samuel 1989; Dixon 1991). Raymond Williams, in *The Long Revolution* (1961), argued on this basis for a transformation of curriculum content; and three years later, in *The Popular Arts*, Stuart Hall and Paddy Whannel argued, more systematically than Blishen had done, and with greater attention to the changing character of post-war society, for a programme of curriculum reworking.

The Popular Arts was the first significant educational attempt to address what had changed in British culture and society since the 1940s. The book established the beginnings of a new agenda, in which the central project was not to educate Wilkinson's 'noble race' – a culturally uniform population, of 'British stock' – but rather to cope with a bewildering collection of changes that had to do with occupational mobility and lifestyle. Hall and Whannel's work, like Blishen's, grew out of the 'sobering' experience of teaching in urban secondary moderns – in Brixton in Hall's case – when they had become 'acutely aware of the conflict between the norms and expectations of formal education and the complexities of the real world which children and young people inhabit' (Hall and Whannel 1964: 13). A revolution in communications, centring on the development of television as a mass medium, had linked with 'changes in the attitudes of young people' based on their increased involvement in consumption and in commercially organized leisure, to transform social life. There was now a 'teenage culture', an area of 'common symbols and meanings shared in whole or in part by a generation' (p. 273): Britain had changed and what happened in youth culture was both the best index of change, and a central part of it. It was a transformation which was reshaping the lives of students, yet schools were ill equipped to make curricular sense of it. They still demanded of students a conformity to traditional values: they expected students to accept particular gender roles, or occupational positions, or moral attitudes whose grip had been loosened by social and cultural shifts. But this was an impossible task, and the attempt to carry it out left teachers 'unmercifully exposed' (p. 22). Their characteristic response had been a negative one: they blamed the difficulties of the school on the providers of mass culture, and sought through censorship and rigid control to suppress its influence. This was a dead-end. The only productive educational strategy was one which, rather than picking a hopeless fight with the influence of 'modern forms of communication', sought to engage in classroom exploration of it. As another South London teacher, John Dixon, put it, 'there exists not merely this sort of elite culture... but some different kind of culture which it is necessary to seek out by going into other people's experience' (Dixon 1961: 315). The process of 'seeking out', which amounted to a willingness to recognize, positively evaluate and make sense of working-class youth cultures, was to influence greatly the generation of teachers entering urban secondary schools in the later 1960s.

Cultural pathologies

These emerging positions, though, were not the main kind of response to cultural and social change. Culturally, educational practice set itself against the new, particularly when it spoke in an American accent. The NUT strongly supported a campaign in the early 1950s against the import of American horror comics (Barker 1984) to which Edward Blishen offered his own kind of support: he tore up the comics that his students brought to class, 'signs of the forces that made Stonehill School so reluctant to be educated' (Blishen 1955: 91). Later, in 1960, R. A. Butler, by now Home Secretary, spoke of the 'evils' which accompanied prosperity, and of a 'moral crisis in the young' (Butler 1961: 5). In this he was joined by the NUT, whose General Secretary depicted 'schools and homes' as 'oases constantly threatened by the surrounding desert' (Hall and Whannel 1964: 21), while in Scotland the Educational Institute of Scotland (EIS) brought out a troubled pamphlet on 'Sex and violence in modern media' (1961). In Wales, the movement to establish separate Welsh-language schools as a central part of the state system also drew strength from fears about the effects of a modernity that was borne along by Anglicization. In all of these responses, the school was defined as the custodian of traditional values, against the new. But, as Mays suggested, this was something of a hopeless role. The school might try to embody and communicate a version of national tradition, but 'how many of the older girls, dressed in their uniforms during the day, don tight-fitting skirts and go out jiving in the evenings, and what do they then think of country dancing and songs about cuckoos and Linden Leas?' (Mays 1962: 91).

Nor did mainstream education share the impulse of Hall and Whannel, Dixon and Blishen to enter into dialogue with the cultures inhabited by students. On the contrary, in the understandings of most educators, working-class culture inhabited the lower depths: 'you've struck the bottom of the barrel here,' teachers at Lumley told Hargreaves (1967: 86). Mays thought that the school, seeking to 'transmit the generally accepted national culture', was 'fighting against both social conditions and the related attitudes of inhabitants' (1962: 10). The Newsom Report in 1963 coupled its observations about an 'unrealized pool of talent' among students with the insistence that what left this talent unrecognized and untended was the masking effects of 'inadequate powers of speech and the limitations of home background' (1963: 3). Basil Bernstein, the most influential educational sociologist of the 1960s, produced in his early work an account of cultural difference – stressing the conflict between the 'restricted' linguistic codes of working-class life and the 'elaborated' codes of middle-class and public discourse – that was equally structured by a model of deficit (Bernstein 1971). It was these positions, rather than more dialogic ones, which matched the attitudes of most teachers.

Nowhere was the conflict between a normative school culture and a pathologized school population demonstrated more clearly than in attitudes towards migrant students from Ireland, the Caribbean and South Asia. To many of those living in an established and relatively homogeneous culture, the presence of newcomers was literally shocking. When the Guyanese teacher Beryl Gilroy eventually found a job in a London primary school, the first class she met 'uttered a gasp' and dived under their tables (Gilroy 1976: 46). Elsewhere, responses were less ingenuous, and took on a hostile edge – as Ian Grosvenor's account of the politics of race and education in Birmingham graphically demonstrates. Irish children, complained the local NUT association in 1963, 'lacked any social training or habits and appear to be allergic to the truth and also to soap and water'. West Indian students, wrote the city's Chief Inspector of Schools in 1965, spoke a 'base patois'. They lacked 'culture in the home', and as a result did not 'understand our wider conception – the inner cohesion of a co-operative, self-governing community, based on trusting and mutually respectful ... relationships' (Grosvenor 1997: 121, 119). In positions like these, the ideal educational community of the 1940s lived on, but now less as a social ideal than as a xenophobic marker of

Britishness. Conflicts around 'proletarianized' generational values had already weakened the capacity of the school to live up to its cohesive ideal. Now migrant groups presented a new challenge, and posed questions about education's capacity for responding to cultural and linguistic difference. The initial responses of educators were panicky in tone and assimilationist in content. Teachers' unions and local policy-makers were agreed that immigrant children should be dispersed through the school system so as to reduce pressures on individual schools, so that they did not become 'purveyors of an immigrant instead of a British culture' (Chessum 1997: 423). Head-teachers refused to accept more than a handful of migrant students, even though there were spare places at their schools (Chessum 1997). At a national level, this position was endorsed – the proportion of migrant children at a school was not allowed to rise above 30 per cent – and accompanied by an insistence that 'a national system cannot be expected to perpetuate the different values of immigrant groups' (Commonwealth Immigrant Advisory Council (1964), quoted in Grosvenor 1997: 50).

Dispersal of migrant children was implemented without regard to parents' wishes, and led to resistance from migrant organizations – the Indian Workers Association saw it as 'a policy to destroy the national and cultural identity of the immigrant children' (Grosvenor 1997: 168). Later in the decade, Caribbean parents in Haringey organized their own protests, pointing out that 'assimilation' involved an assumption that black children *en masse* were ineducable, and that black people could only be integrated if they were in minorities and prepared to give up their cultures (T. Carter with Coussins 1986: 85–6). These were probably the first explicit, argued, politically organized responses to the mono-culturalism of English schools. Their emergence added to the pressures that the post-1944 system was now beginning to face – not only for expansion, and for the end of selection, but also for curriculum reform that would respond to cultural change and diversity, and in doing so require of the school a new cultural role.

Matters Unresolved

The legislation of 1944–7 had sketched many possibilities – some more firmly than others. In the two decades following the legislation, it became clear which possibilities would be developed, and which would remain as mere sketches, never to be realized as central parts of the new system. Into this latter category fell technical education:

part-time compulsory education in county colleges for young workers was a promise that was not kept; the technical schools never became an important part of the system, least of all in Scotland, Wales and Northern Ireland. Likewise, the modern school – the school for the mass of the student population – did not attain the parity of esteem which its designers had imagined, and the relationship between academic success, occupational destiny and social origins remained almost as strong as ever. In other terms, the more far-reaching elements of settlement rhetoric were substantially modified by enduring features of British social and political life: the preferences of elites for an academic curriculum, rather than a technical one; the status enjoyed by the grammar school even among Labour local authorities; the routines of mass education and the beliefs of teachers. For most students, and most teachers, schooling was about the basics of literacy, numeracy and socialization. It was endured without enthusiasm; it was a place riddled with teacher–student antagonism; it was something if not as Taylor suggested to be run away from, then at least to be left quickly behind.

But the dominant features of the system were none the less subject to a further dynamic of change, pointing towards a revision of the post-war settlement. The 1944–7 legislation may have embodied the hierarchies favoured by administrative elites. But the context of its implementation was a social and political situation in which forces antipathetic to elitism remained strong. Wartime had consolidated the strength of the labour movement: the demands for social security and opportunity that were at the core of trade union and Labour policies were rarely translated into bold demands for particular institutions and procedures, nor into active campaigning, but they constituted all the same a threshold of expectation below which even Conservative governments could not let provision slip, as well as a political resource upon which those pressing for more radical educational change could call.

At the same time, there grew, alongside the social and political presence of the labour movement, a different kind of uneasiness with the system that 1944–7 had created. Although parents of grammar school students consistently and vocally opposed comprehensive reform, other parents – probably the majority – were much less satisfied. Parental opinion was not explicitly motivated by issues of social justice, but it was shaped by an increasing discontent with the limited opportunities for certification, and therefore for social advance, that the secondary modern schools offered. Conservatism, however much it maintained a public belief in the virtues of the grammar school, would not ignore this persistent level of discontent, and tried to find ways of accommodating it within the tripartite system. But in this it was unsuccessful, and until well into the 1970s lacked a credible programme. In its effective absence, other forces dominated.

There was a further unintended consequence of post-war expansion that served to unravel the alliances established around the 1944–7 legislation. The public-sector teaching force grew in size – in England its numbers rose from 175,000 in 1946 to 294,000 in 1964 (Simon 1991: 579). Its members lived with the daily consequences of under-funded reform, in the context of chronic difficulties of teacher supply. In this situation their trade-unionism became stronger, fed by a slowly increasing discontent, especially over salaries – relative to comparable groups of workers, teachers' levels of pay declined in the 1950s (Seifert 1987). Grievances in this area intersected with others: com-pared with professional groups such as lawyers and doctors, teachers lacked both a cohesive corporate identity and any power to determine what constituted professional standards and qualifications. During the 1950s, therefore, teachers' unions – the EIS in Scotland, the NUT and NAS in England and Wales – began to edge away from the conservatism of the immediate post-war years, when the only major industrial action threatened by the NUT was against the efforts of a Labour Council in Durham to make teachers join a trade union (Seifert 1987). The year 1961 saw the first substantial strike action since the 1920s, organized by teachers in the west of Scotland. Their protests concerned pay – which was always a central focus – and a cluster of other issues that related both to the conditions of their work and to wider issues of status: the lack of a general teaching council that might secure self-governing status; unsatisfactory negotiating arrangements that seemed to undermine the role of teachers' unions as effective collective agencies; pension rights; government proposals for increased non-graduate entry to teaching. In the same period, teachers in England and Wales organized milder forms of protest, over pay. Thus teachers pursued a 'partnership' with government – through which they sought to influence aspects of reform, especially those concerning teachers' status, training and autonomy – at the same time as they became more inclined to take trade-union forms of action over immediate issues. This unplanned and to some extent contradictory combination of strategies was central to educational politics in the 1970s and 1980s and was partly responsible for setting teachers and governments at odds with each other.

Finally, the 1944–7 settlement was dissolved by a strange articula-tion of economic and cultural change. The dynamic of educational expansion was to draw students from previously excluded groups into schooling, and into the system of certification at some level – the school as a system of containment and mass non-certification could not endure. This was not to say that policy-makers and teachers embarked between 1951 and 1964 on large-scale reform – they did not, and inertia was one of the distinctive features of the secondary system. But schools were nevertheless drawn into a process of cultural encounter, which occurred in parallel with the growth of professional influence: some kinds of power, especially over curricula and pedagogy, were available to teachers. Sections of the teaching force, and those who educated it or strove to establish educational agendas, were committed to finding classroom-based ways in which schools could respond to the cultures and interests of students. What occurred when they did so was a kind of cultural transvaluation. From being regarded as a problem and a deficit, the cultures of subordinate groups became for some sections of the teaching force, especially those linked to the developing left intelligentsia, a resource which pedagogy and the curriculum had necessarily to take into account. In the process, what counted as education was no longer taken as given: the confidence of an Eliot, or a Holmes, that elite education embodied central human values, was not shared by those who worked in mass education for radical change, and education's twin cultural role, of inculcating elite cultures and of organizing the mass of students round a version of the national culture, was called into question. And in these slender signs – constructed in individual classrooms, popularized in some sort in conference interventions, school textbooks, theoretical statements – lay more seeds of future conflict.

3

Expansion, Experiment, Conflict

Throughout the 1960s, and well into the 1970s, education in the 'developed' world still inhabited the golden years. Public expenditure on education rose rapidly in almost all advanced capitalist countries. Britain's educational growth rate was less spectacular than many northern European states but was significant none the less (Aldcroft 1992: 23). Its share of the national income was 4.1 per cent in 1965, more than double what it had been in 1940 (Halsey 1988: 241). For the next ten years, it continued to rise, faster than ever. In real terms, education spending in 1975 was three times higher than in 1948 (Aldcroft 1992: 22). Much of this increase was explained by the extra numbers which the system catered for, with an expansion in higher education, the raising of the school-leaving age to 16 in 1972, and a steady rise in the numbers of students involved in education to 18. But expansion also involved higher levels of spending on each student. Teacher–pupil ratios were much lower in the new comprehensive schools, which the Labour government encouraged from 1965, than in the secondary moderns that they replaced (Simon 1991: 581).

As we have seen, expansion involved new kinds of education, as well as quantitative development. The project of educating the mass of students to a higher level than previously entailed a rethinking of educational programmes, so that they could more effectively respond to what Papadopoulos calls 'the diversified needs of their vastly expanded and variegated clientele' (1994: 59). Rethinking required experimentation, both in the sense of the mapping out at national level of untried policy directions, and in terms of the local development of curricula and pedagogies, in ways that were prompted by national policy guidelines, but which were also inspired by a diversity of social, cultural and educational objectives not fully compatible with government intentions. Government marshalled resources for education, and decided the kinds of institutional structure in which schooling took place. But beyond this, as Papadopoulos recognizes, education developed under its own dynamic, with the theme, ethos and detail of policy being shaped, if that is not too definite a term for the diffuse forms in which change took place, by professional communities – especially teachers, teacher educators and local authorities. In Britain, this policy drift was institutionalized by the councils and committees set up in the 1960s which formalized professional influence over the curriculum, and other aspects of teaching.

The years of this chapter saw the revision of the 1944–7 settlement. The period of compulsory education was extended to 16 in the early 1970s; with the introduction of the Certificate of Secondary Education (CSE) and Standard Grade exams, much larger numbers of secondary school students were entered for public examination. Tripartism ceased to be the dominant model of secondary education. In most parts of Britain selection at 11 or 12 was ended: in 1965, 92 per cent of students in state secondary education were in schools organized along tripartite lines; by 1976, comprehensive schools accounted for 76 per cent of the secondary population. These changes, of course, stemmed from government decision. But, in addition, there developed in the period covered by this chapter a much stronger local and sectoral activism. Activism here should be understood in a broad sense as including not just campaigns directed towards specific political goals, but also activity of a less politically articulated kind, at the level – for instance – of classroom practice or cultural action. From this point of view, the involvement of parents in campaigns for or against selection, of school students in youth subcultures, of teachers in classroom reform, of Welsh-speakers for bilingual education and of activists of various kinds in 'free school' initiatives outside the state system can all be seen as examples of a decentralized and many-sided agency which was just as much a characteristic of the period as government-level reform.

But by the end of the period, this revision, in both its government-centred and its more decentralized aspects, was itself being questioned. In some respects, the achievements of reform looked secure. In 1979, Labour was in power, as it had been in 1964. Though Northern Ireland retained selection, comprehensives provided the near-universal form of state schooling in Scotland and Wales, and Labour had introduced though not implemented legislation which would have ended the resistance of those local authorities in England which still clung to tripartism. The curriculum was still, in practical terms, a matter for local decision. The Schools Council, set up in 1964, still existed; likewise the Consultative Committee on the Curriculum in Scotland. Teachers' unions still had important influence at both local and national level. But in other respects, especially but not only in England, a sea-change had occurred. The institutions, beliefs and practices of the 1960s had all become increasingly fragile, and the rationale for their expansion, and even in some cases for their continued existence, had been undermined. In the process, discourses about schooling had also changed; they were less areas of broad consensus than battlegrounds where a defensive left and an ascendant right fought over education's meanings, methods and purposes.

Explaining this great transformation, and describing the extent of the changes that it involved, which ultimately affected schooling at every level from national policy to the micro-processes of the classroom, are the central purposes of this chapter.

Labour's Turn

The most obvious reasons for the shift were economic and international. All advanced capitalist economies experienced in the mid-1970s a 'second slump', as powerful in its long-term effects as that of the 1930s. Rates of profit and growth declined, while rates of inflation rose. Against a background of social turbulence, governments cut public spending and imposed policies which sought to restrict the rise in incomes which workers had achieved in the 1960s; unemployment increased, especially among youth, and in most Western countries the slow rundown of heavy industry increased in pace, as governments presided over the eradication of unprofitable sectors. As part of the drive towards austerity, public spending was cut, first as an immediate response to crisis, later as a considered strategy for the restoration of profitability. Again this was an international tendency, but it was particularly marked in Britain: Britain and Italy were the only advanced economies in which public expenditure as a percentage of GDP was lower in the mid-1980s than it had been twenty years earlier (Aldcroft 1992: 23). In later years spending on education recovered, but never, proportionately, to the level of the early 1970s: reviewing the record of the Labour government of the late 1990s, Howard Glennerster noted that public spending on education fell as a percentage of GDP from 6.7 per cent in 1975–6 to 4.7 per cent in 1987–8, before rising to 5.2 per cent in 1995–6 (Glennerster 1998: 318).

From a British point of view, the political impact of these developments can be best grasped by considering the events of September–December 1976. Two years earlier, a Labour government had been elected, on the crest of a wave of trade union militancy, promising in the midst of economic crisis an 'irretrievable shift in the balance of wealth and power towards working people and their families' (Labour Party 1974). By late 1976, Labour was signalling a decisive shift away from this objective. Under strong pressure, both from the USA and from its own right wing, James Callaghan's government agreed to the terms of an International Monetary Fund (IMF) loan, and moved to cut public expenditure in ways guaranteed to worsen provision and to increase unemployment. In doing so, Callaghan emphasized to the Labour Party conference that his government was making a definitive break with the post-war past – a break that embraced not only financial policy but the social and political order that economic growth and full employment had enabled:

> For too long we postponed facing up to fundamental choices and fundamental changes in our society and our economy.... The post-war world we were told would go on forever, where full employment could be guaranteed by a stroke of the Chancellor's pen.... We used to think that you could just spend your way out of recession.... I tell you in all candour that that option no longer exists. (Callaghan 1987: 425–6)

In this broad sense, Callaghan's judgement was representative of that of many Western politicians, both social democrat and conservative. He was also typical in stating that there should be a shift within social programmes towards policies that would foster economic efficiency (Callaghan 1987: 427). What was exceptional was the immediacy with which Labour's turn on economic and financial policy was reflected in education. In October 1976 Callaghan made at Ruskin College in Oxford a speech on education which outlined a verdict on the past three decades and announced a change of direction. According to Callaghan, governments between 1944 and 1976 had been the overseers of a system which was neither uniform in its practice nor capable of delivering high standards. Decentralization of educational control was a problem, not a solution. Education policy should be guided by economic imperatives; students should be prepared for the 'world of work'; existing classroom practice should be subject to critical scrutiny, central influence over educational change asserted. Over the next decade, this general outline of policy, drafted in the Department of Education and Science, rather than being simply the work of Callaghan himself, guided the increasingly detailed interventions of central government into schooling (Chitty 1989). The interventions began in the form of spending cuts and developed into a strategy for relating education to a large-scale programme of social and economic restructuring: the education revolution of the 1980s and '90s had its origins in the conflicts, crises and realignments of the 1970s.

This transformative programme was powerfully motivated, not least by a resurgent educational right, and those who have supported its subsequent development have often been inclined to present it as something ineluctable, as an inevitable response on the part of education to social change (Barber 1996). In fact it was nothing of the sort. The social changes to which it responded were not pre-ordained, but were themselves the result of sharp political contestation. Nor was the programme itself pre-planned in all its details; it, too, was shaped by, and took advantage of, circumstance, and reflected the success and failure of particular groups of contending educational actors. Because of this, it took different forms in different parts of Britain, a process which demonstrated the importance of 'local' influences – alliances, traditions and conceptions of educational and social purpose – on the shape of educational provision.

Change and controversy were sharpest in England, which was the heartland of educational discontent. It was there that the most dramatic educational scandals and confrontations occurred, there that media coverage of education's shortcomings was at its most intense. In England, too, strong public school and grammar school sectors embodied an older and seemingly better sense of educational purpose, and helped supply a new account of education's problems and prospects, elaborated by impassioned and skilful right-wing critics. These latter criticisms combined a number of themes, from the damage wreaked by progressive education to the links between inadequate schooling and economic decline. The economic crisis of the 1970s was grist to the mill of those who made such connections – economic crisis was utilized to make a point about schooling's ineffectiveness – yet in other parts of Britain, where the effects of decline were even more sharply felt, the arguments of the right had much less resonance, even when education's failures were openly recognized (Reynolds 1990). In Wales and Scotland, there remained a cohesive alliance that broadly supported the post-war educational settlement, and schooling enjoyed, especially in Scotland, a high level of popular confidence. In Northern Ireland, the circumstances of war meant that British governments did not seek to duplicate there their mainland programme (Benn and Chitty 1996).

Fifteen Years Earlier...

The Labour Party came into government in 1964 committed to a second wave of reform, centring on economic regeneration. Planning mechanisms would co-ordinate public- and private-sector activities. Government would promote and subsidize technological change. Regional planning would ensure that resources were transferred to the old industrial areas, so as to diversify their economic base and end their decline. Education, at all levels, would be a focus of investment and a site of reform, which would create the culture of a new age. Thompson, quoting from the speeches of Harold Wilson, Prime Minister from 1964 to 1970, sets out the connection between economic and technological change and educational reform in these terms:

> It was in the 'white heat' of a planned technological revolution that the 'New Britain' was to be forged, and the language used to conjure up this vision was equally the language of revolution and science. This revolution would see the triumph of a new class: the 'sweeping away' of the 'grouse-moor', the 'Edwardian establishment, the small minority of ... British people' who in consequence of 'their family connections and educational background' saw themselves as having a 'unique right to positions of influence and power' and whose incompetent 'amateurism' was at the root of the nation's economic failings. Their place would be taken by 'those previously held down', namely the 'millions of products of our grammar schools, comprehensive schools, technical schools and colleges' ... What would be created would be 'a Britain based on public service, not a commercialised society where everything has its price'. (Thompson 1996: 185; Wilson 1964: 10–14)

The general themes of this programme – economic growth through state intervention, economic and technological innovation and social and cultural modernization – were the common sense of several western European governments, and indeed of sections of British Conservatism. Where they differed from Conservatism was in a stronger emphasis on state intervention, and on the public sector as a source of the dynamism and collective social purpose that could bring the 'New Britain' into existence. This last point needs particular stressing: to an important extent, Labour was the party of the public sector; it took the advice of a 'new educational establishment' of sympathetic journalists and academics and of what Kogan called 'an articulate group of practitioner-advocates' who argued for reform (Boyle and Crosland with Kogan 1971: 46); it encouraged the growth of 'an informed educational public', organized through lobbying groups that supported expansion and reform (Crosland, in Boyle et al. 1971: 176); it valued the expertise of public-sector professionals and relied on them – not least in education – to carry through the detailed work of change. In turn it was influenced by public-sector organizations, including trade unions, along a path of decentralized initiative, improved working conditions, higher levels of spending and policies that connected education to wider social reform. It was this aspect of Labour's programme – the extent to which it had, allegedly, succumbed to 'producer capture' and developed policies which were aligned more to the interests of professional groups and trade unions than to the general good – which was singled out for criticism by Conservatives in the later 1970s, who in doing so were in their own way analysing something essential to Labourism's second wave.

The radicalism of Harold Wilson's rhetoric was muted in office. His government was reluctant to pursue its objectives in the face of opposition, whether from international finance or from the British Civil Service. Thus the sterling crisis of 1966 led to a deflationary turn in economic policy and the collapse of attempts at co-ordinated and directive economic planning. In education, the government considered but drew back from reform of the public schools; and the advice of its civil servants led to a dilution, in England at least, of long-held plans for comprehensive reorganization (Simon 1992). Nevertheless, taken as a whole its education programme brought about important change. The difference cannot be measured only by reference to legislation or achieved policy. It must also be understood in wider terms. The reforms that Labour instigated, or continued, had important effects on the dynamics of educational change: they strengthened the capacities of some groups of social actors; they weakened, or aroused the opposition, of others; they created especially in the form of the comprehensive school new and lasting sites of initiative and conflict; they embedded an understanding of the connection between education and wider social reform.

Labour's most distinctive project – the one which distinguished it most clearly from Conservatism and served as a symbol of the ways in which it sought to combine economic efficiency and social justice – was secondary school reform. This was pursued in different ways across Britain. In Northern Ireland, which was ruled until the early 1970s by a Unionist administration with little interest in change, Labour's programme was blocked, even after the introduction of direct rule from Westminster in 1974. The Cowan Report of 1976 talked of the government's 'national commitment' to comprehensive schooling, but also of the need to 'govern Northern Ireland in the interests of its people, and in doing so to take full account of its particular and special characteristics' (Cowan Report 1976: 1). These peculiarities included a grammar school system which was unusually inclusive: the ratio of grammar to secondary modern (intermediate) schools in the mid-1960s was roughly 2:3; most middle-class children attended grammar schools and demand for private education was much less than in England (Atkinson 1969). But, as in Wales, the neglect of the majority who were not academically successful was striking: there was no examination below GCE level established in Northern Ireland until 1973, nearly a decade after the introduction of the CSE in England. The British government could note the injustices that this entailed, but, confronting high levels of armed conflict and popular mobilization throughout the 1970s, it did not want to open another area of conflict. It would not be until the late 1990s that comprehensives would again make a serious appearance on the educational agenda.

In England, Michael Stewart, briefly Labour's Secretary of State for Education in 1964–5, aimed at first to proceed in line with the explicit policy of his party, which required local authorities to end selection at 11. Several local authorities, including Manchester, Bradford and Leeds, had already moved in this direction, well before Labour's 1964 election victory (Rubinstein and Simon 1973). But making such change mandatory would have involved immediate conflict with locally entrenched Conservative interests, which had already demonstrated their ability to delay or divert reform. It was also viewed without enthusiasm by many civil servants at the Department of Education and Science (DES). Although sections of the DES had come to favour in general terms the expansion of opportunity (Boyle and Crosland with Kogan 1971: 24), there remained a tendency that believed no more now in 1964 than in the 1940s in the possibilities of high-level mass education, especially in urban schools. Their concerns were of a different sort: comprehensives in cities would bring together in one place students with 'acute' problems of motivation. They would do little to resolve a 'worsening problem' of slum schools, which were already adversely affected by the impact of Commonwealth immigration. What was needed in this view was less a disruptive organizational change than the devising of a curriculum whose focus was some way removed from Wilson's rhetoric of radical change: for the civil servants whose memoranda have been explored by the historian Gary McCulloch, the essential task of the urban school was to to convey the 'fundamentals of our social and political order' (McCulloch 1998: 139–41).

Advised otherwise by its Civil Service (Crosland, in Boyle and Crosland with Kogan 1971:189), the Cabinet rejected the party's position, and instead relied on a policy of persuasion, embodied in the DES circular 10/65 in which Anthony Crosland, Stewart's successor, 'requested' local authorities to develop schemes for reform which followed one of six options (Simon 1992). From the beginning, therefore, comprehensive reform in England was implemented in an uneven way. It lived in the shadow of selective education and in many cases perpetuated selective arrangements. It had no single institutional form. Some comprehensives included post-16 students; many did not. Some comprehensives had formerly been grammar schools, with all that implied for their internal culture and their status; some had been secondary moderns. Some schemes of reorganization actually involved the preservation of at least one grammar school, in a nominally comprehensive local system (Crook, Power and Whitty 1999: 14). The result was that disparities of esteem and outcome continued to be important, and issues of choice and privilege remained. Particularly in the south, grammar schools, protected by local education authorities which opposed 10/65, thrived, and direct grant schools, given the opportunity by Labour legislation, opted out of the state sector to become public schools (Rae 1981). Meanwhile, schools formally designated comprehensive – particularly those 11–16 schools which lacked a sixth form – often found that they were less an equal part of a uniform system than the bottom rung of a complex new hierarchy. Their students more often came from manual working-class backgrounds, had significantly lower scores on ability and achievement at age 11, and achieved less in academic terms at 16 than their counterparts in 11–18 institutions (Kerckhoff et al. 1996). As the headteacher of the new Archway school, formed out of the same secondary modern school that Blishen had called 'Stonehill Street', noted in 1965: 'our problem is that the old secondary modern tag still sticks' (McCulloch 1998: 144). English schooling was marked thus by institutional diversity, in ways that weakened the possibilities of comprehensive success.

In Scotland the process of reform was different. In the 1950s, loyalties to the selective system and the senior secondary school were strong. For Labour politicians in local government the system embodied 'equal opportunity' in a classically meritocratic form: it provided equality of opportunity for children of equal ability irrespective of their social origins. As one local Director of Education put it, the system 'recognized merit as opposed to influence or social standing' and thus offered the talented working-class child as good an education as their middle-class counterpart (McPherson and Raab 1988: 366). McPherson and Raab note that this myth of an egalitarian system pervaded the 'assumptive world' of Scottish policy-makers, with the effect that in the 1950s at least there was little Scottish pressure on the Labour Party to support comprehensive reform. In the early 1960s, the situation changed. The generation which came to power in the Scottish Labour Party in the 1960s saw the selective system not as providing 'just desert' for working-class children selected on the basis of intelligence, but rather as operating to exclude the great majority of working-class children from access to higher levels of schooling. Moreover, the new generation was willing to use the structures of the Labour Party both to establish the principle of comprehensivization and to achieve rapid local change – pushing aside if necessary those who adhered to selection.

By 1964 there was strong party support for comprehensivization, sometimes following upheavals in local constituency parties. Operating, too, on the basis of a national tradition in which central authority made decisions that were applicable to all, Scottish reform proceeded on the basis of a single institutional model for secondary education – the 12–18 school – and worked at a much faster pace than the English LEAs. Even so, complete institutional change took more than a decade. Glasgow remained strongly selective until the mid-1970s and in Edinburgh in the same period about a quarter of students attended fee-paying secondary schools of one kind or another (Public Schools Commission 1967; Fitchett 1975). But by 1979, although public schools still educated around 5 per cent of the secondary population, the state system was a fully comprehensive one. Moreover, unlike reform in England, change at the level of institutional structure was accompanied by the promotion of reforms internal to the school: the Scottish Education Department recommended, throughout the second half of the 1960s, that secondary students in their first two years should be taught in mixed-ability classes, and by 1972 this had become a norm (McPherson and Raab 1988: 393). In England, by contrast, mixed-ability grouping was the exception, not the rule (Rubinstein and Simon 1973: 121). Young had described in the 1950s how the first comprehensives, eager to win the support of middle-class parents, had 'continued to abide by the segregation of ability' (1958: 41). From such a starting-point, change could only be slow.

Wales, like Scotland, moved towards almost total comprehensivization; but it did so without modifying central aspects of the grammar school tradition. Precisely because a relatively high proportion of Welsh students already attended grammar schools – 60 to 70 per cent in some rural areas – it was more likely that the values of the older system would endure into the new. At the end of the 1970s, critics concluded that the Welsh education system was still highly traditional in its narrow academic orientation (Rees and Rees 1980). The 11+ had been abolished, but there were rigid bilateral

divisions within the new schools, and there was no strong comprehensive ethos. In their study of one working-class area in South Wales in
the mid-1970s, Reynolds and Sullivan found that students in the new
schools were performing poorly in academic terms, while the social
role of the schools, in terms for instance of pastoral care and relations
with parents, was underdeveloped (Reynolds and Sullivan, with Murgatroyd 1987). By contrast with Scotland, early streaming was the
norm, and the sixth form of Welsh comprehensives remained open
only to those who were academically successful (Rees and Rees 1980;
Benn and Simon 1972). As a result, the effects of comprehensive
reform were less marked in Wales than in England: or, to put it
another way, the demand for schooling had not increased at the
same rate in a Welsh economy that was still organized around occupations that did not require high levels of qualification. In 1966, the
proportion of Welsh 17-year-olds still at school was 17 per cent; the
figure for England was 12 per cent, and even in the south-east it was
only 15 per cent. By 1977, the Welsh advantage had been eroded:
21.7 per cent of 17-year-olds now stayed on, but this compared with
19.2 per cent for England as a whole and 23.9 per cent in the south-
east (Rees and Rees 1980).

Primary Education

Comprehensive reform entailed changes in curricula and pedagogy
throughout the school system, though the pace and reach of change
was very uneven. Its most immediate effect was on primary schools.
The abolition of selective examinations at 11 or 12 had a rapid effect
on the ways in which primary schools were organized: at the start of
the 1960s, most primaries were streamed; by the end of the decade,
most were not. At the same time, progressive educational ideas grew
in influence. The Scottish Education Department's *Primary Education
in Scotland* was published in 1965. The Plowden Report – *Children
and their Primary Schools* – came out in England in 1967, and the
Gittins Report (*Primary Education in Wales*) in the same year. These
official documents called for new kinds of teaching and learning in
primary schools – a call underpinned by what Plowden described as a
'recognizable philosophy of education' (Plowden Report 1967: 187),
owing much to the philosophy of Jean-Jacques Rousseau and the
psychology of Jean Piaget (Darling 1999). The reports became what
Bernstein and Davies called the 'semi-official ideology of primary
education', systematically expounded to trainee teachers (Bernstein
and Davies 1969: 56; Darling 1999: 31). All endorsed the 'child-

centredness' and 'activity-based' teaching, which became the official value system of primary education. But, as progressives themselves noted, this philosophy was hardly the rule in schools. Streaming may have diminished but, as Gittins put it, few teachers had so far been able to 'shake themselves free of the grip' exerted by the examination: the primary curriculum was not 'forward-looking' (Gittins Report 1967: 6). 'Forward-looking', for all three documents, meant 'experiential' (1967: 6): a successful curriculum would be one which related to the interests of the child. 'The acquisition of knowledge and skills,' suggested *Primary Education in Scotland*, was less important than 'the fostering of intellectual curiosity' (Scottish Education Department 1965: 18). If this was achieved – if the school 'devised the right environment for children' – then they could 'be themselves and develop at the pace appropriate to them' (Plowden Report 1967: 187). The child was 'the agent of his own learning' (p. 194); children learned through 'individual discovery, first-hand experience and opportunity for creative work' (p. 188). In such an environment, which would not be a narrowly focused 'teaching shop', children would have 'some hope' of becoming 'balanced, critical, mature' adults (p. 187).

Plowden's approach to primary education has been criticized on many occasions. Two years after its publication, an eminent collection of philosophers and sociologists attacked its 'biological' conception of child development, which under-stressed social determinants of learning, and 'rather crudely dichotomized' 'being told' and 'finding out' as alternative modes of learning (Bernstein and Davies 1969: 78). Later, radical, critics argued that the report's conception of 'the child' and of 'natural modes of learning' was highly normative – presenting middle-class subjectivity as a universal rule and in the process neglecting the ways in which class and gender affected processes of learning (Walkerdine 1984). From a different perspective, influential research in the 1970s alleged that the 'informal' styles of teaching that Plowden promoted were less successful than formal teaching methods (Bennett 1976). This latter research had enduring effects; Bennett's work launched two decades of criticism of the culture of primary education, for which the 'progressive' reports of the 1960s were held responsible: from this perspective, the professional culture of primary education was insufficiently focused on 'direct instruction' of students, did not value 'high cognitive performance' and embodied teachers' systematic 'low expectations' of those whom they teach (Campbell 2001: 37–8).

These latter criticisms, and the policies to which they were connected, will be explored in a later chapter. For now, what is more important is to grasp the significance particularly of the Welsh and

English reports in terms not just of pedagogy but of the issues of culture, opportunity and decentralization which were central to the dynamic of policy pre-1976. The Scottish Education Department (SED) document, published two years in advance of the others, was less informed by the social agenda of the mid-1960s, and had a more exclusive focus on classroom practice and a more centralist grasp of policy development. But for Plowden, and in a different way Gittins, the agenda was broader. Both documents tried to rethink the relationship between students' learning and the social and cultural conditions of their lives outside school; Gittins, in broad terms, emphasized national culture, and Plowden, class. Gittins understood 'culture' in an anthropological rather than a high-cultural sense, very different from that of English conservatives such as T. S. Eliot (see chapter 1), and very close to that of the Welsh cultural theorist Raymond Williams (1961). Culture was 'the ways of life, the social institutions, the values and beliefs of a people' (Gittins Report 1967: 212). The child living in Wales 'should be able to experience his identity as part of a particular community and socio-cultural tradition – its language and history, its institutions, and its literary and musical culture' (1967: 207). Of these traditions, the report focused particularly on the Welsh language, spoken as a mother tongue by about 16 per cent of schoolchildren (p. 257). Believing that the language was crucial to Welsh identity, the report made proposals that came to form the basis of future policy: it 'endorsed the principle of a fully bilingual education' and recommended that 'the effective teaching of Welsh, as first or second language, should be ensured' (pp. 544–5). It had very much less to say about other aspects of Welsh society and culture. It did not apply its theories about culture and identity to the largely anglophone and industrial south, despite the vibrant history of the coalfield; and it had little to say about social disadvantage, except in rural contexts. In this it perpetuated a long tradition of thinking about education and national identity in Wales. Writing of the 'imperial Wales' of the early twentieth century, the historian Gwyn Williams remarks that the 'educational drives' organized by the Welsh middle class were 'rescue enterprises directed at a minority rural Wales in a permanent crisis of depopulation' – enterprises that never properly recognized 'the complex reality of industrial Wales which came to embrace an overwheming majority of the population' (G. A. Williams 1985: 234–6). Gittins remained within this tradition; it would not be until the 1990s that questions of culture and Welsh identity would be presented in more inclusive ways.

Plowden had a less positive evaluation of popular culture: as Mortimore and Blackstone note (1982: 43), it popularized the idea of 'cultural deprivation', a condition caused by such factors as poverty, poor mother–child relationships and insufficient linguistic stimulation. But it had a much more developed social programme – it was 'the first attempt by an official committee to come to terms with the problems set for schools by poverty and deprivation' (Glennerster 1995: 136). It connected its efforts to understand the social conditions of learning with a concern for questions of resourcing. In both respects, it sought to broaden the terms of the post-war settlement, recognizing that stronger measures were necessary to compensate working-class children for social disadvantage. Thus in terms of resourcing it argued for 'positive discrimination' to 'favour schools in neighbourhoods where children are most severely handicapped by home conditions', with nursery education expanded and salaries raised to retain teachers (Plowden Report 1967: 465). At the same time, it suggested that raising levels of achievement among working-class students involved reorganizing both classroom modes of learning, and the relationship between school, parents and community. In this latter respect, it took educational debate and practice considerably beyond the terms of the earlier post-war period. As Halsey pointed out, the implication of Plowden was that 'access' was not enough. To open nursery schools, or to abolish selection at 11 or to raise the school-leaving age were from this point of view necessary measures, but not sufficient ones. There needed to be other changes too – in the content of the curriculum, in resources, in the capacity of the school to earn the support of students and parents, and in the 'home circumstances' of students and their families. In all these senses, Plowden did much to broaden debate about the meaning of 'equal opportunity' (Halsey 1972: ch. 1).

Plowden and Gittins and to some extent *Primary Education in Scotland* helped also to ensure that the rethinking and broadening of equal opportunity were carried forward in ways that encouraged decentralized or professional initiative. Government's role in funding local post-Plowden reform was crucial. But no political agency shaped definitively the content of the reports. *Primary Education in Scotland* was written by a committee consisting of three college staff, eight teachers and eight inspectors (Darling 1999) and was later endorsed, and in no sense limited, by the Secretary of State for Scotland. Likewise, Crosland, who wrote the customary ministerial foreword to Plowden, did not 'regard either himself or his officials as in the slightest degree competent to interfere with the curriculum' (Boyle and Crosland with Kogan 1971: 173). In the absence of such interference, the three reports took the ideas developed by progressive educators over the previous century to the height of their influence.

The conditions for their prominence were provided by the post-war drive to expand education, and to draw into the system students from all social classes. But Plowden and the other reports were far from being expansion's necessary outcome. They represented rather the influence that teacher trainers, inspectors and local authority advisers – a whole cadre of educators, some of whom in Wales were also members of a cultural-nationalist intelligentsia – had achieved within an education system in which central control was relatively weak. The significance of Plowden especially was thus not only the stimulus it gave to particular forms of classroom practice, but also its endorsement of educational aims that did not derive exclusively from a project centred on economic growth. Plowden's emphasis on learning through play, on the emotional life of children, and on a concept of the curriculum as 'activity and experience' rather than of 'knowledge to be acquired and stored' (Plowden Report 1967: 195) seemed to many of its critics to imply a lack of interest in outcomes more definitely related to the skills requirements of the future workforce. (Gittins's cultural nationalism, and pride in the character of Welsh education, was open to similar criticism on rather different grounds.) For those seeking ten or fifteen years later to overturn the 1960s' revision of the post-war settlement, 'Plowden' was a term that condensed all their criticisms, and they were right to assert its importance, for the report signified not just a high point of progressive influence, but also the opening of a wide gap between the social and economic design for education that was favoured by long-established elites, and the preferences of educators. 'What are the foundations of civilized life?' asked one distinguished educationalist at a Schools Council conference. 'Love, sympathy and respect for others,' was his first answer. He did not mention the economy (Morris 1967: 7).

Secondary Education

Developments in secondary education were not supported by statements of such an authoritative and wide-ranging sort. They tended to be instead the result of a variety of influences, the most co-ordinated of which was examination reform. The Certificate of Secondary Education (CSE), introduced in England and Wales in 1965, was an equivocal initiative. On the one hand, it was the lower tier of a two-tier 16+ exam system, and for a period strengthened tendencies towards streaming between 'academic' and 'non-academic' students. Within comprehensives, GCE students were placed in different teaching groups from CSE students, while in the secondary modern school studied by Hargreaves students who were deemed capable of CSE entry were separated from those who were not (Hargreaves 1967: 82). But at the same time CSE had the effect of stimulating school-based curriculum development. In England – though less so in Wales, which was much more conservative in its approach to curriculum change – many schools took up the opportunity offered by the CSE for designing and examining localized teacher-designed 'Mode 3' syllabuses: the proportion of CSE subject entries under Mode 3 rose from just over 12 per cent in 1969 to just over 26 per cent in 1978 (Whitty 1985:121).

There were similar developments, up to a point, in Scotland. Until 1964, the great majority of secondary students were in effect denied any opportunity of national certification (McPherson and Raab 1988: 248). After 1962 the introduction of a Standard Grade exam, taken at 15, extended the opportunity of certification to about half the year group (1988: 308). This, like the English reforms, was both a response to popular demand, and an attempt to keep existing hierarchies in place. But, by contrast with England, it did not stimulate local-level reform; the Scottish system, suggest McPherson and Raab, operated on the basis of shared assumptions about what comprised a good schooling (1988: 304). England did not. There was no commonly held myth of English education that could serve as a reference-point for evaluating good practice, and England experienced as a result sharp arguments and polarities around educational values and objectives. There were teachers, for example, for whom the significance of CSE Mode 3 went beyond its function of devolving the assessment of students' work to school level – for them, it also provided a means of establishing a more radical curriculum, closely related to local interests, outside the traditional framework of examination. In Murdock's terms, it could 'encourage pupils to develop and articulate their own particular sense of themselves and their situation, over and against the definitions imposed on them from the outside' (Murdock 1974: 101). But, as Whitty makes clear, such radicalism did not go unchallenged: the university-controlled boards through which GCE examinations were conducted were unhappy with a proliferation of local schemes, which seemed to call into question the validity of school examining as impartial, objective and related to externally assessed criteria. From the mid-1970s on, both GCE and CSE examining boards were more reluctant to approve Mode 3 courses (Whitty 1985: ch. 6). In this area, curriculum reform began to reach its limits, and to be held in check by forces that questioned the effects of decentralization on educational standards. In the same way, for some writers, the introduction of the GCSE in the mid-1980s was in part an attempt to impose 'tight control from the centre' on the curriculum (Broadfoot 2001: 145).

The same pattern of English polarity is plain also in other areas of curriculum reform, from the working papers and research projects of the Schools Council, to less formalized curriculum movements. In Scotland, the pace of reform in both primary and secondary education was dependent upon the capacities of the national centre – of the SED and the Inspectorate – to give a lead. In England the emphasis was on local initiative; there was no question of looking to a national centre for direction. This was something about which curriculum innovators were both explicit and committed. Thus the 1965 Schools Council Working Paper on English stressed that 'development must be school-based and co-operatively organized' with 'no hierarchy of initiative or control' (Schools Council 1965: 9). The insistence on autonomy was underpinned not only by a belief in the capacities of teachers, but by a theory of learning. Good English teaching 'arises from an interaction between the pupils' and the teachers' experiences'; it depended on 'spontaneity in the creation of appropriate learning situations'. It was therefore dependent above all on the teacher's ability to 'understand and respect the nature of the pupil's previous experience' (1965: 20): teachers were required to become sympathetic interpreters of students' lives. In English, especially, this position became an orthodoxy, albeit one that was inflected in very different ways. In the influential Anglo-American manifesto for a new English teaching, *Growth through English*, the emphasis was placed on sensitivity to the individual child, and respect for the complexity of learners' achievements (Dixon 1975). In other work, the emphasis was retained, but placed in a more broadly social context: the need for sensitive 'interpretation' was understood to apply not only to individual patterns of learning but to cultural contexts. In the process, culture was revalued. Ken Worpole was not untypical in arguing that 'the majority of people have never been allowed an opportunity to speak, and have been considered invisible or hidden from history' (Worpole 1974: 193). New practices and technologies of English teaching – the student autobiography, the tape-recorded interview, the story published and circulated in the community outside the school – could bring this invisibility to an end (1974: 193). Thus, as Hewitt suggests, in the practice of many English teachers, working-class speech and story came to be presented as evidence of a 'common working-class culture', disconnected from the 'powerful institutions and high-cultural traditions of society' but rooted instead in a community, and possessing qualities of depth and resistance (Hewitt 1989). This revaluation was strongly linked to the social conflicts of the period. As we shall see, it drew from a wider radicalism outside the school, while at the same time it served to provoke a militant, right-wing response to educational change.

Radical Shifts

The initial pace and direction of curriculum reform had been set in the middle 1960s. From the late '60s onwards, other dynamics came into play, so that, as we have begun to see, projects originally framed by a version of the 1944–7 agenda became home to more radical practices and critiques. Between 1968 and 1974, the relative social peace of the golden age came to an end: across western Europe a series of working-class protests and emerging social movements challenged inequalities, claimed rights of participation and recognition, and asserted militant identities. At factory level, workers realized that 'the rises so long negotiated by their unions were actually much less than could be squeezed out of the market', and levels of strike action rose (Hobsbawm 1994: 285). When the Labour government tried to legislate against this movement, localized action was transformed into successful, national protest. New or rediscovered forms of collective action – shipyard occupations on the Clyde, mass picketing by miners in 1972 and 1974 – suggested that working-class insurgency amounted to not just a set of claims on the existing order but an alternative to it, embodying values in which 'community' and 'solidarity' took on more militant meanings. Outside the workplace, other social movements made similar claims: in Northern Ireland, to civil rights; in Wales, for recognition of the Welsh language; among black communities, for freedom from discrimination. Across Britain there were youth movements that forced themselves on the attention of educators, both through new levels of disaffection and disruption, and more explicitly in organizations such as the Schools Action Union – active in the late 1960s in London – and the National Union of School Students (Wagg 1996). At the same time, a libertarian education movement, operating in 'free schools' outside the state system, served as a source of criticism and experiment (Wright 1989).

Teachers themselves participated in these various movements, both through trade union militancy and through their educational activism. Teacher union militancy was mild compared with that of other workers but nevertheless reached a level not seen in England and Wales since the 1920s. In 1969–70 teachers in England and Wales organized what was in effect their first ever national strike action – over pay – and the EIS took similar action early in 1970. In the same period, breaking with professional tradition, the two major English and Welsh unions affiliated to the TUC. But militancy also took other forms, less centred on pay and conditions. Especially between 1968 and 1974, universities and colleges of teacher education were affected by, and themselves generated, movements of protest and attempts to develop new kinds of knowledge and new sorts of social identity. The teachers who graduated from these institutions formed a generation which sought to translate these experiences into an educational practice that could transform the ways in which schooling related to the majority of its students. From the perspective of many of them, comprehensive reform was important, but on its own it was not enough. 'There will be no comprehensive education,' stated the *May Day Manifesto* in 1968, 'until there is a genuinely basic common curriculum, which relates all learning to centres of human need, rather than to prospective social and economic grades' (Williams 1968: 35). From this point of view, an agenda for schooling should include questions of ideology as well as institutions, the content of education as much as broadening the pathways of access to its higher levels. It needed to be alert to the identities and tacit knowledges of excluded groups, and critical of the vested interests embodied in the official curriculum, that had 'emptied education of its potential as a means of self-realization' and rendered it 'primarily a medium of economic exchange' (Murdock 1974: 101). It was in this light that the Stepney teacher Chris Searle wrote of 'the growth of a new methodology and classroom consciousness of working-class students themselves using their own local resources, perceiving their own neighbourhood, families, history and themselves – in short their class – as relevant and proper material to form a basis of knowledge and identity' (Searle, cited in K. Jones 1983: 128).

Searle was widely known; he had published the poetry of his students and been disciplined for doing so, in a case which seemed to dramatize the conflict that Murdock was describing. His work was typical of a practice that combined strong radical assertion with a sense that it was possible to develop, in the space provided by a decentralized school system, an alternative way of working. But radicalism of this sort was never more than a minority commitment. Sheila Rowbotham's autobiography, *Promise of a Dream*, gives a good account both of the 'moment' of educational radicalism and of its conservative context. Writing of her experiences in the late 1960s, she described two worlds of education – a working life that combined supply teaching in secondary schools ruled by the cane with Saturday 'free schools' that raised, chaotically, questions of children's freedoms and the requirement on adults to find new, less oppressive educational roles (Rowbotham 2000). These two worlds coexisted throughout the period of radically inspired grassroots change. No account of the period should underestimate the conservatism of its cultures of teaching. Hargreaves, for instance, emphasizes the deep antipathy of most secondary school teachers to the idea of destreaming, and Darling describes how even the official progressivism of the Scottish primary school was compromised by a heavy reliance on corporal punishment as a means of discipline (Hargreaves 1967: 189; Darling 1999: 35). One of the achievements of the very diverse movement for radical change in education was to challenge and undermine this conservatism at many points, in an attempt to transform the relationship of teachers to those they taught, as well as the connection between the school and wider social change. Yet the achievement was necessarily limited. Minoritarian, operating at the grass roots, and on many fronts, it had no overall programme for reform. Michael Young had described the reformers of the 1950s as 'the planners', a term which was meant to suggest a certain lack of human sympathy in their programme for increasing social mobility through education. No one could accuse the classroom radicals of that; but a relative freedom to develop at classroom level had discouraged them from broader thinking about change. In this sense, their lack of interest in a 'plan' was a problem, for which general statements of opposition to the existing educational order – 'emotionally repressive . . . perpetuating the class divisions of society' – did not compensate (K. Jones 1983: 126).

But this did not mean that radicalism was an isolated position. Radicals were often ferocious in their criticisms of Labour's policies – the Fife headteacher R. F. McKenzie was not alone when by 1970 he had arrived at a despairing judgement on Labour: 'those of us who imagined that the Labour Party would make fundamental changes in our society, and particularly in our education system, now see their efforts overborne like an irrelevant eddy in a stream' (McKenzie 1970: 67). Nevertheless, despite frequent denunciations of this sort, in some senses educational radicals functioned not in furious isolation but as the left wing of a reforming movement, located within established networks for change, which had begun to criticize the educational preoccupations of earlier decades and to develop alternative positions. At their most explicit, these positions had two main elements, well expressed by Halsey and his colleagues. First was a shift from 'equality of access' to 'equality of achievement'. In this new interpretation 'a society affords equality of opportunity if the proportion of people from different social, economic or ethnic categories at all levels and in all types of education are more or less the same as the proportion of these people in the population at large. . . . The average woman or negro [sic] or proletarian or rural dweller should have the same level of educational attainment as the average male, white, white-collar suburbanite. If not there has been injustice' (Halsey 1972: 8). Second was a realization that education, in itself, was only a minor element in the system of social stratification. 'The major determinants of educational attainments [are] not schoolmasters but social situations, not curricula but motivation, not formal access to the school but support in the family and the community', wrote Halsey (1972: 6).

Arguments like these were voiced not just on the fringes of educational debate, but at its centre: Halsey was a close adviser to Crosland and his critique of orthodox policy was published by the DES, no less, in 1972. Materially, they contributed to initiatives such as the positive discrimination projects which followed Plowden. More generally, they contributed to a sense that educational reform was an unfinished business, whose successful conclusion depended on a deeper radicalism. In this respect, they connected back to classroom radicalism and school-level change in the curriculum. So far as the relationship between education and wider social reform was concerned, critics of the existing school system could do little except apply political pressure to government. But in a decentralized system there were immediate opportunities for curriculum change, and here those teachers who sought action found legitimization among researchers and policy advisers. In the twenty years after the Second World War, writes Whitty, 'British sociologists... were largely concerned with the problem of increasing access to schooling, rather than with the nature of the education which they sought to distribute more widely' (1985: 9). In the later 1960s, however, a number of researchers began to explore the internal processes of the school, and the ways in which curricula and institutional procedures such as streaming contributed to the failure of working-class pupils (Hargreaves 1967; Lacey 1970). Hargreaves, for instance, suggested that the abolition of streaming by ability, linked to a 'fundamental rethinking of teaching methods', was virtually a precondition of productive change (Hargreaves 1967: 190). At the same time, policy advisers were arguing that comprehensive reform would not be complete without the development of a new 'common curriculum' that could appeal to 'members of all social classes': the ideals of the grammar school 'were not the only educational ideals worth pursuing' (Halsey 1965; Halsey et al. 1980: 214). These incitements to further change, made in some cases from positions near the top of the educational hierarchy, converged with the radicalism that was increasingly affecting its lower levels.

Race

Conflicts around race and education demonstrate the dynamic very clearly. The willingness of educators in the early 1960s to demand of migrant communities that they assimilate to British ways of life at the expense of their own cultural identities had later been tempered by more pluralist policy recommendations. The 1966 Local Government Act made resources available for schools with significant numbers of ethnic minority pupils. Plowden made similar recommendations; it was critical of previous assimilationist policies, such as the dispersal of ethnic minority students across the schools of an LEA, and wrote of the 'cultural enrichment' which such students brought to their schools (Plowden Report 1967: ch. 6). As the Swann Report noted, 'integration' began to replace assimilation as a policy goal, and references to diversity, tolerance and equal opportunity begin to punctuate policy texts, which now 'attempted to give at least some recognition . . . to the backgrounds of ethnic minority children' (Swann Report 1985: 191). At the same time, the funding targeted at ethnic minority communities, even though it was justified in terms of limited goals such as the teaching of English, helped bring into being specialist groups of teachers and advisers who developed new agenda focused on remaking schools as multicultural institutions rather than forcing-houses of assimilation. This process of change intersected with political mobilization. The 1968 speeches of the Conservative politician Enoch Powell, asserting Britishness against the alien cultures of migrant populations, had politicized the question of race. Migrant communities, already discontented with what they saw as the exclusionary tendencies of the school system, increased their activity. Education became a central target of their campaigns. Local authorities continued to design policies for the dispersal of black students on the basis of assumptions about their lower levels of educational capacity; special schools – for the 'educationally subnormal' – were populated by West Indian students in disproportionate numbers (T. Carter with Coussins 1986: 89–90). Between 1969 and 1971, organizations of black parents and teachers campaigned against these procedures. Raising questions that went beyond the immediate focuses of their discontent, they attacked the institutional racism of education and argued for a new kind of curriculum for black students, based on 'identity, pride and belonging' (Coard 1971). Throughout the 1970s, popular campaigns about youth and schooling – around deportations, mobilizations against fascism, the policing of youth, racist attacks – provided a context which both encouraged policy-makers to seek educational means of ameliorating conflict and stimulated some teachers to devise curricula that could explain racism in socio-economic terms, or encourage expression of black identities. In the process, the student identities which schools had previously sought to promote, and the curricular and pedagogic means by which they did so, were called into question.

Gender

The same pattern is apparent in the gender politics of schooling, where again official reform intersected with activity 'from below'. Women's increasing involvement in paid labour, without amendment to their burdens in the home, created new pressures and discontents. The expansion of higher education had increased the numbers of women students, who graduated to face an occupational world in which they were allocated subordinate roles. The Edinburgh teacher Lesley Hills, looking back on the 1970s, documented an educational world that was rigidly segregated and male-dominated. Other commentators have presented the Scottish policy community as a force for reform, pushing steadily from the 1960s onwards to extend opportunity. Hills (1990) makes clear the limitations of this perspective: in the local policy community, a male membership system operated, based on appointment and patronage, which was impervious to the experience of female teachers and students and resolutely masculine in its approach to the education of boys, who were beaten regularly. Hills's account demonstrates how anger at the closing of particular structures of opportunity to women spilled over into a general discontent with male domination. In this, it is typical – the women's liberation movement raised with great force and appeal questions that related the shapes of women's discontent to the patterns of male domination, in all areas of life, public and personal. Out of these experiences came a new, diverse set of educational practices, from campaigns for increased nursery provision to intense critiques of the school. For feminists, the school's role was not the benevolent enabling of ever-greater levels of opportunity, but the perpetuation of oppression and inequality. Anne-Marie Wolpe, for instance, noted that secondary school had a negative effect on girls' achievement: between 11 and 14, their levels of attainment declined at the same time as the school's emphasis on their destiny as wives and mothers increased (Wolpe 1977).

There was nothing unitary about the women's movement in this period: it had no single set of demands and no one focus. Its activities were usually local and small-scale, even if they relied upon a wide network of curriculum initiatives, trade union caucuses and school-level women's groups (Arnot et al. 1999). It was partly as the result of its pressure that Labour introduced a Sex Discrimination Act in 1975 that – *inter alia* – made it unlawful for schools directly to discriminate against students, by barring them on gender grounds from taking particular subjects. But this was less the culmination of the movement's activities than a spur to further work: the SDA 'has not broken down prejudice and discrimination in schools', argued two feminist teachers at the end of the 1970s. The 'mores' of the school needed to change as well, and all aspects of the way in which schools assigned sex roles to students and teachers had to be questioned (Saunders and Marsh 1980). Immediately, what were at stake in such a campaign were issues of access and discrimination – the ways in which girls were denied formal access to particular subjects or levels of education, or else informally excluded from participation even where access had been granted. It was this sort of issue which fed most easily into an overall politics of educational reform. But feminism also raised a great number of other questions about the ways in which schools contributed to the forming of gendered identities; these questions, which connected to issues of sexuality and power, proved less easy to assimilate.

Like teachers concerned with issues of race and class, the minority of teachers who addressed questions of gender worked not from a blank slate, but with the familiar child-centred ideas of progressivism. They retained a stress on 'activity', 'discovery' and 'relevance' but gave these terms a focus that related much more to questions of culture and collective identity than to learning needs understood primarily as individual. This perspective entered into the mainstream of reform. When the Bullock Report into language and learning declared that 'no child should be expected to cast off the language and culture of home as he crosses the school threshold' (1975: 75), this was from one point of view a repetition of a progressivist respect for individuality. But it also made a wider call, for schools to engage with languages and cultures which had not, traditionally, been their own. This capacity for turning progressivism towards the social was a general trend of the period, which had several strands. In some versions, it stressed the recognition of home cultures via a curriculum that was castigated by its critics as 'saris, steelbands and samosas'. In others, it assumed an explicitly anti-racist or feminist dimension, hostile to the established curriculum and finding its subject matter in an attention to popular culture that matched that of Hall and Whannel. As in Hall's own work, though, 'popular culture' had acquired in the 1970s a new meaning: it was assumed to be based on resistance, implicit criticism of the status quo and a latent realism and good sense which classroom experience could make articulate. Whatever its variants the cultural turn of the later 1960s and '70s created a link between the work of the school and the challenges to established forms of identity, knowledge and power that were developing outside it.

New Social and Economic Priorities

On the eve of Callaghan's 1976 Ruskin speech, schooling in England was both radical and conservative. It was home to curriculum experiment, yet in primary schools, ten years after Plowden, it was still dominated by a traditional pedagogy and a narrow, highly traditional, focus on reading and writing (Department of Education and Science 1978). It was based on a commitment to equal opportunity yet continued to produce large numbers of unqualified school-leavers. It was claimed by government and assumed by professionals to be developing in line with popular demand, yet was subject to increasing criticism for its remoteness from parental opinion (Department of Education and Science 1977b). Though often justified in terms of an expanded, remade system's contribution to economic growth, it was nevertheless increasingly seen by business as an obstacle to national efficiency (Weinstock, cited in Chitty 1989: 61). Resting on the belief that public spending was necessary for equality and cohesion, it confronted an electorate whose purchasing power was declining and which was reluctant to pay more taxes (Glennerster 1998: 309). Finally, still regarded by many in the new educational establishment as incomplete, schooling reform had by 1976 appeared to its ever more prominent right-wing critics to have reached the point where it threatened both standards and social stability.

Schooling, in other words, was inchoate and disputed, rather than unified around a common set of objectives; its content, purposes and systems of control were called into question from many sides and, as we shall see, were the objects of a succession of controversies and scandals. Yet what brought about the fundamental changes signalled by 1976 was not so much an accumulation of local or particular reversals as a sharp and lasting change in government's understanding of education's priorities and procedures. In this sense, post-war reform died from the top: there was still life after 1976 in the various limbs and branches of the system, but it was slowly, through the 1980s, extinguished, as a new educational order, created by law-making rather than decentralized initiative, emerged. In the process, the relations and alliances established between reforming Labour governments and its 'partners' at various levels of education, from LEAs to professional pressure groups, to teacher trade unions, were severely weakened. It proved impossible for such governments to pursue their new course and at the same time maintain old systems of partnership.

In the summer of 1976 Callaghan commissioned a balance sheet of post-war education – a document produced in the DES, supposedly confidential but in fact widely circulated, known as the 'Yellow Book' (Secretary of State for Education and Science 1976). It brought to the surface the DES's longstanding unhappiness with the direction of state education, and with the positions of the main social actors who were driving change. The principle that 'no one but teachers has any right to say what goes on in schools' was challenged. Primary education, the report observed, was under the 'general influence' of child-centred approaches, even if they were fully developed only in a small number of schools. Streaming had been abandoned; group work rather than whole-class teaching had become the norm. Aesthetic subjects and 'free expression' were now more prominent. 'In the right hands' this approach was capable of producing admirable results. But for 'less able and experienced teachers' it represented a trap; some 'had allowed perfomance to suffer' (para 12). The time was therefore 'almost certainly ripe for a corrective shift of emphasis' (para 13).

But far more was at stake here than an issue of pedagogic method. The DES aimed not just at reshaping practice through judicious advice, but at bringing to a halt what seemed to be the spontaneous and deep-seated tendencies of the school system, towards localized, piecemeal, unsupervised, professionally led and progressive-influenced reform – in primary schools and throughout the state system. Thus the report moved on to a dismissal of the Schools Council, which, despite all the resources available to it, had 'scarcely begun to tackle the problems of the curriculum as a whole' (para 50) and had done nothing to reform the examination system. Secondary schools, in 'an almost desperate attempt to modify styles of teaching and learning so as to ... enlist the co-operation of their more difficult pupils', had possibly been 'too ready to drop their sights in setting standards of performance' (para 23).

Schools and social order

The criticisms were in part a continuation of the old fears of those at the centre of an education system that was increasingly escaping their influence. But several factors gave them a new salience. The reforms of the 1960s had clearly encountered social limits – in the resistance, for instance, of students now compelled to stay at secondary school until they were 16. These problems were likely less to disappear than to worsen, since, with the onset of economic crisis, the youth labour market had collapsed. In its absence, there immediately arose problems of social control, as a volatile section of youth left school to no clear destination and without the disciplining effects of the workplace. At the same time, the spectacular political presence of youth haunted policy-makers: the riots at the Notting Hill Carnival of 1976, the punk movement, the large and aggressive anti-fascist mobilizations of the mid-1970s all appeared as signs of a fragmenting social order which policy needed to address in new and systematic ways that were beyond the capacity of schools. In fact, some aspects of schooling seemed to add to problems of control.

Events at William Tyndale Junior School in Islington seemed to confirm such a reading. Teachers there implemented a radical version of a progressive curriculum, centring on free choice and the celebration of unauthorized cultures. Criticized by the educational right, and caustically inspected by the Inner London Education Authority (ILEA), the teachers went on strike. The subsequent ILEA inquiry into events at the school served as a dramatic condensation of issues of teacher autonomy, child-centred pedagogy and the politicization of schooling (Gratton and Jackson 1976; Ellis et al. 1976). It was a condensation which provided the material for the first great educational scandal of the post-war years, and marked the beginning of intensive, spectacular popular media coverage of schooling. From now on, as the educational right quickly understood, what was perceived as a crisis in education would be played out under the spotlights of press and television. On such a stage, the influence of professionals could be cancelled out by the ability of hostile media to set an agenda in which teacher autonomy appeared not as a rational solution to problems of curriculum development but as the central factor in the crisis of the school (Corner House Bookshop and School without Walls 1978). Newspapers like the *Daily Mail* established a style of educational coverage which linked issues of 'standards' and those of 'politicization': schools were failing, now, not because they were dealing with intractable problems of social inequality, but because the ideologies of progressive educators and the political commitments of a section of the teaching force were driving them away from common sense and traditional understandings of schooling's purposes and procedures.

Schooling and 'economic facts'

Other factors were less local, connected to the great political shift of the mid-1970s, as governments in the advanced capitalist countries responded to the end of the golden age and the beginnings of a period of profound economic restructuring by insisting that education be more cheaply and effectively delivered and more clearly targeted on areas of economic need. There were, said the Government Green Paper which followed Callaghan's Ruskin speech, 'hard and irreducible economic facts' that dictated change (Department of Education and Science 1977a: 24). The educational system was 'out of touch with the fundamental need for Britain to survive economically in a highly competitive world' (1977a: 2). It had to become not just more attuned to the specific requirements of business in respect of occupational skills; it had also to change its entire ethos, so that 'preparation for the world of work' was placed near its centre. In speaking so, Labour inaugurated an as yet unbroken process of 'economizing' educational discourse (Kenway 1994). Justifications for change centred on economic arguments, and connected to demands that educators focus on objectives set by government's reading of national economic goals. At the same time, and consequently, government provoked enduring tensions with its public sector base, including teachers, who feared both for their autonomy and in some cases for the future of their preferred models of teaching and learning.

Continuities of Reform

After 1976, then, the Labour government made a sharp turn: reforming tendencies were in many important respects brought to a halt; other priorities began to dominate. Yet the policy shift was never a complete one. Principles of access and opportunity were extended into new areas. Issues of ethnicity and gender were increasingly taken up by local authorities and at national level, the Warnock Report, commissioned by Labour, though reporting to its Conservative successor, argued for a redefinition of 'special needs', so that many more children so described could be integrated into mainstream education, with their learning needs recognized and – it was hoped – adequately resourced (Warnock Report 1978). Comprehensive school reform presented an equally complex picture. On the one hand, in the climate of the 1970s it was not well resourced. Purpose-built comprehensives were much less likely to be built in the 1970s than in the previous decade because funding from national government was less available, and many comprehensives, in terms of accommodation and student intake, were little more than redesignated secondary moderns (Kerckhoff et al. 1996: 185–9). But if the reality of comprehensivization was uneven and under-resourced, then at least in legislative terms Labour attempted to complete the work of comprehensive reform in England, and, after unsuccessfully attempting to use existing procedures to force comprehensivization in all LEAs, eventually legislated to compel comprehensive provision. (The legislation was immediately repealed by the incoming Conservative government in 1979.)

Private education

Overall, however, the more radical and wide-ranging aspects of reform were dropped, most notably in the case of private education, whose development in the 1970s provides an excellent example both of the problems of reform and of the revival of modes of education that seemed at some early points of the post-war period to have become obsolescent. In its period in opposition between 1970 and 1974 Labour had moved to the left on several issues, private education included. The party conference called for its eradication and Roy Hattersley, Shadow Education Minister, warned headteachers of 'our serious intention initially to reduce and eventually to abolish private education' (Rae 1981: 13). Hattersley aimed finally to redress what Crosland, writing twenty years earlier, had called the 'glaring injustice' of the public schools. The schools had been unaffected by the government-directed reforms of the 1960s. Unable to devise a policy that would bring them within the state system without – it was thought – affronting rights of parental choice, the Labour government had left them outside the framework of reform. But they changed none the less, in what was perhaps the most successful example of modernization in the period. From the early 1960s, the major public schools, organized through the Headmasters' Conference, carried out a concerted programme of self-transformation. They deliberately distanced themselves from a past associated with the provision of recruits to church, armed services and empire. They obtained substantial funding from industry to resource science education, and emphasized academic attainment to a much greater extent than previously: as Halsey recognizes, between 1960 and 1980 the proportion of 17+ students at public schools declined from 29 per cent to 19 per cent, but nearly a third of students obtaining three or more A levels were from the private sector. The schools were achieving more, from a proportionately smaller base. They were assisted in this by one of the significant by-products of comprehensive reform. Direct grant grammar schools were academically the most successful sector of secondary education in England and Wales. When Labour insisted, after its re-election in 1974, that they choose between joining a largely non-selective state secondary system, and leaving the state sector, most schools took the latter option. When they did so, the private

sector acquired another asset, and at the same time a sizeable proportion of middle-class parents – the direct grant schools were predominantly middle-class institutions – turned away from the state
and towards the private sector.

Public school culture was also transformed. Many schools had
already, in the 1950s, begun what one headteacher called 'the process
of making the community of the school more civilized': fagging was
abolished, along with beating, cold showers and elaborately distinctive uniform; art, craft, music and trips overseas all aimed to supply a
richer and more 'modern' education without altering the fundamentally segregated character of the school (Rae 1981: 95–6). In the late
1960s, another wave of cultural change hit the schools. Public school
students, particularly in boys' schools, took up some of the themes of
generational revolt. They objected to the rules on uniform and hair
length, resisted attendance at chapel and refused to join school cadet
corps. The schools, on the whole, negotiated with these challenges
rather than entirely suppressing them. John Rae, headmaster of Westminster, describes the movement towards a 'more flexible and informal attitude on the part of the school authorities, for whom the
opportunity to jettison the more regimented elements of public school
life fitted well into a modernizing programme in which academic
success was more important than the moulding of particular, now-
outdated models of character' (1981: 114). The schools, in other
words, were beneficiaries of cultural change, to which they adapted
successfully.

After 1976 the government's interest in pursuing the kinds of
reform initiated in the late 1960s for the most part ended. After
1976, the private sector was safe: Hattersley's position was not supported. Likewise, sponsorship of radical, locally based reform concluded with the closing down of Community Development Projects
in the late 1970s. The effects of social class on educational opportunity no longer occupied policy-makers: the stream of government-
commissioned reports on the issue, which had begun in 1954, came
to an end. After Bullock in 1974, there were no more official reports
to argue that relations between home and school should be central to
educational practice. Instead, as we have seen, new themes emerged,
which, representing a consensus among policy-makers in government
and representatives of business, cut at the heart of the purposes and
alliances that had developed since the mid-1960s. However, these
themes were not the only ones that were being deployed to shape a
new agenda. Since the late 1960s, and with increasing success, a
refounded educational right had managed to convert its discontents
with change into the outline of an alternative programme, and into an

effective challenge to the hegemony of reform. It is on the nature of this new challenge that we now focus.

Conservatism Reborn

By the late 1960s, Conservatism's educational programme was a self-acknowledged failure. The centrepiece of its post-war policies had been defence of the tripartite system, and step-by-step the unsustainability of such a defence had been forced upon its leaders – who by the mid-1960s were echoing reformers' claims that 'intelligence' was something to be acquired rather than inherited and whose 1970 election manifesto, recognizing the deep unpopularity of the 11+, made no commitment to its restoration (Boyle and Crosland with Kogan 1971). In government between 1970 and 1974, Conservative policy continued to be reactive rather than innovative. Margaret Thatcher, as Secretary of State for Education, continued against her will to approve local schemes for comprehensive reorganization, though wherever possible she preserved in them some degree of selective education (Simon 1991). The Government's main statement of strategy reiterated Labour's commitment to expansion, and notably lacked an interest either in a more directive style of policy implementation, or in linking education to the economic objectives which were beginning to be reasserted by other governments (Department of Education and Science 1972; Organization for Economic Co-operation and Development 1974).

But between its electoral defeat in 1974 and its return to office in 1979 the educational politics of Conservatism were transformed. The party developed the basis of a programme radically different from any other in the post-war period, and via polemic and the brilliant exploitation of the scandals produced by the crisis in educational reform it made itself a force in the popular politics of education. When Callaghan made his Ruskin speech, it was as much a response to Conservatism's achievement in placing 'educational failure' and 'low standards' at the centre of popular debate as a statement which emerged from Labour's own policy reflections.

The rebirth of radical, non-consensual Conservatism in education is usually traced to 1969, when public opinion was first stirred by new rightist intervention. In fact, its origins lie deeper, in the discontent of sections of right-wing opinion with the whole direction of post-war educational change. The intellectual resources of which conservatism began to make use in the 1960s came not out of deliberations on economic restructuring and social change but from the re-emergence of old concerns, to which the crisis of the 1970s allowed what one

Conservative intellectual called a 'second wind' (Cowling 1987). As chapter 1 suggested, Conservatives such as Richard Law and Angus Maude had never accepted the legitimacy of the post-war settlements – Law claiming that it involved the 'collapse of all moral values', Maude criticizing the new, professionally dominated order in education. Until the 1970s, dissent like this appeared to contribute no more than a footnote to post-war history. What gave it a new relevance was the election in 1975 of Margaret Thatcher as Conservative leader. Thatcher's programme took the form of a war against the post-war settlement, the economic and social policies on which it rested and the labour movement and public-sector influences which had done so much to bring it about. It was also of course a war against those tendencies in the Conservative Party which had accommodated themselves to the settlement – tolerating trade union influence, high levels of public spending and an economic policy centred on full employment. Far from accepting this settlement, Thatcherism set out to destroy it. In the process, it legitimated the prejudices of Conservative activists and rejuvenated the anti-settlement Conservative right.

The New Right of the 1970s addressed a very wide range of issues, but possessed no single coherent programme for dealing with them, and the 'solutions' adopted by its various components were often mutually contradictory: the political authoritarianism of some was hard to reconcile with the market-based enthusiasm of others. Nevertheless, in the context of Conservatism's growing hostility to the post-war settlement, its different parts made common cause. The market, not the state, tradition, not innovation, became the uneasily coupled motifs of Conservative policy, and from the mid-1970s onwards Conservatism became less a force for stability than one which sought restlessly to impose these principles on a recalcitrant social order. In many important respects it succeeded, but did so – as the next chapter will show – only at the expense of its own coherence.

At the economic level, the rejection of consensus grew into a bold programme for privatizing nationally owned industry, introducing market-based change to the welfare state and eradicating trade union interference with the free working of the market. To this extent, Conservatism was compatible with programmes adopted by other governments in Europe, North America, and Australia and New Zealand, which likewise sought to dismantle the welfare regimes of the golden age. But in other areas of social, political and cultural life the changes fought for by the right expressed concerns which were peculiarly English: they had deep cultural roots within English society, but little resonance elsewhere, even in Britain. This peculiarity needs some attention.

England and the right

The post-war educational settlement was a response to an endemic conflict between a system based on restrictive educational institutions and the pressure for the entrance of non-elite groups on to the educational scene. Like other legislation of the period, it provided only a partial resolution of the conflicts it addressed. Nevertheless, it helped bring about a post-war shift of cultural power away from Conservatism. In recognizing the principle of secondary education for all, in establishing local authority control and in allowing a strong measure of teacher influence on the curriculum it set up an institutional framework in which some educationalists were able to reshape curricula in ways that were both critical of received definitions of culture, and responsive to pressures arising from important cultural changes in the post-war period, which had to do with generation, class, ethnicity and gender. This process went further and faster in England than in other parts of Britain. It was in England that control of the curriculum from the centre was at its weakest, and in England that discontent among a section of the teaching force with the embedded traditions of schooling was at its strongest. In Scotland and Wales, by contrast, there existed a greater level of satisfaction with what were seen as the inclusive characteristics of national education systems; and in Scotland a more powerful and coherent approach to curriculum change expressed itself in the Munn and Dunning Reports (1977) which, anticipating by several years English attempts to rethink curriculum and assessment issues, combined, within the context of support for comprehensive schooling, both the introduction of a core curriculum and proposals to strengthen differentiation between students of different ability groups. In these countries, too, although it experienced a minor electoral revival in Wales in 1979, Conservatism was in terms of votes, parliamentary seats and influence a declining force. It lacked the political leverage easily to reshape systems which by custom or a slow post-1945 process of administrative devolution had consolidated a character different from that of England. Equally as important, England was the home of a right-wing intelligentsia fiercely attached to a national heritage, to elite education and to the myths of excellence and leadership that clustered around it. Thus it was in England, centre simultaneously of progressive experiment and of bitter discontent with post-war reformism, that the heartland of the New Right was located.

In 1969 the first of a series of essays was published on the perils of educational reform. It immediately became both notorious and a bestseller – 80,000 copies were sold of its first two issues. *Fight for Education: A Black Paper* was edited by two university lecturers in English, Brian Cox and Tony Dyson. Cox, whose influence on the five Black Papers, published between 1969 and 1977, was the greater, had been a Labour voter in the election of 1966, but like many intellectuals of the period he combined a belief in social reform with a deep attachment to the imagined educational community of the past, a world of 'boundaries, limits and enclosures' in which disciplined classes, sharing a common culture, worked to achieve a knowledge whose values were not contested (Cox 1992: 8):

> The emphasis was on service and self-discipline, a true attention to the realities of the social world.... At Nunsthorpe [the elementary school Cox attended] we were invited, indeed compelled, to submit ourselves to the disciplines of study. The rules we learnt were a means of understanding the demands of the outside world, and of controlling them in the service of the community and our own desired forms of personal fulfillment.... I learned that outside myself there existed an invulnerable world of learning and aesthetic pleasure, available for consolation even at the darkest moments of sickness and failure. (Cox 1992: 19–21)

For Richard Law, writing of Shrewsbury in the 1900s, the point had been to evoke the tranquil and now utterly lost world that privilege enabled. Cox, likewise, found his reference points in a vanished past, but for him the values created there were recuperable, in a state system purged of progressive influence – to which end his energies for the next ten years were devoted. Cox was deeply unhappy about the 'revolutionary' cultural and educational changes over which Labour presided. 'Anarchy is becoming fashionable', the initial manifesto of the Black Papers declared. 'Plowdenism' in the primary school destroyed the ordered community of learning, in favour of 'free choice'. The 'grammar school concepts of discipline and hard work' were being 'treated with contempt'. In the wake of the events of 1968 in France, and the movement against the Vietnam war, universities had become sites of 'egalitarianism and destruction' (Cox and Dyson 1969, cited in Cox 1992: 144–5). These shifts were not just the outcome of a temporary extremism among the young; they stemmed also from a lack of belief among policy-makers in the role of education. Gripped by a 'bankrupt romanticism', they forgot that teachers must be above all 'exponents of the great achievements of past civilization' and urged them instead to 'decode the radical critique of the young' (Cox 1992: 144–6). Labour was not extending educational reform, but undermining its essentially meritocratic character; it was betraying the interests of the bright working-class child, who was cut off by progressive relativism and licence from the standards and the culture which were not only valuable ends in themselves, but also the prime means of individual empowerment (Halsey et al. 1980: 8; K. Jones 1992: 12).

The Black Paper critique was thus based initially not so much on a Conservative rhetoric of national decline than on a disillusioned judgement, made from within the tradition of equal opportunity reform, of Labour's achievements: it was the first popular, effective critique of post-war welfarism and its capture by a producer class (K. Jones 1989). But from the beginning the Black Papers offered a home to other voices, those of Conservatives such as Angus Maude and Geoffrey Bantock, who had been long-time, frankly elitist critics of reform. By 1972, Cox himself had joined the Conservative Party, and the Black Paper project became a part of the work of developing a new programme for Conservatism in education.

Conservatives had fought and lost the election of 1974 with educational policies which largely centred on questions of expenditure, but within the party there was a rising interest in questions of standards and values (Knight 1990). From 1975, with Thatcher as leader, this emphasis became stronger, and was linked to a wider politics. The polemics against the cultural damage effected by the comprehensive school and by progressive primary education remained. But they now took on more general meaning: what reform threatened were not only the established and successful educational cultures evoked by Cox in his memoir of Nunsthorpe, but also the wider systems of meanings and values that constituted English culture. Educational conservatism linked itself with wider controversies about national identity.

Conservatism, culture and race

This shift can only be understood against a wider background. In 1968 Enoch Powell had launched what was in effect a movement against black immigration, in the name of the defence of English identity. Powell's political impact was massive: his call for opposition to entry to the European Common Market in 1974 swung millions of English votes away from his own party and towards Labour – though it is notable that his influence was much less in Wales and Scotland (Johnson 1997). Powell's conception of politics was in important ways a discursive and linguistic one: it was about 'trying to provide people with words and ideas which will fit their predicament better than the words and ideas which they are using at the moment' (Powell, quoted in Shepherd 1996: 297). The 'predicament' which

Powell imagined in 1968 was that of working-class English people, faced with threats to their homes, their jobs and their identity from an inexorable process of inward migration. The language he used was that of nation, conflict and danger: the government's liberal attitudes to immigration amounted to 'the nation building its own funeral pyre' (1996: 347). The cultural transformation of his West Midlands constituency was in some ways worse than the experience of war: 'acts of an enemy, bombs from the sky' people could understand, but now they faced an 'invasion which the Government apparently approved' and which left them bewildered.

It is impossible to understand the English politics of education in the 1970s – and later – without appreciating the ways in which it was shaped by cultural meanings and conflicts in which questions of 'race' and 'nation' played a central part. The right responded to school-centred multiculturalist and anti-racist policies with a populist and potent discourse. Profoundly influenced by Powell's objective of discovering a language in which experience could be voiced, evaluated and connected to action, it sought constantly to redescribe education in terms of threatened tradition, identities unsettled by reforming projects, and cultural crisis; and in this process to identify a new danger, that of multiculturalism. Multiculturalism – according to the Black Paper contributor Edward Norman, Dean of Peterhouse College, Cambridge – rested on the myth that England was a pluralist society. It was not: however much intellectuals might 'put the values of their society up for sale', working-class and lower-middle class England 'showed few signs of religious or moral diversity' (Norman 1977: 103). The school curriculum should reflect such uniformity; educational reform which tried to do otherwise was a betrayal of identity.

Norman's position amounted to a call for intervention to halt the slide towards cultural degeneration – in other words, for strong action by the state to organize social cohesion around established and traditional norms, in which questions of Englishness would be central. This would be the hallmark of Conservative policy for the next twenty years; it would supply many of the resources for the right's attempts to create a popular politics of education, and ensure a profound if not always explicit racialization of educational discourse.

Market thinking

But it was not the only theme. Law and Maude, whose influence on the Black Papers was noted by Conservative activists, had an economic as well as a cultural position. They were what Hobsbawm calls 'old believers', people for whom state influence on economic life was practically disastrous and ultimately totalitarian, and for whom the only rational form of economic organization was one in which prices, levels of employment and decisions about output were left for market forces to determine. For thirty years after 1945, these ideas had seemed redundant. After the collapse of the economics of the golden age and the inability of welfare state societies to sustain economic growth, low rates of inflation and high levels of employment, they re-emerged. From the mid-1970s on, Conservatism sought a programme to arrest the drift of post-war policy towards ever more extensive social reform and greater levels of public ownership. In education, groups such as the National Council for Educational Standards and the Institute for Economic Affairs elaborated the concrete, sectoral detail of such an agenda. It reached a wider audience in the *Black Paper* of 1977, where Stuart Sexton, later to be an adviser to the Secretary of State, set out to 'sketch a new system for secondary education'. Its basis would be 'absolute freedom of choice by application': parents and children would no longer be allocated to schools by local authorities. Where schools were oversubscribed, they would select students on the basis of 'ability and aptitude'. Where they were undersubscribed, they would face the possibility of closure unless they improved the service they offered. The system would thus have some but no means all of the characteristics of an educational market (Tooley 1999); but it would be regulated by an 'effective and independent inspectorate' and a stipulated 'minimum curriculum' with specified 'minimum standards' (Sexton 1977).

The programme sketched in a couple of pages by Sexton was slow to be developed – it was not until the Education Reform Act of 1988 that it became the basis of policy. But its presence in the 'educational space' – the arena in which objectives, values and procedures were publicly argued over – meant that from the mid-1970s onwards the schooling system that had developed in England after 1944 was now facing three distinct kinds of challenge. Cultural restorationists demanded that established definitions of knowledge and hierarchies of schooling should be reasserted. Civil servants at the DES, supported post-1976 by the Labour leadership, sought a more decisive role for central policy, organized around the relation of school to the world of work. Advocates of the free market sought reforms that would make parental choice the operative principle of the school system. In the two decades after their victory in 1979, Conservatives would draw from the repertoires of all three tendencies in a restructuring of education whose pace and tensions would have consequences throughout Britain.

4

Conservatism: Triumph and Failure

The Conservative Programme

The overall themes of the Conservative programme are best condensed in the title of Andrew Gamble's book, *The Free Economy and the Strong State* (Gamble 1988). Economically, British Conservatism was in the vanguard of global neo-liberalism. Its deregulatory policies helped create the global financial markets of the 1990s; its monetary policies accelerated the closing down of unprofitable industries and promoted a profound social and economic restructuring. Change of this radical kind was necessarily accompanied by political confrontation and transformation, which produced the strong state of Gamble's title. Conservative legislation sought to drive neo-liberal principles into the heart of public policy. An emphasis on cost reduction, privatization and deregulation was accompanied by vigorous measures against the institutional bases of Conservatism's opponents, and the promotion of new forms of public management. The outcome of these processes was a form of governance in which market principles were advanced at the same time as central authority was strengthened.

In the first and earliest instance, economic restructuring was connected to employment policy. Conservatism normalized the use of unemployment as a strategy against inflation: the number of unemployed doubled between 1979 and 1981, and rose to 3 million by 1982. It declined to 1.8 million by 1989, by which time a substantial occupational shift had occurred. Accelerating the trends of the 1970s, manufacturing employment fell and employment in the service sector rose. In the first four years of the 1980s, Britain lost 25 per cent of its manufacturing capacity: by 1988, just over 5 million were employed in industry, compared with 15 million in services, one-third of them part-time and the majority female (R. K. Brown 1990). In the process of this restructuring, Conservatism lowered wages to the point where British labour was significantly cheaper than that of other major European economies; and where for a long period in the 1980s the youth labour market scarcely existed (Cohen 1997). At the same time it defeated working-class militancy, breaking the miners' union and legislating decisively to suppress picketing and solidarity strike action. Its privat-ization of public utilities set an example to governments worldwide, abolishing public corporations and reducing public-sector support for services such as housing, welfare and education. Its policy of cutting public expenditure and subjecting the remainder of the welfare state to a market-influenced system of organization undermined the main element in the system of post-war reform, and contributed to widening inequalities between rich and poor, documented by the Rowntree *Inquiry into Income and Wealth* (Rowntree Foundation 1995). Polit-ically, its most significant achievement was to force Labour into the abandonment of its own historic programme and into accommodation with the Conservative agenda: the Labour Party that finally achieved office in 1997 was one which was reconciled – or committed – to a market economy, a scaled-down public sector and a much less powerful role for trade union interests.

By the end of its first decade Conservatism had presided over and in some sense provoked a major change to the social character of post-war Britain: the workforce of 1989 was not that of 1979 and the ways in which its housing, health, welfare and economic life were organized were likewise vastly different. As Hobsbawm suggests, the class-consciousness of the pre-1979 period, based partly on collective organ-ization in trade unions and communities and partly on sharp segregra-tion between the working class and middle class in housing, life chances and patterns of consumption, came to an end. Cracks had widened between different sections of the working class. For some, restructuring meant increased prosperity, access to better-paid jobs in parts of the service sector and – in some respects – choice. Home-owning, private health provision and higher education all experienced significant growth in the 1980s. For others, it had an opposite meaning: millions were relegated to an insecure existence on the margins of employment. At the same time as disparities of earnings became more marked within the working class, the gap between the income of the richest tenth of society and the poorest tenth grew in the 1980s, as the share of the rich increased and that of the poorest fell (Glennerster 1995: 172, 230). 'Society', wrote Will Hutton in 1995, 'is dividing before our eyes, opening up new fissures in the working population.' It had split into three groups – the 30 per cent who were 'absolutely disadvantaged', the 30 per cent who were 'marginalized and insecure' and the 40 per cent whose 'market power has increased since 1979' (Hutton 1995: 107–8). Hutton's judgement was that this new alignment of poverty and relative privilege constituted 'a new and ugly shape in British society', whose existence amounted to an indictment of post-1979 Conservatism. But he also acknowledged that, from another angle, it amounted to a political success: substantial social groups had benefited from Conservative-driven change, and had a vested interest in maintaining the new arrangements. Conservatism could not have governed for eighteen years without such a constituency.

Nevertheless, such changes, and the means by which they were pursued, created enormous social stress: the casualties of Conservative policy were many, and the conflicts it provoked were substantial; mass strikes, protest, riot and the breakdown of cohesive social relations under the impact of mass, regionalized unemployment, were strong characteristics of the period. In this context, government attempts to reassert social cohesion were – as Gamble's title suggests – often very strongly authoritarian. Inasmuch as these attempts were a means of dealing with fierce opposition to the effects of free market policies the authoritarianism was rational. In other ways, it was destabilizing – not least to Conservatism itself. Conservatism had always offered itself to supporters and opponents as a social philosophy built around continuity rather than sudden change, pragmatism rather than rigorous doctrine. According to Anthony Quinton, Conservatives see society in terms of a 'texture of inherited customs and institutions'; and for Roger Scruton 'Conservatism arises directly from the sense that one belongs to some continuing and pre-existing social order' (Quinton 1978: 16; Scruton 1984: 21). Even in the 1990s, after the shock of Thatcherism, the MP David Willetts contrasted these preferences with the 'very different vision of the human condition' possessed by socialists, for whom the ideal was a movement for change that would sever all such customary ties (Willetts 1992: 69). The companion of this social philosophy was a gradualist political outlook: grandiose schemes for social transformation are suspect in principle, since they threaten to disrupt the social order out of which cultural and political cohesion arise.

Problems of Conservatism

In the conditions of the 1980s, this disposition became anachronistic. Conservatives found it difficult to square their reverent picture of social cohesion and continuity with the permanently unsettling effects of market-driven economic upheaval, in which 'dynamism' came to be valued above custom, and global impact above the consolidation of national identity. Likewise the militant assertions of national interest and national identity which had served Mrs Thatcher well in her offensive against foreign domestic enemies did not provide resources with which Conservatives could successfully deal with questions of European and domestic policy. Britain's relationship with the rest of the European Union was the issue which ultimately brought Mrs Thatcher down and destroyed the unity of Conservatism in the 1990s. Similarly, around questions of race Conservatism had difficulty in accepting changes that had become integral to British society since the early 1970s; both its leaders and its activists were reluctant to recognize the legitimacy of black grievances and the full citizenship rights of black people. In the same way, as Mrs Thatcher eventually acknowledged, Conservatism had difficulty in handling relations between the component 'nations' of the United Kingdom (Thatcher 1993: 618–24). The social, economic and political basis of post-1979 Conservatism was, very clearly, southern England: other parts of Britain provided fewer votes, and reaped fewer benefits. Proudly on record as declaring, 'I'm an English nationalist and never you forget it', Thatcher championed a version of national identity and social solidarity that drew heavily on specifically English traditions, and did nothing to close the growing gap between the mindset and social basis of her politics and the condition of the rest of the United Kingdom. Conservatism had begun to dismantle the nation to which its idea of 'national identity' had historically been attached. It became more evidently recognizable as an English, rather than a British movement: when its leaders and intellectuals discussed 'tradition', 'heritage', 'identity' and the other nation-related concepts that became part of the political discourse of the 1980s, it was clear that their references and frameworks were nearly always Anglo-centric. To the strains arising from free market economics were added those produced by the cultural project of 1980s Conservatism.

Wales, Scotland, Northern Ireland

In Wales and Scotland, national movements had grown stronger in the 1970s as a result of the perceived failure of the centrally directed post-war settlement to safeguard jobs and social welfare – 'evidence that the state was no longer working in the interests of the nation' (Paterson

1998: 60). Harvie notes that the recession of the early 1980s created 'instant post-industrialization' in Scotland, carrying away most of the 'industry expensively induced to settle there' by the development grants of the 1960s and '70s (Harvie 1993). Similarly, in Wales the decline of traditional industry set off a chain reaction of economic, political and social consequences, which undermined both local communities and habitual political allegiances (Rees and Rees 1980). Conservatism responded to these problems from a weak position: what was seen as its responsibility for unemployment and welfare cuts reduced its local political standing to the point where, by 1997, it held not a single parliamentary seat in Wales and Scotland. But its absence of local influence did not lessen its determination to impose radical, market-orientated policies devised in Whitehall on national polities which were seen as bastions of redundant collectivism. Noting that 70 per cent of Scots in the 1980s lived in public housing, Mrs Thatcher inferred that this was evidence of a 'dependency culture' which sustained 'socialist politics' (1993: 620). Her attempts to break this culture, by centralizing policy initiative and proceeding on the basis of administrative decree rather than popular legitimacy, provoked massive opposition. 'There was', she acknowledged, 'no tartan Thatcherite revolution' (p. 618). In fact, Thatcher complained, Scottish Conservatives had colluded with their collectivist opponents, so that 'feeling isolated and vulnerable in the face of so much . . . hostility, they regularly portrayed themselves as standing up for Scotland against me' (p. 619). Conservatism combined attempts at centralization with concessions to nationalist sentiment in ways whose political and institutional outcomes were contradictory.

There were similar paradoxes in Wales. At one level, Conservatism involved 'a highly assimilationist drift', which subjected large sectors of Welsh public life to 'rule by Westminster-appointed quango' rather than by elected local government (Bradbury 1998). At another, Welsh Conservative politicians worked to increase the powers of the Welsh Office – nowhere more so than in education, where Conservative-endorsed curriculum change promoted the Welsh language – in schools if not in Higher Education (Snicker 1998; R. Jones et al. 2002). The decline in the numbers of Welsh speakers which was so marked a feature of earlier post-war decades slowed almost to a halt between 1981 and 1991, as a result not of rural renewal, but of the growth of what Aitchison and Carter call a 'new bourgeoisie . . . with a substantial and influential Welsh-speaking element' (1999: 93). This 'bourgeoisie', strongly based in the public sector, owed its rise to Conservative sponsorship of new institutions – schools, media, quangos and public-sector bodies. Yet its allegiances continued to lie elsewhere, in nationalism or in social democracy.

In Northern Ireland, conservatism faced problems of a different kind, but even here centralist authority was mitigated by policies which aimed in some way to negotiate with local interests. Mrs Thatcher sought the military defeat of the IRA, and rather than compromise with nationalism was willing to see the hunger-strikers of 1981–2 fast themselves to death. But, at the same time, Conservatism's Northern Irish policy was marked by an attempt to develop some alternative to 'sectarianism' as a basis for social organization: to this end, there was a massive outflow of funding from London to Belfast to sustain welfare services, and within education, tentatively, the Conservative administration came to support some degree of non-denominational schooling, and of curricular recognition for nationalist traditions (Dunn 2000). Republicanism was quick to point out that these measures were intended to weaken the political force of nationalism, even as they made symbolic concessions to it, and 'to make good West Brits of us all' (O'Connor 1993). Nevertheless, they necessarily involved Westminster in a dialogue around identity and tradition whose outcome – as we shall see – was more pluralist than that arrived at in England.

Schooling and inequality

Education bore the marks of both the economic and the social impact of Conservative policy. According to Glennerster, public expenditure on education as a percentage of GDP had fallen under Callaghan's government from a high point of 6.5 per cent in 1975–6 to 5.4 per cent in 1978–9. After a slight rise in the early 1980s it fell to 5.3 per cent in 1983–4 and remained below that level until virtually the end of Conservative rule in 1995–6 (Glennerster 1998: 37). Capital spending on schools fell to a point where by 1993–4 it was less than half its mid-1970s level. After rising in the 1980s, when student numbers, especially in primary schools, decreased, spending per head of the school student population fell steeply in the 1990s (Smith et al. 1997: 127). The system was subjected not only to financial constraint but to the pressures of social polarization: in 1979 an estimated 10 per cent of children lived in poverty – i.e. in households whose income was less than half the national average; by 1993, the proportion had risen to 33 per cent (Oppenheim and Lister 1997: 24). Education reflected these divisions. As the resources available to the wealthy increased, the fee-paying sector grew in size, reversing a century-old trend: in 1979, it attracted 5.8 per cent of the British student population; by 1991, the figure had risen to 6.7 per cent. Nearly all students in this sector could be assured of entering higher education, whereas only one in four of state school students in the mid-1990s gained a university place (Glennerster 1998: 38; Wilby 1997: 142). Within state education, poverty and educational failure were strongly correlated. In secondary schools, for instance, statistics which demonstrated an overall rise in levels of attainment served to conceal a widening disparity between examination success rates in rich and poor areas (Smith et al. 1997:135). As a 1997 Ofsted survey reported, state schools with heavy concentrations of poor children were by far the worst performers at GCSE level.

In some senses, there was nothing new in this. Stratification by social class and the crystallization of class differences in institutions hugely differing in the status and resources they command were – as we have seen – long recognized as the central 'tragedy' of British education (Tawney 1973a). What was new about inequality in the Conservative period were the ways in which it was sustained by the interrelationship between the increasingly diverse and complex forms adopted by the state school system and the opportunities offered to privileged groups to pursue educational advantage within this diverse system through the greater exercise of 'choice': in the terms of Gewirtz et al., 'choice systems privilege[d] certain sorts of family and disadvantage[d] others' (1995: 22). To understand these forms, we need to analyse three strands of Conservative policy, distinct in terms of their motivation and argument, and interwoven in practice – modernization, marketization and tradition-centredness.

Modernization

The modernizing strand in Conservative education policy accepted the commonplaces of the international policy community – not unlike those of Callaghan's Ruskin speech – which by the 1980s had rejected the equation between educational expansion, of an undifferentiated kind, and economic growth. There was instead a much greater attention to specifying technical and economic needs. As Papadopoulos explains, the OECD had long since ceased to believe that educational investment was itself producing economic benefits. Education's economic role – that is, in OECD terms, its major role – was now seen more precisely, in terms of its capacity to assist or to hinder economic restructuring: its focus should be on 'updating skills and competences of individual workers', an 'essential requirement for the development of flexible labour markets capable of responding to continuous change' (1994: 171). Since, as Kovacs puts it, 'the skills needed to function competently in everyday life are very different today than they were one or two decades ago', the curriculum required modification; and, since 'the knowledge and qualifications thresholds for jobs have risen', there was a need for a rapid rise in educational standards, as measured by performance in public examinations (1998: 222–3). All this required a more detailed kind of intervention by government in education.

Positions like these became a commonplace of policy discourse, especially in relation to the themes of 'education for the world of work' which burgeoned in the 1980s. Nevertheless, modernization troubled Conservatism. Much of the force of the right-wing critique of post-war reform had been based on a sense that 'excellence' resided not in the raising of the level of mass education, but in retaining established, elite educational institutions, whose success was a function of their selectivity. 'More will mean worse', Kingsley Amis, the novelist convert to Conservatism, had warned in 1967 (Amis 1981: 167). But it was with exactly the supply of 'more' that Conservatism was occupied. The number of under-5 children in state schools rose from 17 per cent in the early 1970s to 55 per cent by 1995/6 (Glennerster 1998: 43). The number of 17-year-olds attending schools and colleges full-time rose from less than 24 per cent in 1979 to over 60 per cent in 1994–5 (Glennerster 1998: 46). Post-16 education and training thus became the experience of the majority of students – especially of girls, 75 per cent of whom were in 1995 taking full-time courses post-16 (Arnot et al. 1999: 16). Higher education expanded rapidly: at the end of the 1970s, 12.7 per cent of the post-school age-group were in higher education; by 1990, age participation rates had topped 20 per cent (Ainley 1994). By 1987, the separate two-tier exam system at 16+ had been brought to an end, and a common examination, the GCSE, introduced. In 1988, the Education Reform Act established the national curriculum, a universalistic form of provision which ensured that the curriculum provided for girls no longer denied them access to scientific and technological education. In all these respects, Conservative-led changes significantly increased curricular and institutional access, in ways that seemed to conform to the classic pattern of post-war schooling, and even to speed up the processes by which it expanded provision and certification to new age cohorts and social groups.

At the same time, Conservatives increased the interventionist capacities of the state. For Hobsbawm's 'old believers', the ideal form of state was one in which central powers were minimal, and autonomous institutions determined their own objectives, values and procedures. In the course of the 1980s, the impossibility of this perspective became plain. Keith Joseph, a politician who in opposition had done more than any other to rehabilitate free market ideas, found himself as Secretary of State commanding an apparatus that was now increasingly involved in specifying the everyday practice of schools. So, while the Centre for Policy Studies, the think-tank he set up in the 1970s, promoted ways of thinking about education whose inspiration was traditional, and whose institutional model remained the autonomous and self-governing school, Joseph, like the ministers who succeeded him, organized in the name of 'effective education' a vast new complex of regulations and regulators that would measure and direct the processes and outcomes of schooling. Ofsted, the Office for Standards in Education – created in 1992 – was in one sense the product of two decades of Conservative critiques of state education, but in another it was the very reverse of their ideals.

Marketization

The modernization of schooling was articulated with a second major trend in Conservative policy, marketization. Pierson writes that 'the original and "authentic" aspiration of the new right was to replace states with markets' (Pierson 1998: 168). As Tooley regretfully points out, this was not what happened in education. For him, the defining features of a market are an absence of state provision and funding, minimal regulation, easy entry for new suppliers, and the operation of a price mechanism responsive to supply and demand (Tooley 1999: 11). Conservative policy from this perspective is better seen as a set of 'choice' reforms, the chief feature of which is that 'parental choice is permitted within a heavily regulated, state provided and funded system' (1999: 11). Within this system, market norms do not properly apply. Parents do not pay for the essentials of schooling, new schools cannot easily appear in response to parental demand and government has no intention of lessening its powers to regulate the curriculum and monitor performance. But to emphasize as Tooley does the limitations of Conservative change is to under-emphasize their novelty and force. 'Marketization', understood in the sense of reforms that strengthened competition and differentiation within the school system, brought about major shifts in the management and cultures of schools and the behaviour of large groups of parents and school students.

On the supply side of schooling, Conservative governments worked to increase the diversity of provision. Following the failure of Labour's tentative plans for universal comprehensivization, some 10 per cent of pupils in England in the 1980s continued to be educated in grammar or secondary modern schools (Simon 1991: 587). The number of students in private schools rose, and the private sector was strengthened in 1980 by the Assisted Places Scheme, which subsidized places for 30,000 students at 'independent' schools. From 1986, the government encouraged and part-funded the development of fifteen selective 'City Technology Colleges', outside the local authority system (Whitty et al. 1993). But it was the Education Reform Act of 1988 that did most to increase diversity of provision. It allowed schools to 'opt out' of the locally-controlled system and to become 'grant-maintained' – that is, administratively self-governing, and funded, with striking generosity, by the central state. By 1997, 16 per cent of secondary schools in England and Wales had become grant-maintained, with intakes that were notably more middle-class than those of LEA comprehensive schools (Benn and Chitty 1996). In the 1990s, other categories of school were created: specialist schools, permitted to select 10 per cent of their intake on grounds of ability; technology schools, funded at a higher level than the norm (Halpin 1997). Thus, while the secondary system in England and Wales remained nominally comprehensive, the reality, especially post-1988, was different. Once church schools, the remaining grammar and secondary modern schools, grant-maintained schools and other new types of institution were excluded, it had become clear by 1997 that the number of locally controlled comprehensive schools – that is, schools recruiting from across the ability range – had been reduced to only 40 per cent of the overall total (Fitz et al. 1997). Pre-existing patterns of diversity had been accentuated to create a complex and subtly differentiated hierarchy of schools, whose status, reputation and achievement levels varied considerably.

Diversity was accompanied by a degree of financial autonomy. After 1988, schools managed their own budgets, with their income depending in part on the number of students they attracted, as 'customers' of their services. Customers, or their parents at least, would make choices between schools on the basis of performance indicators, in the form of examination and test results. The impact of these changes on the school was to induce the development of a new managerial culture, adopting private-sector models of management, and intended to bring about what Fergusson calls 'a more far-reaching overhaul of the methods and purposes of service delivery' than could be achieved by central direction and regulation alone (Fergusson 1994: 95). Among parents, according to Gewirtz and her colleagues, the effect of choice-based reform was to accentuate the patterns of advantage and disadvantage between parents who possessed the resources, cultural capacity and know-how to make informed choices in the new system, and those who did not (Gewirtz et al. 1995).

The Conservative programme for education, even where it expressed strong expansionary and in some sort universalizing tendencies, characteristic of 'modernization', was thus implemented through a medium – marketization, or choice-based reform – which tended to accentuate differentiation between schools and between groups of students and parents. This outcome was intended, and promoted, by government directive as well as by the logic of the market and was further strengthened by other aspects of the Conservative programme. Thus Keith Joseph contrasted the supposedly 'levelling' tendencies of education policy in the previous period with his own commitment to differentiation (Knight 1990: 152). Differentiation ran through most aspects of Conservative modernization: the GCSE was remodelled in the 1990s to create higher and lower tiers of entry. In the 16–19 sector, a significant numerical expansion was accompanied by the development of a curriculum and examination system which maintained strong boundaries between academic, vocational and 'general' low-level qualifications (Ainley 1998); and the growth in the number of university places in the 1980s occurred alongside the accentuation of distinctions in the status and resourcing of degree courses (Ainley 1994).

Market-centred change was much stronger in England than in other parts of Britain. In this it differed from modernization, which in varying forms was a preoccupation of policy communities throughout Britain. Welsh policy-makers accepted from the late 1970s onwards that, whatever the past splendours of a grammar school system much more open to working-class students than its English counterpart, education in Wales was more recently characterized by a very high level of failure, which policy needed to address. 'By far the most distinctive feature of the education system in Wales', wrote Rees and Rees in 1980, 'is its ability to turn out over a quarter of its pupils with no tangible benefit from their five years or so of secondary schooling' (1980: 77). The Welsh policy debate of the 1980s had thus as one of its major themes the apparently exceptionally poor performance of Welsh secondary schools, and the means by which they might be modernized (Gorard 1998). Scottish policy, meanwhile, had moved swiftly, via the Munn and Dunning reports of 1977, to address questions of curriculum and assessment reform (Pickard 2000). There was a consensus in mainland Britain therefore around the necessity of reshaping systems so as to enable higher levels of attainment, and work around such themes proceeded throughout the Conservative period. Marketization, however, was in some respects a peculiarity of the English, designed by policy elites much more strongly committed than those of Wales and Scotland to selective education, legislatively enabled by a Conservative Party strongly rooted in the south of England, and implemented most enthusiastically in those areas of the south-east that benefited from the growth of finance and services that were distinguishing economic marks of the Conservative period. In Wales and Scotland, the number of grant-maintained schools was very small; local education authorities retained a stronger role; local ideologies of education continued to stress more egalitarian goals, and – as we shall see, especially in Scotland – opposition to what were seen as distinctively English educational policies took a militant form. Although the operation of parental choice in Scotland did have some effects on class-based differentiation between Scottish schools (Munn 2001), it was in areas like London that market effects were strongest: in mid-1990s London one-third of parents did not obtain their first choice of secondary school (Audit Commission 1996).

Tradition

The same centrifugal pattern emerges in relation to the third theme of Conservative policy – tradition. The impact of tradition, at least in its Conservative form, was felt much more strongly in England than in other parts of Britain. As we have seen, the New Right of the 1970s, especially in education, expressed itself in neo-Conservative terms, focused on 'problems of declining social control and public authority' (Pierson 1998: 143) and sought solutions in which strengthened conceptions of national identity, as well as government activity to shape the deviant behaviour of individuals, played an important part. These approaches to questions of social cohesion were markedly different from those of the two decades before 1979, in which the dominant assumption had been that the most effective means of creating a common, cohesive culture was a greater degree of equality in social provision. They had a considerable impact on the views of Conservative activists and, by the late 1980s and early '90s, on government itself. Their outcome was what Hall has termed a 'regressive modernization' (Hall 1988). Modernization was articulated with tradition so as to produce discourses and policies that, though politically often effective, were at odds with many of the most powerful tendencies that arose in the course of the social and economic restructuring of British life that occurred in the Conservative period. Thus, in curricular terms, state schooling in England was organized by 1990 around strong centralized control of provision, through a national curriculum which stressed nation-centred themes and which embodied opposition to local diversity, and in particular to any strong response to ethnic or class-based subcultures. The rhetoric of education ministers, particularly between 1991 and 1994, centred on a defence of tradition against innovation and nation against cosmopolitan influences; it exemplied a strong preference for print-centred culture, and a rejection of new media cultures (K. Jones 1994a). John Patten, Major's Education Secretary in the most triumphalist phase of educational Conservatism, expressed these attitudes in their most striking form:

> I am afraid that the interests of children are not served either by some of the examination boards. One recently defended the use of a hamburger advertisement in a public exam by claiming that it provided just as important food for thought for children as our great literary heritage. They'd give us Chaucer with Chips, Milton with mayonnaise.... I want William Shakespeare in our classrooms, not Ronald McDonald. (Patten 1993).

Yet there was a disparity between this approach and the principles of cultural organization which operated in other areas of social life: there, cultural regulation was slackening and 'choice', as exercised in new forms of cultural consumption and lifestyle, was growing. New forms of communications technology proliferated; the regulated duopoly in television was brought to an end by deregulation and channel multiplication; the audience for mass media fragmented; and cultural hybridity became – at least in some cultural sectors – a norm. Conservatism attempted to resolve the difficulties that arose from the tensions between its educational project and developments in other sectors of society by a militant and centrally directed programme of curricular transformation that tended to see the diversity of contemporary culture less as a product of social and economic change than as the effect of political influence, especially that exerted by public-sector professionals and local, left-wing politicians.

Tradition-centred policies provided an essential resource for the right's campaigns. In England, 'tradition', alongside 'standards', became the slogan in whose name Conservatism pursued its campaigns against progressivism and what it saw as the politicization of the curriculum. Since the middle 1970s, the right had sensed the popular attractiveness of campaigns around 'moral traditionalism' and public order (Epstein and Johnson 1999). The National Viewers' and Listeners' Association, led by Mary Whitehouse, had linked a collapse of sexual morality to the influence of public-service television (Tracey and Morrison 1979). The popular press had connected a supposed crisis of law and order to the presence of migrant communities (Hall et al. 1978). The public-sector strikes of 1978–9 were memorably presented in the press as a 'winter of discontent' in which trade union power threatened the fabric of community life. Conservatives thus possessed by the 1980s a discursive repertoire from which to draw, in depicting educational change and its problems and conflicts as instances of a more general social crisis. It was in this light that they sought to represent and battle against the paths taken by educational reform in the post-1979 period.

There was much to fight about. Sex education; religious education; spelling; the 'promotion of homosexuality'; the defence of A levels; 'race'; peace education; police involvement in schools; teacher militancy; corporal punishment; media studies; British history – these were among the issues viewed by Conservativism from the impassioned perspective that a defence of 'tradition' supplied. But its grasp of social change, and of its own role in promoting it, was narrower than the range of issues it addressed. Even as some of its policies served to increase women's participation in the labour force, or to raise the levels of achievement of large numbers of female students, Conservatism at another level sought to hold in check the multiplicity of gendered identities that such change tended to support, and to insist, in the face of change, on the maintenance of a narrow and domestic idea of the feminine (Arnot et al. 1999). The débâcle of John Major's 'back to basics' campaign, when the Conservative politics of the family finally discovered the nature of contemporary sexuality in the form of the indiscretions of its own MPs, was the culmination, and the endpoint, of twenty years of moral traditionalism (McRobbie 1994). It was matched, almost simultaneously, by the failure of traditionalist educational politics: the 1993–4 teachers' boycott of national curriculum testing was motivated in large part by the archaism of the Conservative programme. After 1994, 'tradition' dropped from the practical agenda of the right.

In other parts of Britain concerns with 'tradition' took a different, non-Conservative form. They stressed not the imperative of purging the destructive influences that sought to infiltrate a national culture seen as fixed and 'given' by heritage but rather the need to develop curricula that stressed national distinctiveness much more strongly than previously, while adopting socially inclusive and relatively pluralist definitions of national cultures. The Scottish 'National Guidelines' on English language, for instance, insisted that 'the common experiences, activities, history and artefacts of the people of Scotland constitute an identifiable and distinctive culture', but at the same time spoke of the 'diversity of the community' and its histories (Scottish Office Education Department 1991: 68, 3). 'The curriculum and ethos of schools in Wales,' affirmed the Curriculum Council for Wales in 1989, 'will need to reflect the *varied nature* of the Welsh identity' (cited in B. Jones and Lewis 1995: 23). In Northern Ireland, the government combined repression of Republicanism with the sponsorship of reforms intended to promote the reconciliation of Republican and Unionist communities. Established traditions – which had created a schooling system consisting of 'religiously polarized institutions serving each major cultural group' (Murray 1985: 51) – were increasingly seen as a problem. Rather than celebrating Britishness and the Union, Westminster supported the efforts of a section of educators, who aimed to celebrate both 'traditions' in Ireland. It thus found itself supporting culturally pluralist approaches that it would have rejected in England, in the name of a strategy that was 'healing' in the view of some, Machiavellian in the judgement of others (Rolston 1998). In England 'tradition', operationalized via a literary canon, an emphasis on standard English, and nation-centred topics for the history classroom, was firmly monocultural; in Northern Ireland, by contrast, it was defined in terms of the dual legitimacy of 'Catholic' and 'Protestant' heritages. And, by the same inverted logic, Northern Ireland saw the Conservative government responding sympathetically, and with financial resources, to campaigners aiming to establish new, integrated primary and comprehensive schools.

Stages of Conservative Policy

The history of Conservative-driven change is one of acceleration. In the early 1980s, change was piecemeal and hesitant; by the middle 1990s, it had become hectic and continuous, as government revised not only the legacy of post-war reform but also its own earlier legislation. What permitted the acceleration was the growing sense of government, and of the lobbyists whose policy initiatives fuelled new legislation, that opposition to right-wing change was weakened to the point where there were few limits to the policies that Conservatism could pursue. In the 1980s, some of its most obdurate opponents – teacher unions in England and Wales, local education authorities – had been defeated. By the 1990s, the Labour Party had edged towards acceptance of the combination of centralizing and market-based changes which Conservatism had introduced. In this later climate, Conservative policies developed qualities of 'excess' – especially in the ways in which they promoted selection and championed a right-wing version of tradition. But this triumphalist moment did not last. In many areas – funding, assessment, selection – Conservative policies had provoked strong oppositional movements, for which the principles of equal-opportunity-orientated reform were plainly an issue. Conflict with such movements proved damaging for Conservatism, which by the mid-1990s faced protests over low levels of education spending in the English shires, large-scale opposition in Scotland to 'Thatcherism' in education, and a boycott by teachers in England and Wales of national assessment procedures. Thus, a peculiar double movement was in process: even while the basic building blocks of its system were assimilated into a two-party consensus, in other respects Conservatism's educational policies were contributing to the electoral débâcle of 1997.

Early stages

The Conservative manifesto of 1979 was, by later standards, a modest one, and where it promised most it least delivered. The real significance of Thatcher's Conservatism for education was clearer elsewhere – in the implications for spending of its declaration that 'public expenditure is at the heart of Britain's economic difficulties' (White Paper 1979); and in its realization that policies such as the sale of council housing could by consolidating anti-collectivist trends in society create new constituencies of Conservative support. But in direct terms of education policy, the manifesto offered little: repeal of legislation that would have abolished selection in the state system; some measures to increase parental choice; a new attention to basic skills and, most radically, a national system of testing at 7, 11 and 14.

The proposals on testing would have led to an early confrontation with the entire educational establishment – that grouping of local authorities, academics, policy experts and teacher unions which at the end of the 1970s was still, though with some reservations, committed to the objectives and the institutional procedures associated with the post-war settlement. Such a confrontation would have added to the problems that Mrs Thatcher's government – intensely unpopular in its first three years in office – had to face. Mark Carlisle, Secretary of State for Education from 1979 to 1981, spoke accordingly of the need for a 'conciliatory rather than provocative approach' (Knight 1990: 138). The DES continued to push forward, albeit slowly, some of the centralizing themes that had been established by Callaghan's Ruskin speech: it began to play a role in co-ordinating

LEA curriculum development; it promoted initiatives designed to encourage technical and vocational education in schools. Likewise, other aspects of Labour's agenda retained a place – most notably the insistence of the Warnock Committee, embodied in the 1981 Education Act, on the integration of children with 'special needs' into the mainstream education system. New policy, embodied in the 1980 Education Act, centred on a narrower range of measures than those suggested by the manifesto. The Assisted Places Scheme provided subsidies for students transferring from state schools to the private sector. The publication of schools' examination results – A and O level, CSE – helped operationalize the principle of professionals' accountability for their work. Parental choice was extended by legislation to give parents the right of appeal against a local authority's choice of school for their children, and the power to send their children to schools across local authority boundaries. The welfare measures associated with the post-war settlement, in particular the provision of school milk, meals and transport, became discretionary rather than compulsory elements of LEA provision.

These were significant challenges, applied much more firmly in England and Wales than in Scotland, to post-war trends of educational governance and provision: they strengthened the private sector, reduced the welfare element in schooling, challenged the non-accountability of schools and weakened local authorities' capacity to control admissions to schools; they defended these changes in the name of parental choice, standards and financial necessity. But their scale was limited. The Conservatives had yet to imagine, in any practical sense, the full possibilities of an education system that combined market principles with central control. More importantly, political conditions made a project like that of Sexton in the 1977 *Black Paper* seem unrealistic. The years of Carlisle's Secretaryship were the low point of Conservative fortunes. The recession provoked by Thatcher's anti-inflationary policies was at its deepest; her cabinet was packed with ministers who were strongly critical of the effects of her strategy on manufacturing and fearful of the social consequences that it might provoke. Trade union militancy was still at a high level, and educational opposition to Conservatism strong. That this situation changed was the outcome of a number of different conflicts and strategies, few of which could have been foreseen at the time of Carlisle's first cautious steps. From 1981, the immediate effects of recession eased. A series of adversaries – miners in the strike of 1984–5, Argentinians in the Falklands / Malvinas war of 1982, local councils, the anti-nuclear movement which sought to prevent the stationing of Cruise missiles in Britain – were defeated. The distinctive features of Conservative economic restructuring – including the privatization of state-controlled industry – began to fall into place. Opposition from Conservative sceptics died away, and the influence of New Right ideas became more pronounced. There began a process of reshaping institutions, and the practices of those who worked in them, so as to fit them for their part in a new social order. It is in this context that the accelerating pace of educational change in the later 1980s needs to be understood.

Conservative militancy

As it took shape after the general election of 1983, the overall programme of Conservatism under Margaret Thatcher emerged as a design for the destruction of the post-war settlement and the ways in which it organized social, economic and political life. Struggles that addressed so fundamental a set of issues could not be won simply through legislative action or state diktat, central though these were to the operation of Conservatism. They also required victory in what Stuart Hall called 'a battle of hearts and minds', through which a Conservative hegemony could be established (Hall 1988). To win its campaigns, Thatcherism summoned up aspects of Conservatism – the passions of grassroots activists, the anti-statist commitments of right-wing intellectuals – that in the golden age had been sidelined as obstacles to consensus. In the late 1980s and the early 1990s, these features of Conservatism enjoyed their time in the sun, and contributed to the party's victory over a range of opponents – not just the radical activists of the post-1960s generation, but also the professional interests which had taken root in the institutions characteristic of the post-war settlement.

Education – or the educational space – was one of the main sites on which these battles were fought out. What happened in education had importance not only for the preparation of the workforce and citizenry of the future, but also for the ways in which social ills might be explained and social futures imagined. Conservatism sought to represent the problems of schooling as a kind of condensation of all the worst effects of post-war history. Schools dramatized the British disease: bureaucracy stifled enterprise and prevented the exercise of choice; unaccountable professional power fuelled an insatiable demand for increased funding, drove down standards, politicized the curriculum and created a gulf between what parents and business wanted from the school and what the school actually provided. But struggles over schooling could also demonstrate the reviving power of

Conservatism, as it worked to exorcize professional influence and implant new cultures in the school that would serve tradition and enterprise alike.

Newspapers and think-tanks

In these struggles over the meaning and purpose of education, a new set of educational actors emerged. As we have seen, Kogan (Boyle and Crosland, with Kogan 1971) identified two kinds of network which influenced policy after 1944. The first – comprising teacher unions and local education authorities – he termed the 'old educational establishment'. Their influence on education policy and practice was complemented in the 1960s by the work of public intellectuals, such as the sociologists who advised ministers like Crosland and explained to a popular audience the necessity for change. This activity, linked to the work of pressure groups and 'practitioner-advocates', created an educational space dominated by questions of access, opportunity and social justice. Conservatism had no such resources to draw on. At no point did it command a sizeable number of activists. Yet by the 1980s, Conservatism succeeded in greatly diminishing the influence of both the old and new 'establishments', and in suppressing educational radicalism at school and local levels. Important to its success were two kinds of actor: first, the think-tanks and pressure groups which constituted a Conservative establishment of intellectuals and political activists; second, the popular press, especially the *Sun* and the middle-market *Daily Mail*. The think-tanks like the Institute of Economic Affairs, the Centre for Policy Studies (CPS) and the much smaller Adam Smith Institute (ASI), enabled small numbers of Conservative intellectuals to 'effect a transformation in the views of a strategic policy-making elite' (Desai 1994: 31). Conservative-supporting national newspapers, making use of the ideas of the think-tanks, worked to create popular perceptions of a crisis in schooling and a climate in which equality-orientated educational projects came to seem not just illegitimate, but – in an adjective which became part of the currency of policy argument in the 1980s – 'lunatic'.

The initial focus of the think-tanks was economic: an early member of the CPS, in the late 1970s, saw its prime function as the 'preparation of an alternative economic strategy' (Desai 1994: 53). Likewise, the ASI's *Omega File* of 1984 was an early advocate of choice-based reform (K. Jones 1989: 47–8). But the same organizations which argued for market influences and decentralization also defended 'traditionalism' in the cultural field and called for immediate centralized action to reverse the drift of policy towards egalitarianism. In one sense, these paradoxes reflected the incoherence of the Conservative programme. In another, they displayed its tactical astuteness: it was often on cultural grounds that Conservatism succeeded in discrediting the legacy of reform.

Opponents

The strengths and the limitations of Conservative strategy became particularly clear around issues of 'race'. At governmental level, Labour post-1976 had re-prioritized educational reform, displacing questions of equality from their central position, focusing policy on vocational themes and seeking to implement change through a greater measure of central direction. However, the project of post-war reform was much too diffuse and localized to be affected in its entirety by changes decided at the level of central government, and anyway there was still space in the ensemble of Labour's policies for some continuing focus on equal opportunity issues. Moreover, the perceived failure of Labour in government to make progress towards social justice stimulated many of its activists to pursue radical reform at local level, so that the emphases of national policy did not match a developing, centrifugal pattern of change. In a number of English cities, local authorities, influenced both by social movements and by cadres of Labour activists new to local government, initiated new kinds of educational project. These grew out of a critical attitude to past failures to develop effective policies of equal opportunity. They focused in part on the achievement of working-class students, but also involved, for the first time, an emphasis on feminist and anti-racist education (Inner London Education Authority 1983b).

By the early 1980s, it had become plain that the school system was failing large sections of ethnic minority students. The Rampton Report of 1981 identified considerable underachievement on the part of 'West Indian' students compared with whites and Asians. Rather than explaining this failure as earlier documents had done (Department of Education and Science 1971) in terms of the linguistic deprivation of learners, it attributed it in part to the – often unintentional – racism of teachers, inappropriate curricula, and the discouraging effects of discrimination in the labour market (Rampton Report 1981). Another government report (Swann Report 1985) confirmed the finding of underachievement, and again attributed it in part to 'unintentional racism'. It further suggested that there needed to be a cultural shift in all schools, towards a 'redefined concept of what it means to live in British society': schools needed to be less ethnocentric and more multicultural (1985: 8).

The claim that failure was linked to racism was echoed in much school-based research, which in some ways repeated in regard to race the conclusions of earlier research about the social relations of the classroom and their impact on the achievement of working-class students. Green's work, published as an annexe to the Swann Report, suggested that the 'ethnocentricity' of teachers expressed itself in the way they interacted with children of different ethnic groups (P. Green 1985); Troyna (1993) suggested likewise, and Mac an Ghaill (1988) showed how racism prompted the resistance of black and Asian students. Research findings of this sort fed into the discourse and practice of what Hatcher calls 'a dense undergrowth of journals, school and local authority policy documents, teaching materials and policy statements by campaigning organizations and teacher unions' (1998: 272). By the middle 1980s, some twenty-five English local authorities had appointed advisers on multicultural education; two-thirds of LEAs had produced statements of policy. Organizations such as ALTARF (All London Teachers Against Racism and Fascism) and NAME (National Anti-Racist Movement in Education) had established a network of curriculum activism, linked to anti-racist activity outside the school. Within this undergrowth, there was no single viewpoint. Most LEAs limited themselves to working for a greater degree of multiculturalism. Others, such as the London Association for the Teaching of English (LATE), argued that racism 'is endemic in our society, enshrined in laws, in the daily life of communities, in educational policy, in school curricula and organization, in the way teachers teach and in the things children learn; no teacher can duck this fact' (LATE 1982). Schools must eliminate institutional racism – embodied, for instance, in their admissions and exclusions policies – and promote curriculum change, in which recognition of the histories and cultures of excluded groups should have a central part. In the process, they should form links with social movements outside the school, since change in teachers' practice was 'brought about first by the voice of black pupils and the black community, and second by overt racism on the streets' (LATE 1982).

This activity represented in one sense the high point of two decades of curricular radicalism, in which the classroom-based developments of the 1960s and '70s were now connected to the policies and spending commitments of local authorities. In another sense, it amounted almost to that radicalism's final stage. Eighties Conservatism – Thatcherism – was strongly focused on the securing of social cohesion through the promotion of English national identity. It was affronted by the Swann Report, whose pluralist recommendations it did little to implement. Its response to anti-racist radicalism was one of outrage, mixed with tactical calculation. Conservative educational policy by the mid-1980s was very broad in scope, and had reached the point of conceiving a complete redesign of the schooling system. The radicalism it encountered in some urban local authorities was only one part of what it intended to dismantle and replace. But confrontation with local authorities usefully served to prepare the way for the wider project. By presenting to the middle ground of public opinion the spectacle of a schooling system in which unaccountable professional interests were apparently creating a curriculum that broke with national tradition, Conservatism could do much to legitimize its programme of change. The press were crucial to this strategy: mass-market newspapers were the channel by which the polemics and blueprints of the Conservative right (e.g. Palmer 1986) reached a wider readership. It was in these newspapers that Conservatives honed what Stephen Ball (1994) called a 'discourse of derision' – a means of presenting the projects of educational reform as extreme, un-British, bureaucratic, politicized and a distraction from the central tasks of schooling (K. Jones 1989: 54–64). The *Sun* made much out of an allegation that two London councils had banned the children's rhyme 'Baa, Baa, Black Sheep' from their nurseries (Searle 1987); and the *Mail on Sunday*'s successful campaign against a local race-equality programme, introduced by the headline 'Race spies in the classroom', was instrumental in discrediting much local authority reform.

Thus, prompted and supported by powerful media campaigns, and urged on by right-wing lobbyists, the government, well before the Education Reform Act of 1988, legislated or took executive action in a number of areas relating not just to 'race', but also to gender and sexuality. The 1986 Education Act gave school governors, rather than local authorities, power to determine the nature of sex education. In response to the attempts of some London education authorities to introduce to the classroom 'positive images' of lesbians and gay men, the 1988 Local Government Act prohibited local authorities from 'promoting teaching in any maintained school of the acceptability of homosexuality as a pretended family relationship'. By 1988, much of the case for the sweeping changes of the Education Reform Act had been made to rest on the extremism of teachers and local authorities. The deployment of traditionalist themes of nation and family had done much to enable this success. But, as we shall see, its agenda, though well equipped for cultural agitation, was less adequate for the work of reconstruction. The vision of the forces which sought to discredit progressive reform was informed both by free-market enthusiasm and by cultural nostalgia; and so Conservative-driven change moved forwards with its eyes fixed firmly on the past. In the process the New Right overlooked what might be called the rationality of the progressive project – its attempt to develop an education practice that was sensitive to cultural and economic change. Cheered and spurred on by a popular press and a collection of lobbyists who championed traditionalism, Conservatism headed towards what became, in the 1990s, one component of its nemesis.

Local authorities and curriculum activists were joined as culprits by unionized teachers. From 1985 to 1987, teachers in England and Wales organized a pay campaign that depended for its effect not only on strike action, but also on a refusal to cover for absent colleagues. In this latter respect, it involved therefore a struggle with managements for control over conditions of work. The campaign had a considerable impact, not least on parents, upon whom fell the duty of caring for children sent home from school. But the teachers' unions were not united. Since 1970, the dominance of the NUT had been challenged by the growth of the NAS/UWT (National Association of Schoolmasters/Union of Women Teachers), which presented itself as a defender of teachers' sectional interests rather than a force concerned also with education policy; and by AMMA (the Assistant Masters and Mistresses Association), formerly a union confined to grammar and public schools, which had extended its reach among teachers alarmed at the growing militancy of the other teachers' organizations. In the 1985–7 dispute, tactical differences between the unions, accompanied by competition over recruitment, proved disabling. By 1987 teachers' energies were exhausted, their divisions considerable, their public support dwindling. The government was able to present the teachers' action as evidence that, like other public-sector workers, they had abandoned traditions of professionalism and required, consequently, a strong degree of policing. The 1987 Teachers' Pay and Conditions Act provided such control: it abolished national pay negotiations, replacing them with a review body on which the unions had no say; it also specified in considerable detail the duties of a teacher, and made 'cover' for absent colleagues, along with attendance at after-school meetings, a compulsory part of teachers' work (Pietrasik 1987). The struggle for control over conditions of work was settled in favour of school managements; there developed what one group of researchers called 'a more concentrated and explicit control over the teacher labour process, with the introduction of practices to intensify work, contain staffing levels, and use more flexible employment contracts including casualization' (Sinclair et al. 1996: 42).

In Scotland, these conflicts took a different course, and their outcome was much less decisive. In the mid-1980s, a long period of teacher militancy, again over pay and conditions, received public support. This was partly because Scottish teachers possessed in the EIS a single union, and partly because the teachers were able to present their campaign as a national struggle against a government hostile to Scottish institutions and traditions. 'Could it be', an EIS official asked, 'that George Younger is no longer Secretary of State for Scotland, but the minister applying English education policies to the Scottish education system?' (D. Ross 1986: 85). Nationalism linked to united teacher action was a potent strategy. Teachers retained their negotiating rights, and union influence – exerted through the EIS, a much more powerful union than its English and Welsh counterparts – remained strong. Other subsequent aspects of the Conservative programme were muted in Scotland: no national curriculum was introduced; attempts were made and defeated to introduce the universal testing of primary school students in ways that would allow the construction of league tables of school success and failure. If anything, the Conservative effort to export the English model to a semi-autonomous country, where levels of support for the right were very low, only increased the demands for a break with London.

The ERA and After

If Labour after 1976 had signalled moves towards the centralization of policy, and the eclipse of equality as one of policy's major goals, then during the 1980s Conservatism had continued this work, both by beginning to achieve command of the teaching force, and by restricting or deterring local initiatives, especially those of a broadly egalitarian kind. In terms of the revision of the post-war settlement, these were important, if negative, achievements. But they did not of course represent the full extent of the Conservative programme; this only began to take shape after Thatcher's third election victory in 1987. It was formalized in the major achievement of educational Conservatism, the Education Reform Act of 1988.

The ERA was part of a set of changes, in housing, education, health and social security, that between 1988 and 1990 effected a 'decisive break' with post-war social policy (Glennerster, Power and Travers 1991). Not only did it change the institutional pattern of schooling, but it also substantially modified its social relations and reshaped its values, meanings and objectives. To put things more strongly, it destroyed the educational culture which had developed between 1944 and 1979, and began the work of creating a different one, in which old 'social actors' were marginalized and new ones rendered powerful. What it created was successful: it established enduring ground rules for schooling in the 1990s and beyond.

The provisions of the Act, as they affected schools, embodied all the tangled themes of Conservative policy – modernization, marketization and tradition. The most obvious modernizing element was the national curriculum. All students between the ages of 5 and 16 in state schools were to follow the same 'broad and balanced' subject-based curriculum; the curriculum would be specified by government-appointed committees and approved by the Secretary of State. Students' progress through the curriculum would be monitored by national tests, which would enable measurement of the performance of individuals and of schools. In these ways, it was argued, both entitlement and accountability would be secured, and the 'inconsistencies and inequalities' which had historically affected schooling in England and Wales would be mitigated (Moon 1991; A. Green 1990). Moon remarks that these goals were in some sense shared across the political spectrum, with many educationists accepting that 'the logic that underpins the provision of free and compulsory schooling [should] also extend to what is taught' (Moon 1991: 10–14). Similarly, writing of 'special needs', Dyson and Slee note that with the national curriculum 'for the first time [measures] were introduced which constituted an entitlement for all – or very nearly all – pupils... Moreover, the guidance... issued on the implementation for children with special educational needs promoted a strongly inclusive view of the curriculum, emphasizing the importance of "access"... rather than segregation' (Dyson and Slee 2001: 180). As we shall see, similar arguments have been made in relation to the national curriculum's effect on the examination performance of girls, especially in relation to science, where the new entitlement opened up areas which had previously been a male preserve (Arnot et al. 1999).

But modernization was combined with strong archaic elements. The curriculum was designed on a subject basis, and in its essentials replicated the grammar school curriculum of the earlier part of the century (Simon 1988). This had difficult consequences for primary schools, especially. As intended, the subject emphasis of the curriculum worked against child-centred practice, but the large number of compulsory subjects actually reduced the amount of time that teachers spent on literacy work, so that one of the major objectives of the 'standards-raising' policy Conservatives had pursued since the

1970s was compromised (Campbell 2001). In addition, the content of the curriculum at several important points reflected the traditionalist, ethnocentric preferences of ministers and pressure groups. Hence there was an emphasis on British history, European art and music and English literature, matched by an unwillingness to acknowledge cultural diversity: minority languages, except, in Wales, Welsh, were not recognized; standard English was highly valued, at the expense of non-standard dialects. In the 1990s, these influences were for a time to grow stronger, contributing to a complex pattern of reform – a universalism with strong archaic elements.

Outside England, however, 'tradition' conveyed other meanings, and was developed as an educational theme in markedly different ways. Since the partial implementation of the Munn and Dunning reports in the middle 1980s, Scotland had stronger guidelines on curriculum and assessment than were possessed in England. Partly for this reason, and partly out of deference to the strength of Scottish opinion, Conservatism made no attempt to apply a national curriculum north of the border. National guidance did become more specific, however, and exercised a strong homogenizing influence on schools. In cultural terms, this involved both the identification of a national tradition in subjects such as literature and history, the rediscovery of the repressed popular elements in that tradition, such as the language / dialect of Lowland Scotland, and for the first time, according to Arshad and Dinez, an attention to issues of multicultural diversity and racism (1999: 881). There were similar developments in Wales, where since 1979 Conservatism had presided over institutions which had become steadily more devolved, under the patronage of a sympathetic Minister of State – Wyn Roberts – and an 'ambitious bureaucracy' at the Welsh Office (G. E. Jones 1992: 101; Snicker 1998). The ERA, which in England served to centralize Civil Service control over the curriculum and to restrict cultural diversity, in Wales led to the introduction of stronger national institutions, separate from those of England, and operating with a different cultural programme. The Curriculum Council for Wales (CCW), established by the ERA, produced curriculum orders not only for the teaching of Welsh, but also for important aspects of other subjects, including history, geography, music and art. There were undoubtedly elements of a specifically Welsh cultural restorationism in this programme, concerned as it was with the distinctive culture and heritage of the country, but as we have seen it argued in other respects for a much greater degree of cultural pluralism than its English counterpart: pointedly, the CCW emphasized that communities, including national communities, consisted of varied groups whose plural existence raised 'issues of diversity, equality and prejudice'; and that the curriculum should reflect and explore such issues (CCW 1991, quoted in Phillips and Daugherty 2001). Thus Wales, like Northern Ireland, interpreted 'culture' in ways which set itself aside from an English model. By asserting so strongly the relationship of culture to nation, Conservatism, in the increasingly devolved British polities of the 1990s, had encouraged the development outside England of projects very different from its own.

Modernization, entwined with archaic elements, was further complicated by its relation to market-orientated change. It was the establishment of a market, or quasi-market, constituted by schools which operated in some ways as autonomous units under the leadership of managements deploying techniques intended to improve a school's market position, which was meant to supply the local dynamism that would complement centrally directed reform. To this end, the ERA implemented a set of interrelated changes. 'Local Management of Schools' (LMS) transferred control of school budgets from local authorities to heads and governors. With control went power – over staffing levels, material resources and policy choices – which was shifted from the LEA to the level of the school governing body: LEAs were compelled to release a high and growing proportion of their budget directly to schools. Alongside LMS, the Act introduced another form of autonomy: parents could vote on whether to take schools out of LEA control altogether, and, thus becoming grant-maintained (GMS), to receive direct funding from government, at a level that turned out to be much higher than the average (Halpin 1997). Under both LMS and GMS the size of the school budget was affected by the number of students on the school roll, and limits on school numbers imposed by LEAs that had aimed to equalize student intakes between schools were lifted. By linking budget levels to student intake, the Act created a context in which schools had to act in ways that were attentive to issues of supply and demand. Parents and students were to be provided with market information about the school in the form of test and examination results; the Standard Attainment Tests (SATs) established by ERA thus served both to supply government with information about levels of performance, and to facilitate the development of local 'markets' – in which of course some schools, by reason of their intake and already-established status, were particularly advantaged. The devolved school system was steered and regulated by new agencies created by the ERA and subsequent legislation in 1992–4. Ofsted, the Office for Standards in Education, carried out detailed and often unsympathetic inspections of schools; the Teacher Training Agency produced detailed specifications for what was in effect a national curriculum for teacher education; the Schools Curriculum and Assessment Authority stipulated the school curriculum and provided for the national tests. In addition, competitive bidding for status and funding – in relation, for instance, to specialist school status – helped create a system in which there was incessant pressure for change, motivated in the name of raising standards but producing also other effects.

That the ERA system fostered the creation of local hierarchies of schools, linked to social class differences between their populations, is well known. State schooling had always been affected by powerful segregating tendencies, in which the ability of middle-class groups to prepare their children for entry to higher-status schools had interacted with the housing market to produce sharp distinctions between different schools, connecting location, social class intake and academic success (Lowe 1997). After 1987, these tendencies became more pronounced. Benn and Chitty suggest that by 1994 policy was 'fuelling polarization rather than resolving it'; funding arrangements ensured that extra resources went to schools that were already 'doing well' in terms of intake and achievement, while in other schools there developed a pile-up of social and educational problems (1996: 226). Whitty, Power and Halpin, on the basis of work that compares reform in England with other national experiences, concluded that marketization 'might well have damaging effects' (1998: 128). Gewirtz, Ball and Bowe go further, to speak of a 'decomprehensivization of secondary schooling', and to provide a stark account of market-orientated reform in areas of London:

> Working-class children who...are most likely to fail the covert and overt tests of ability and motivation and children with emotional, behavioural, language or learning difficulties are on the whole likely to be ghettoized in under-subscribed, understaffed, low-status schools. At the same time, middle-class parents are most likely to apply and have their children selected for the oversubscribed, favourably-resourced, favourably staffed high-status...schools. (1995: 164)

Such research suggests that the 'universalism' claimed for ERA is severely compromised by its segregating effects. But, as Gewirtz and her colleagues recognize, the ERA was a design for modernization, as well as marketization – in fact a design for modernization *through* marketization, The transfer of budgets to schools, the introduction of performance indicators like SATs and the measures to enable parental choice were meant to facilitate the emergence of strong, change-orientated, market-responsive school managements which would develop not only financial abilities, but also the capacity to change the cultures of their schools. In 1988 the accounting firm of Coopers and Lybrand, asked by government to advise on the management of the post-ERA system, were insistent on this deeper role: 'What is required is a fundamental change in the philosophy of the organization of education [at school level].... The changes required in the management process are much wider than purely formal' (quoted in Gewirtz et al. 1995: 91).

The ensemble of measures instigated by the ERA, combining national direction and local managerial initiative, amounted to the 'fundamental change' that Coopers and Lybrand had called for. It provided a means for the dismantling of the regime – the system of relationships and cultural patterns – established in the years after 1944, and for the creation, in some depth, of a new educational order that reshaped the objectives, processes and cultures of schooling. It was effective, through separate legislation and policy diffusion, in all parts of Britain, even though not all its components were replicated elsewhere. Scotland, for instance, had no provision for the publication of test results and almost no grant-maintained schools; its relatively higher level of confidence in professional judgement was expressed in a weaker role for governing bodies in relation to school budgets, and the strength of teacher organization reduced many of the problems of workload of which teachers in England complained. (Riddell et al. 2000; Clark 1997). But all the same, as Echols shows, the introduction of choice-based reforms did increase social-class-based differentiation between schools (Echols et al. 1990); and, as Fairley and Paterson make clear, devolved management and the managerialist practices that accompanied it had become by the mid-1990s a norm (Fairley and Paterson 1995).

The old and the new

These effects of the ERA can be more closely specified in terms of their impact on teachers, students and parents as well as on the 'educational space', and the setting of research and development agendas. The most obvious changes among teachers involved the weakening of their unions, a sharp increase in both their workload and the monitoring of their work by line managers, heads and inspectors and the loss of much of their classroom autonomy. More generally, the introduction of the national curriculum affected what Reay (1998) calls the 'strategic activity' of teachers – their capacity to initiate, shape and popularize curricular practice. The authoritative status of the national curriculum tended to foreclose arguments about educational purpose: especially as the testing system developed, questions of purpose and process became less a centre of debate initiative and controversy than a set of matters that had been pre-decided, outside the school. Likewise, with the decline of effective trade-unionism, teachers' capacity to affect decisions about the disposition of resources and the daily routines of the school was constrained (Gewirtz et al. 1995: 98). When one researcher talked in 1995 to teachers at a London comprehensive which had formerly enjoyed a reputation for union militancy and radical curricular initiative, she found that teachers 'made hardly any mention of present engagement with wider political struggle as educational activists.' She read the disappearance of this engagement, once the hallmark of radicalism, as a sign of the times, and noted its replacement by a discourse organized around 'accountability, access and achievement' (Reed 1995: 94). Even in Scotland, researchers noted that, by the mid-1990s, the trend towards market-influenced managerialism had 'reduced resources' and contributed to 'low morale among teachers, parents and pupils', particularly in working-class schools. This meant that 'the energy' which had previously gone into – say – anti-sexist education was 'instead used in maintaining the basic functioning of the school' (Turner, Riddell and Brown 1995).

The Conservative programme also reshaped the lives of school students. This was in some measure due to the regime established by the ERA, but it also had more general causes. Up until the 1970s, most students left school with low levels of certification, but with a confidence in the strength of the youth labour market. The collapse of this market, the decline of apprenticeship and continuing presence of radical influences on school cultures had produced turbulent results. Looking back in 1992 over the previous fifteen years, Chris Richards listed 'the broader protests in which London school-students had involved themselves':

> 1976–80: participation in protests against ILEA's programme of secondary school closures and amalgamations; 1979: protests against the effects of teachers' industrial action (the closing of schools at lunchtimes); 1981–88: participation in protests against successive proposals to abolish ILEA; 1984/5: action in Newham and Tower Hamlets against racist attacks; 1986: walkouts in support of *Militant*-organized strike against the Youth Training Scheme; 1985–87: sporadic support for teachers' industrial action over pay and conditions. (Richards 1992: 93)

By the early 1990s, such protests had come virtually to an end: as with teachers, the sporadic connections between students and social movements became attenuated, while regulative pressures increased. Influenced by vocational educational initiatives, a new kind of pedagogy had developed that encouraged students to turn their aspirations towards the world of work, and to 'abandon their outmoded identities and aspirations' (Arnot et al 1999: 82; Cohen 1984). The ERA's emphasis on performance, the establishment of a common 16+ examination in 1985–7, the opening up of higher education to a much larger number of students and the evident occupational shift away from industry, strengthened trends towards certification and participation. In the process, a new student culture, in which successful examination performance had a central part, came into being: the new structures, rhythms and expectations of education exerted an influence on students that was both more extensive (involving greater numbers) and more intensive (encouraging a greater subjective investment in schooling). Particularly significant here were the opportunities presented to female students. Feminism in the 1970s had spoken of the inadequacies of girls' education (Deem 1978; Wolpe 1977; Weiner 1997): the curriculum excluded the experiences of girls and women; sexism was a blatant everyday problem; the relatively high achievement of girls at primary level not maintained in secondary schools; boys had higher occupational aspirations and were more successful in the labour market. By the early 1980s, in the then still-decentralized system, a 'range of local authority and school-based strategies had developed to counter these inequalities' (Weiner 1997: 6; Arnot 1991). The ERA ended this period of local initiative. Yet, despite its demise, the outputs of schooling changed in unexpected ways, as a combination of a reformed 16+ exam system and a national curriculum which demanded that *all* students took maths, science and technology opened new opportunities for girls. By 1996, in most subjects at 16+, the performance of girls surpassed that of boys; at 18+ the gap between male and female performance closed considerably (Arnot et al. 1999). In higher education, the proportion of women entrants rose from 30 per cent in 1970 to more than 50 per cent in 1998 (Mackinnon et al. 1996: 177; DfEE 1998a: 77). These achievements were strongly class-related – working-class girls still had only the most limited chances of access to university (Plummer 2000) – but they meant all the same that Conservatism had presided over a historic rise in the achievement of girls. Whereas traditionalist Conservatism had sought to reinforce established identities, educational and occupational change had undermined its efforts: education had become an arena in which gendered occupational destinies and social roles were called into question.

This was a shift that had implications for boys as well as girls. In 1977 Paul Willis's classic ethnography, *Learning to Labour*, had detailed – and, for some critics, over-celebrated – the resistance to the schooling of working-class 'lads'. Confident that jobs awaited them, Willis's students refused any kind of collaboration with school – one boy set himself a performance target of completing the year without writing a word. By the 1990s, following the collapse of the youth labour market and the development of a performance culture in schools, this kind of subculture had come to be regarded less as resistant than perverse. Policy-makers focused on the 'problem' of working-class boys, who were seen as a social group left stranded by economic history: technological change had eliminated the jobs that once they would have taken. Now, according to the dominant discourses of policy, they were involved in a culture of academic failure, indiscipline and potential criminality (Epstein et al. 1998). The problem was seen as their own. From being a class whose failure had seemed emblematic of the injustices of an entire system, they had become instead a minority, a deviant group, whose failure seemed anomalous rather than typical.

Thirdly, the ERA had implications for parents. Across Britain, post-1987 Conservatism sought to reshape institutions and to demolish professional networks of interest that were deemed bureaucratic. Rhetorically, 'parent power' played a major part in this project: governing bodies had been opened up to parents, increasing amounts of information about school performance made available and ministers – such as Michael Forsyth at the Scottish Office – habitually appealed for support over the heads of professionals to parents as consumers (Humes 1995). The ERA, by allowing the creation of grant-maintained schools on the basis of a ballot of parents, institutionalized parental will as a formative local force. But it was as individuals, rather than as a group of voters, that parents were intended to exert their most powerful influence: by exercising their right of choice, they would apply a market pressure upon schools. Thus change in local patterns of schooling would occur not, as often in earlier decades, through a contentious process of public and collective decision-making, but through a series of private decisions. Given opportunities by the ERA, and aware of the rewards attendant upon good decision-making and the dangers resulting from uninformed choice, larger numbers of relatively privileged parents – throughout Britain, even in 'collectivist' Wales and Scotland – became 'skilled choosers' (Gewirtz et al. 1995), attentive players in the differentiated system. This did not prevent movements of protest at low levels of spending on schools, which were politically damaging to

Conservatism in both England and Scotland (Pickard 2000: 233). But it did for the most part direct concerns about educational opportunity along individual, rather than collective, channels.

Finally, there is the complex question of the effects of the ERA on the 'educational space', on the areas of public, policy and academic discussion where agendas are set and the importance or unimportance of particular questions settled. Before 1976, discussion of change in education had focused at the level of policy-making and research on questions of equal opportunity and social class; at the level of curriculum and pedagogy the same issues motivated the classroom work of many teachers, and a significant number of researchers and teacher educators. These focuses produced on the one hand an attention to large-scale, systemic questions – the comprehensive versus tripartism, the status of public schools – and on the other a fine-grained interest in learning and teaching as cultural processes in which issues of power and authority, identity and experience were always at play. With the ERA came a twofold shift in focus. The school system was no longer seen in terms of an increasingly uniform design for increasing opportunity and minimizing disadvantage, but rather as a diverse set of institutions whose effective operation would secure a rising standard of achievement. And whereas earlier positions, of Schools Council innovators (Stenhouse 1967) as much as radical sociologists (Young 1971), assumed the intrinsic difficulty involved in relating the formal curriculum of the school to the experience of (particularly) working-class students, in post-1988 thinking such problems found no place. In the words of the 1987 DES circular which sketched out the national curriculum, the task was to ensure that all students had access to 'the same good and relevant curriculum . . . regardless of sex, ethnic origin and geographical location' (Department of Education and Science 1987: 3).' This double movement, from system to individual institution, and from curriculum as cultural problem to curriculum as product delivered 'regardless of' cultural specificity, enabled the emergence of a new paradigm of research and policy, that of school effectiveness and improvement.

School effectiveness

'School effectiveness' research, which had grown in volume and persuasiveness during the 1980s, argued that the old approaches to reform had been too deterministic in the way that they linked differences in educational achievement to the social class of students (Angus 1993; Hatcher 1998). Schools could 'make a difference' to students' attainment; and the most effective schools, even with working-class intakes, could achieve 'success against the odds' (Barber and Dann 1996). Research and policy could produce for schools a design for improvement by generalizing from the lessons of research into 'the key determinants' of effective practice (Sammons et al. 1995: 1). The technologies of change thus devised provided a repertoire from which the managements of the post-ERA period could draw, in rationalizing and making uniform the practice of their schools. Headteachers were encouraged, in school effectiveness writing and in educational bestsellers like Caldwell and Spinks's *The Self-Managing School* (1988), to become 'educational leaders', setting targets, designing programmes of action to achieve them, and ensuring that the work of teachers was focused accordingly (Caldwell and Spinks 1988). It may well be that such approaches were responsible for some of the improvement in student performance which marked the Conservative years. Yet there was much that they did not address. As their Northern Irish critics pointed out, targeting low-achieving schools for special attention hardly addressed problems arising from the social inequalities of the country, and from the structural inequity of its selective education system (Shuttleworth 1995; McKeown and Byrne 1999). There were also other problems: raising achievement for all did not necessarily entail reducing inequality, and using test and exam performance as indicators of success meant a tacit abandonment of broader curriculum reform in favour of an acceptance of 'limited and culturally specific' understandings of educational value (Hatcher 1998; Slee and Weiner 1998: 6). Nevertheless, in terms of its political, discursive and practical influence, the school effectiveness and improvement movement was successful. Linked to the focus of government and media on standards and results, it helped embed 'performance', understood as the school's capacity for delivering educational outcomes that were not themselves left open to question, at the centre of the new educational space.

Decline or Consolidation?

In 1992 the Conservatives won their fourth successive election victory, a victory which was quickly overshadowed by a currency crisis, a prolonged Conservative schism over the European Union and a succession of corruption scandals. Yet at the same time there began a further hectic and paradoxical period of educational change, which led both to the eclipse of 1980s Conservatism, and to the consolidation of its achievements; to a new rise in opposition to its policies, and to their acceptance as the basis of further change.

From 1989 onwards, the subject working parties which had been charged with designing the detail of the national curriculum in England began to report. The think-tanks and pressure groups which had done much to campaign for central state control of the curriculum were disappointed with the results, and agitated for a revision of the working parties' recommendations. At the same time, they argued for the simplification and 'Anglicization' of the national testing system, so as to emphasize basic skills and the English cultural heritage. This agitation was successful in that it produced a New Right capture of the national councils which oversaw changes in curriculum and assessment, but disastrous in that the proposals which these bodies drew up provoked very strong opposition from teachers, especially from teachers of English, who made what might be seen as one last spectacular appearance on the stage of cultural politics (K. Jones 1994b). In 1993–4, a boycott of the SATs, instigated by English teachers and supported by the teachers' unions, brought the testing system to a halt. The government was compelled to redesign the national curriculum, so as to lessen its detail, and remove the stronger signs of the traditionalist and ethnocentric enthusiasms of the New Right; the project of converting the school into a centre for the promotion of traditional values came to an end. Similar changes were made to the SATs. The 1995 national curriculum thus marked the end of the New Right's curricular influence, at the same time as it helped embed the curriculum, and its associated testing system, at the consensual centre of English schooling.

The same points might be made of marketization. The ERA was strongly shaped by the agitation of the Conservative right. Yet what the ERA led to was not the New Right vision of the autonomous, lightly regulated, traditionally orientated school, but the installation of a centrally guided, locally empowered managerialism as the directing force of change. It was this model that, following the ERA, shaped British schooling. In doing so, it both developed and displaced the impulses of Conservatism: developed, because it took the market-based preferences of think-tanks such as the Adam Smith Institute and gave them a concrete and sophisticated organizational form; displaced, because it allowed little room for Conservatism's cultural passions, and led to a reform agenda which was shaped not mainly by the undiluted preferences for markets and selection of the Conservative right, but by a programme in which a degree of marketization was just one element in a system of effective schooling, in which the position of a strong, directive state had been consolidated rather than diminished. Yet, within this framework, the Conservative commitment to diversity lived on, to the point where it established a binding hold over its successor. When the Education Secretary, John Patten, indicated in 1992 that 'specialization' would be the dominant principle of secondary school organization, and when the (renamed) Department for Education introduced measures for funding 'specialist schools' and enabling them to select a proportion of their students, he was establishing an agenda that would last (Chitty 2001).

Partisan though it was, the ERA would not have endured, then, without corresponding to a logic of education change that ran deeper than the immediate preferences of Thatcherite Conservatism. When a communist teacher called in 1953 for 'systematic', 'clearly defined' programmes of study that would 'take all children together...up to the required standards' or when the socialists Jackson and Marsden criticized the bureaucratic remoteness from parents of the secondary school, they would not have imagined that their calls for change would be answered by a Conservative government (M. Morris 1953: 84; Jackson and Marsden 1962). But in one sense that is what happened. The 1988 reforms can justly be read as a one-sided assertion of monoculturalism, and as introductions of market principles to education. But they were also responses to enduring problems in the post-1944 system, providing right-wing answers to questions that had long been posed by reformers critical of the system's lack of democracy, its low standards and its failure to organize itself around principles of universal access. It was partly for this reason that the 1988 settlement was adopted so readily by Conservatism's New Labour successors. But this striking act of policy adoption depended also on profound shifts in the Labour Party. The government that came to power in 1997 was in most respects unrecognizable from its social democratic predecessors: it was novel not just in its policies, but in the policy contexts it established. 'Old' educational actors, evicted from the educational space by Conservatism, were not readmitted by Labour. In their place, a host of new actors appeared – multinationals, edubusinesses, management theorists – who sought to develop the framework established by Conservatism into a fully coherent system.

5

New Labour: The Inheritors

The Newness of New Labour

In the spring of 1997, the Conservative Party lost its first general election in eighteen years. It won fewer parliamentary seats than at any time in the twentieth century, and no longer represented a single constituency outside England. As it left office, it took with it the more spectacular features of market-centredness, nationalism, cultural nostalgia and tolerance of poverty and widening inequality that had marked the politics of the 1980s and 1990s: there was no longer a Thatcher to announce 'there is no such thing as society', or a Major to champion the unchanging continuities of English life (Raban 1989; Major 1993). It was replaced by a government whose leaders had spent the 1990s reinventing their party under the name of 'New Labour'. New Labour did not possess the hostility towards the European Union that was so marked a feature of Conservative rhetoric; it promised to regulate more stringently the denationalized industries created by privatization; it offered a constitutional programme based on devolution – especially on matters of social policy – to Northern Ireland, Wales and Scotland. It emphasized 'social inclusion' – 'Britain rebuilt as one nation in which each citizen is valued and has a stake' (Blair 1997b) – as a key divide between its own policies and those of Major and Thatcher, and continued to stress its identity as a 'broad-based movement for justice and progress' (Labour Party 1997: 2). At the same time its leaders stressed as a founding principle what other Labour governments would have balked at: that the direction of the British economy would be decided by market developments, with little degree of state intervention. As the Chancellor, Gordon Brown, put it, 'today we know that in a global economy greater competition at home is the key to greater competitiveness abroad. We know that it is the openness of the economy, not its closed nature, that is the driving force in productivity growth' (cited in Owen 2001: 209). New Labour, according to Brown, had learned from the bitter experience of its predecessors that 'any government, be it left, right or centre, depends on its credibility with the markets' (G. Brown 1997: 15).

From these perceptions, much followed. First of all, educational priorities were presented squarely in terms of servicing market-driven growth: Education Secretary David Blunkett told the free-market Institute for Economic Affairs, 'the work of DfEE fits with a new economic imperative of supply-side investment for national prosperity' (Blunkett 2001). Second, market credibility required that public expenditure be kept close to the relatively low level established since the 1970s, something that in New Labour eyes was also demanded by the electorate. Explaining the government's reading of the opportunities and constraints that it faced, Glennerster notes New Labour's belief that raising taxes was politically impossible. Conservatism, through policies that had severely increased poverty and at the same time encouraged many people to opt out of state provisions for health, education and pensions, had created a situation that would make enormous spending and tax-raising demands on any government that tried to introduce a universally available, high-quality welfare system (Glennerster 2001a). What New Labour thought possible was a different sort of system, described by Hills in 1999 as 'selective universalism' (cited in Glennerster 2001a: 286). Selective universalism targeted much new spending on the poorest groups, for instance in relation to the state pension, while relinquishing the idea that it was possible to raise general levels of welfare provision – e.g. for pension levels that would attract middle- and high-income groups away from private schemes. At the same time, however, the principle entailed that in other parts of the welfare state – notably health and education – it was both feasible and necessary to sustain institutions to which the great majority of the population would want access. Hence, following the freeze on public spending levels which lasted for most of its first term in office, the government planned large-scale increases for the period 2000–4, which would take spending on education back to the level of the late 1970s.

The third point about New Labour's dedication to competitive principles is that they applied not just to the share of GDP which the public sector took up, but also to practice within the sector. The government accepted, by and large, the structural reforms of the period 1987–92, which sought to transform the quality, effectiveness and efficiency of the public sector, through the introduction of quasi-market programmes. In education, as we shall see, this meant an endorsement of much of the 1988 Education Reform Act and its successors, in relation both to 'parental choice' and to competition between schools in a diverse and unequal secondary school system. In the school sector, thus, 'selective universalism' meant a system open to students from all social groups, but structured in ways that supported different types of schooling, qualification and outcome, probably according to some important extent to social origin (Robertson and Lauder 2001: 232).

Fourth, New Labour's belief in competitiveness as the driving force of change inclined it to regard the private sector as, in the words of one of its chief policy advisers, a force 'uniquely capable of managing change and innovation' (Barber 1998b). From this it followed that business, equipped with such qualities, should have a strong role in the future development of the public sector, including schooling. New Labour aimed not only to relate public-sector activity more closely to the expressed needs of business, but also to involve private interests more actively in the delivery of social services, again including education.

This strong acceptance of expenditure constraint, business agenda and principles of choice and competitive organization was combined with measures that sought to repair the social damage of the previous two decades. Unemployment in 1997 was lower than in the early 1990s, and very much lower than in the period 1979–83. But the 1997 figure of 1.2 million was in some ways misleading. It excluded, for instance, those who, being categorized as disabled, were not registered as looking for work, and this number had risen sharply during the Conservative years. Moreover, the lower unemployment figures could not be read as the sign of a healthy social order: many of those in work were part-time and/or low-waged; absence from the unemployment register did not mean an escape from poverty, especially in areas which had experienced not just the collapse of job opportunities but the destruction, through crime, addiction, and family and community break-up, of an entire social infrastructure – an experience unforgettably documented by Davies (1998).

As Glennerster has demonstrated, New Labour deployed against poverty a battery of tax, benefit and legal measures – including the minimum wage – which have had some redistributive effect, or at worst have prevented inequality from rising further (2001a: 395–7). It has accompanied these changes with policies designed to address some of the non-economic aspects of poverty and of the wider condition that the government, following the European Commission, calls 'social exclusion'. According to European Commission reports, the concepts of social inclusion and exclusion refer not just to wealth and poverty but to 'the social rights of citizens... to a certain basic standard of living and to participation in the major social and occupational opportunities of society' (cited in Castells 1998: 73). From this viewpoint, employment is important, and so is literacy; and being free of addiction or of the fear of crime is just as much a condition of inclusion as having a certain level of income. It is in this context that the breadth of New Labour's social policy should be understood – stretching from 'sure start' projects for very young children, to adult literacy programmes; from a concern with teenage pregnancy to anti-truancy work. Schooling after 1997 was the site of many such projects.

But social inclusion, as Levitas stresses (1998), is not the same as equality. The attempt to improve the living standards of poor people, and to enable their sometimes enforced 'participation in social opportunity', does not entail a lessening of the advantages of more privileged groups, nor an effort to return to the objective of 'equality of outcome' that many social reformers thought possible in the 1960s and '70s. On the contrary, many of New Labour's policies, especially in education, were designed to allow more advantaged social groups differential access to particular forms of provision – certain types of school, certain groups within the school, certain forms of certification. Conversely, for another section of the school population, New Labour envisaged clearly signposted non-academic routes (DfEE 2001). Marshall's insistence in 1949 that the work of the school was inescapably bound to the occupational order would not have discomfited New Labour. Nor would his conception of the school as a force for the building of citizenship – though, as we shall see, New Labour's understanding of what was involved in such a project entailed government intervention of a much more intense and directive kind than earlier reformers had envisaged.

Knowledge and Globalization

The rather nebulous label of the 'Third Way', which was much used in the early years of the Blair government, was meant to designate the complex of policies outlined above – policies that accepted the creativity, dynamism and efficiency of the market, and attempted to combine such acceptance with a conception of government that found space for regulation of utilities, some measure of redistribution, and active intervention in particularly ravaged areas of social life, even if stronger economic involvement, through public ownership and demand management, was now ruled out. Education took on a particular importance for New Labour because it is positioned in the centre of the 'Third Way' – at the point where market dynamism and government action seemed to meet. From this perspective, if government could create an effective education system – 'modernized' and 'world-class', in New Labour terminology – it could contribute crucially to Britain's success in what was seen as an ever more competitive global marketplace. 'Education, education, education,' replied Blair when asked about his government's priorities – and in doing so he signalled a commitment to highly active *sectoral* involvement in schooling, despite having withdrawn from core areas of economic policy.

In some senses, these ambitions for education and fears about the educational strength of competitors were part of an old tale, and echoed the concerns of Harold Wilson in the 1960s and, before him, of the mid-Victorian reformers who, alarmed at Britain's decline relative to the burgeoning economies of Germany and the United States, voted for the 1870 Education Act. What gives the tale a new twist is a twofold development that can be summed up in the terms 'knowledge economy' and 'globalization'.

'Knowledge economy' is a term used quite loosely in policy documents and economic commentary to designate both ICT companies and a much larger sector 'encompassing the exploitation and use of knowledge in all production and service activities' (Department of Trade and Industry 1998). Castells, using the term 'informational capitalism', offers a more developed analysis:

> Productivity and competitiveness are the commanding processes of the informational . . . economy. Productivity stems from innovation, competitiveness from flexibility. Thus firms, regions, countries, economic units of all kinds, gear their production relationships to maximize innovation and flexibility. Information technology and the cultural capacity to use it are essential in the performance of the new production function. (Castells 1998: 341)

In Castells's account, the workforce of informational capitalism is divided in ways that are strongly shaped by its varying educational capacities. Its leading sectors have 'accessed higher levels of education' to the point where they can 'reprogramme themselves' for the 'endlessly changing tasks of the production process' (1998: 341). Workers of this sort are key to the competitiveness of firms. By contrast other sectors, not engaged in high-value production, are termed by him 'generic labour'. Lacking the capacity to learn new skills, they are as individuals expendable to informational capitalism, though as a class they remain necessary. Governments have a role in seeking to maximize competitive advantage by increasing the supply of reprogrammable labour, of high-value human capital, while also managing the problems of social polarization and precariousness among the rest of the workforce and the rest of society. Education is important in both respects.

The knowledge economy, of course, is an international phenomenon. Discourses about its implications for schooling interlock with another set of policies and discourses that centre on globalization. Both as imperial power and as American client, Britain has always been touched by global flows of activity – episodes crucial to educational development in Britain, such as the sterling crisis of the late 1940s, and the IMF demands of 1976 were effects of trans-continental relationships. In the last two decades these flows have intensified, as states have reduced their capacity to control global movements of capital as well as important areas of the domestic economy – Conservative governments, like those of other European states, lifted restrictions on the free movement of capital, and deregulated or privatized the public sector. The effect has been to strengthen the power of transnational companies, and weaken that of most nation states. Halsey and his colleagues sum up the consequences in these terms:

> Transnational companies will invest in those nations where tax regimes and labour costs are low, while providing the infrastructure of a highly skilled workforce, sophisticated transport and financial communications. In effect, the state has to provide or create the conditions where a sophisticated infrastructure is delivered, while controlling tax demands and the costs of social production. (Halsey et al. 1997: 6)

Much more than Conservatism, which was shackled in some respects by its nationalist and Europhobic tendencies, New Labour is a party which is happy with this perspective; it accepts in full what it reads as the economic, social and cultural consequences of globalization. As Tony Blair wrote:

> Globalisation is changing the nature of the nation state as power becomes more diffuse and borders more porous. Technological change is reducing the capacity of government to control a domestic economy free from external influence. The role of government in this world of change is to represent a national interest, to create a competitive base of physical infrastructure and human skills. The challenge before our party... is not how to slow down and so get off the world, but to

educate and retrain for the next technologies, to prepare our country for new global competition, and to make our country a competitive base from which to produce the goods and services people want to buy. (Blair 1995: 20)

Blair combines a market-based recognition of 'porosity' and the limits of government action with an assertion that governments should act decisively within those fields where directive action is still possible. Alertness to the needs of the knowledge economy is crucial here. Governments must focus on 'creating a fully-educated labour force conversant with the skills necessary to implement the new technology'. Education must be lifelong and it must be technologized, and if this is accomplished then Britain will be transformed not only into a country of 'innovative people' but also into the 'electronic capital of the world' (Blair 1996: 93, 98, 127), capable of responding to 'the emergence of the new economy and its increased demands for skills and human capital' (DfEE 2001: 8).

At this point theories of change shade into questions of political strategy. 'Globalization' is a rhetorical term as much as it is an analytic one. It functions not just as a tool with which to theorize emergent social forms but also as a condensation of a number of wider arguments that relate to the possibility – or impossibility – of political and social change in the contemporary world system. It is thus utilized not only to describe change, but to effect it. It speaks of the inevitability of global processes, and of the necessity of urgent governmental action to respond to them. The preoccupations of New Labour education policy – the attempts to control educational change at a detailed level, the quick pace and short time-horizons of strategies for change, the impatience with the teaching force, the focus on ICT and work-related learning, and even the necessity of social inclusion – all ultimately connect to a reading of the world that is enabled by 'globalization'

This is not only a British phenomenon. As a theory, 'globalization' may well overestimate the ways in which the circulation of capital across frontiers fixes the limits of national economic strategies (Hirst and Thompson 1996). But, as a discourse, it bears out its own truth. Discourses about globalization have become a global phenomenon, and British educational policy takes them as its starting point. As the connections between policy-makers in Britain and international policy elites have grown stronger, there has developed a consensus among international organizations, such as the World Trade Organization (WTO), the European Union and the OECD, both about the nature of change and about the measures that are required of governments to respond to it. The consensus – I shall call it a global policy discourse to indicate both its spread and the object that it speaks of – is evolving rather than static. Its starting point is that there now exists, in the OECD's words, a 'knowledge society' in which routine and low-skilled jobs are no longer in demand. In this dynamic society, where multi-skilling and flexibility are at a premium, schools must 'lay the foundations for lifelong learning', and sustain 'innovation, experimentation and improvement' (Papadopoulos 1994: 175; Johannson, cited in Hatcher 2001b: 45). This is not a society heading towards greater equality, and the task of education-alists is to accept and reflect its fundamental divisions, In fact, the European Commission argues, nothing else is possible:

> Whenever educational systems have been tempted to follow fashion-able utopias that seek to break with [the] ... filtering mechanisms that are founded in a form of individual competition, the experiments have failed: education has disconnected itself both from the business world and, more generally, from our societies, which do not work that way. (cited in Hatcher 2001a)

This position continues to underlie the policies of global and regional organizations. But more recently the orthodoxy has shifted somewhat to emphasize alongside the creation of a skilled and flexible work-force the role of the school in building 'cohesion and social capital', which is now argued by some international organizations to be 'one of the main outcomes on which schools' success is to be judged' (Johannson, cited in Hatcher 2001b: 45). The European Union's gradual turn in the 1990s towards a 'more activist social policy' to complement its financial and economic strategies strengthened such tendencies; social policy has come to be seen as an important productive factor (Dale and Robertson 2002: 24–5).

We can accept here Taylor's argument that 'ideological discourses which frame education policies at the national level might already be globalized' (Taylor et al. 1997: 61). At regional level, we can go on to speak of stronger processes of co-ordination. Dale and Robertson note in the European Union the development of 'Euro-networks of all kinds' – lobby groups, professional associations, conferences, research projects and journals which contribute to 'an enhanced institutional and discursive thickness' (ibid.). The growth in these forms of a 'European educational space' (Lawn 2001) has been complemented by developments at the level of transnational policy. The EU accepted at its Lisbon summit in 2000 the importance of a common framework for education policy, established by 'fixing guidelines for the Union, combined with specific timetables for achieving the goals which they set' (European Commission, cited in Dale and Robertson, 2002: 26). Thus, although, formally, the sovereign capacity of states to determine education policy has not been breached, the EU is having 'considerable effects on how its members exercise their autonomy' (ibid.).

Nevertheless the discourses of educational policy-making and change are quite capacious, and allow for differing inflections of social and economic priorities. These differences are the result of interaction between global, 'travelling' policy and national circumstance (Alexiadou et al. 2001). For, as Held and his colleagues put it, 'the social and political impact of globalization is mediated by domestic institutional structures, state strategies and a country's location in the global pecking order' (Held et al. 1999: 13). This process of mediation becomes especially clear when we turn from global discourse to national circumstances in Britain and Northern Ireland.

Devolution

During the Conservative years, the gap between national educational cultures grew wider, so that when, following referenda in its first term of office, New Labour created devolved assemblies in Belfast and Cardiff and a parliament in Edinburgh, such devolution was less the catalyst of dramatic change than a single moment in what appears with hindsight to be an accelerating, centrifugal process. The exception here was Northern Ireland, where the break with the past was much sharper. It is true that constitutional change and power-sharing gave a new impetus to policies developed since the 1970s that promoted a dual 'cultural heritage' – to that extent there was no rupture, except that the 'tolerance' that featured in earlier policy discourses was replaced by a more positive assertion of rights of citizenship. In other respects, established practice was more evidently interrupted. The end of direct rule from Westminster meant neither a return to Unionist power, nor the assured continuation of selective schooling. The Belfast 'Good Friday agreement' of April 1998 created a power-sharing assembly and meticulously defined arrangements for community autonomy and equality (O'Leary 1998). These included the establishment of a human rights commission, with a brief to protect individual liberty and equality, and strong legal provisions covering a range of equality issues. The agreement made no formal changes to the existing, largely segregated system of schooling, but in other respects its implications were far-reaching. The Department of Education, for instance, now worked to a brief (given it by the Northern Ireland Act of 1998) that required all educational processes to be subjected to scrutiny in the name of equal opportunity 'between persons of different religious belief, political opinion, racial group, age, marital status or sexual orientation'. Legislation could not cancel the legacies of war: the children of Holy Cross School in Belfast found in 2001 that they could attend classes only by running a gauntlet of Protestant anger. But all the same, Northern Ireland's laws were in advance of any other part of Britain. At the same time, with the ending of the impasse on equality issues imposed by Unionism and by direct rule, political initiative passed in some measure to forces with a developed social agenda.

In 1997, after Labour's election victory but before the Good Friday agreement, the Northern Ireland Office had commissioned research on the effects of selection; support for this work continued after devolution had been put in place. The research was published in 2000 (Gallagher and Smith 2000), and identified a number of the undesirable effects of selection, including the existence of a long tail of under-achieving schools and a 'polarity of achievement', as well as the under-representation of children from socially disadvantaged backgrounds in grammar schools (McKeown 2001). With the ending of direct rule, and the lessening of the influence of both the Ulster Unionist Party and the hierarchy of the Catholic Church, there was a political opening for a new approach to questions of selection. Under power-sharing arrangements, the education portfolio was taken up by the Republican (Sinn Fein) leader Martin McGuinness, whose party, like others in the new assembly, was committed to 'engage fully in the overhaul of our education system and begin to redress the injustices of the past' (Sinn Fein, cited in McKeown 2001). Thus for the first time since the 1970s, according to McKeown and Byrne (1999), 'the structure of Northern Ireland's education system' came 'under critical and informed review'. The motivations for the review were mixed. The globalized discourse of policy-making provided some participants in the Northern Irish debate with justifications for change based on the competition-driven need to invest more strongly in human capital; hence the Confederation of British Industry (Northern Ireland) argued that 'Northern Ireland needs to move up the value chain; from a low-skilled and low productivity economy. . . . The implications for education are that the demand for a highly skilled, adaptable and creative workforce will increase' (cited in McKeown 2001: 11).

Positions like these, not uncommonly expressed in the consultation processes which were part of the review, could have resulted in an upgrading of vocational education, rather than a move towards the ending of selection at 11. But, just as in England, Wales and Scotland during the 1960s, changes to the system of secondary education were

influenced by anti-selective arguments, in which egalitarian considerations were a strong element. 'The eleven-plus tests are divisive,
damage self-esteem, disrupt teaching and learning and reinforce
inequality of opportunity,' stated the author of the recommendations
that were put before the Northern Ireland Assembly in the autumn
of 2001 – recommendations whose objective was to end academically based selection at 11 (Learner 2001). Earlier in the year, as a
further indicator of Northern Ireland's policy trajectory, McGuinness
had announced that it would break from the ERA framework to
the extent of no longer publishing the league tables of examination
passes which facilitated a choice-based secondary system (Thornton
2001).

Whether as a result of sudden turns or more gradual developments,
it was plain by 2001 that the education systems of the various polities
of Britain were becoming more unlike – or, at least, that Scotland and
Wales, as well as Northern Ireland, were becoming more unlike
England. No part of Britain had unbeen touched by the politics of
choice and diversity, managerialization and centralization introduced
in 1988. But in several important respects, some having to do with
policy, some with ideological and political influence, it was plain that
England – however much its education system conformed with international models – was in British terms becoming something of an
exception. What could be called the 'deep' dissimilarities between the
systems, which stemmed from the relationship between education and
national identity – as expressed through social and political movements, and as exemplified, often, in the relation beween class, education and attainment – were with surprising speed producing
assymetrical policies. In 2000, Linda Croxford summarized the findings of a major research project into 'home international' compari-
sons between England, Northern Ireland, Scotland and Wales that did
much to clarify these differences (Croxford 2000). She reported that
there were significant differences in the organization of secondary
schools, and the effect of social class – though not of gender – on
the attainment of students. Even though Northern Ireland's system
was thoroughly selective, it was the English system which was the
most diverse. England had a much larger private sector. It retained
grammar and secondary modern schools in some areas. It had a much
higher proportion of students attending denominational schools
than either Scotland or Wales. These differences in school organization correlated with differences in social segregation and in attainment. In the English and Northern Irish systems students from
different social classes were less likely to attend the same school;
England had the strongest correlation between socio-economic status

and educational attainment. Scotland and Wales, with almost fully comprehensive systems, experienced less social segregation than England. Yet the social mixing of students there did not appear to correlate with lower levels of attainment: in terms of average levels of attainment at GCSE, where an exam system common to England, Northern Ireland and Wales provided some means of comparison, there was no difference between the three nations. On these bases Croxford concluded that 'there is less social-class inequality in the two systems which are wholly comprehensive' (2000: 4).

These differences, identified on the basis of a study of a 1990 cohort of 16-year-olds, are effects of the varying national traditions and educational cultures that are described in earlier chapters. They indicate something of the angle from which the changes demanded by the international policy consensus are approached. In no country does the policy-making elite reject 'globalization'. The blend of technology, innovation and inclusive education which Blair sees as the key to UK success is echoed in the other countries of Britain. It was not Blair, for instance, but Rhodri Morgan, First Secretary of the Welsh Assembly, who compressed knowledge economy and globalization discourse into a single sentence by writing, 'Wales must be at the forefront of new ideas and new technologies if it is to transform itself into a prosperous economy in the future' (Morgan 2000). But the impact of the travelling policy of globalization on the four national cultures of education produces significantly different local outcomes. In England, as later sections of this chapter demonstrate, policies designed to enhance competitiveness have the effect of sharpening the differentiation which Croxford notes as a peculiar feature of its education. In Wales and Scotland there is a more complicated picture. The desire to create a knowledge-based economy to replace an obliterated heavy industry is widespread in Welsh politics though in some respects shakily founded – Morgan's ambitions do not easily connect to the social condition of a country in which 25 per cent of the population live in poverty, and which lags greatly behind average English levels of per capita income (Adamson 1999; McLean 2001: 443). Critics have suggested that the vision of a prosperity delivered by high technology has more to do with elite legitimizations of policy than with planning realistic futures in which all can share (Lovering 1996; 2000). But an alternative view would be that it is the Welsh Assembly itself which recognizes the depth of its difficulties, describing Wales in these terms:

We have to face the fact that by comparison with other countries Wales has low economic activity rates; a significant incidence of low skills and

qualification levels... relatively high inactivity in the working population; low pay and low productivity; a low proportion of GDP in high
growth, high value-added sectors. (National Assembly for Wales 2001:
para 6)

Significantly, though, this description of problems at the economic
level is not linked – English-style – with a denunciation of education's
supposed responsibility for decline. The Assembly's first major statement of principle takes another direction. It celebrates 'the
informed professional judgement of teachers'; it envisages a 'fully
comprehensive system of learning', dedicated to 'narrowing inequalities between advantaged and disadvantaged areas, groups and
individuals'; it argues that 'children facing special disadvantage and
provision must be better provided for' than the norm (2001: paras 9,
12). From this perspective, there is an attempt to discourage some
elements of institutional diversity and autonomy: the Assembly and
LEAs attempt to hold back the proportion of funding that is passed
directly to schools; the Minister for Education opposes the involvement of the private sector 'in the delivery of education in Wales'
(Woodward: 2001).

Scotland's economic position is different from that of Wales. The
average income of its inhabitants has since 1979 risen to English
levels, and as a result of the favourable funding arrangements secured
both by popular protest and by the pressure exerted by previous
Secretaries of State, its spending on schools is more generous (McLean
2001: 445). But in many respects it retains with Wales an agenda that
is more inclusive than that of England, even though it has absorbed
more from the global policy context. Managerialism has not passed
Scotland by. From 1992, the devolution of budgets to schools provided a context from which local management cadres emerged, and in
the mid-1990s, under both Conservative and Labour rule, a spate of
Scottish Office documents disseminated ideas and practices concerning 'value for money', performance indicators, customer care and the
rest of the managerial agenda (Scottish Executive 1999). There is a
strong emphasis on mechanisms of performance management, as a
means by which national agenda can be transmitted to school level,
and to this extent Scotland, with its ambition of achieving a 'world-
class' education system (Scottish Executive 1999), is just as recognizable as England in terms of its membership of a global policy community. According to Raffe et al. (2001) managerial approaches have
been responsible, in a deliberate attempt to break from more consensual and gradual processes of change, for accelerating the pace of
Scottish reform – to the point in summer 2000 of the 'Higher Still'

fiasco, when complex changes to systems of post-16 certification were pushed through without adequate consultation and resourcing.

But none of this means that the global discourse of change is reproduced identically throughout Britain. In its English and quintessentially New Labour version, the discourse depends for the depth of its impact on two conditions. The first is the widespread sense that more consensual and 'undirected' kinds of change – essentially, the movement for comprehensive reform – have failed. The second is that teachers are complicit in this failure, and only a strong management of the teaching force can deliver success. Neither of these conditions exists in Scotland. In Scotland, public support for the common system of secondary education is strong, and the EIS, with a long history of securing popular mobilization behind its campaigns, is a much stronger union than its counterparts south of the border. It has been able to prevent the implementation of performance-related pay – a system which has also been criticized by the Welsh Assembly – and to organize a more effective defence of teachers' working conditions. Likewise, with the exception of the Private Finance Initiative there is less emphasis on the role of the private sector in educational reform, little belief that differentiation among schools is a pathway to higher achievement and a much higher confidence in the capabilities of teachers. 'Inclusiveness' tends to be regarded as a valuable goal in itself, as well as a historic property of the Scottish system (Ozga 1999), and 'equality' figures as one of the national priorities of the Scottish school system (Scottish Executive 2001). From this position, New Labour's 'modernization' can appear in some respects as the problematic intrusion of a specifically English project (Ozga 1999). Westminster-based New Labour sets the pace of change, elaborates the master-discourse of reform, reflects most enthusiastically an international consensus, and affects the lives of the greatest number of teachers and learners, but it is not the only version of education policy at work in Britain.

New Labour and History

So far, this chapter has attempted to place New Labour education policy in relation to spatial factors of globalization and the developing pattern of differences within Britain, and in relation to the overall tendencies of its economic and social policy. In this section, the placing is of a different kind. Its focus is temporal; it concerns New Labour's relation to the past, and in particular to the two traditions of policy – the one orientated towards equal opportunity and decentralization; the other towards choice-based reforms and centralization –

which have been discussed in earlier chapters. These are relationships with which New Labour itself has been preoccupied, since its identity as a party depends upon its ability both to distinguish itself from previous political formations and to claim aspects of their traditions as its own.

New Labour has constructed a version of post-war history whose first purpose is to draw a line between itself and the Labour governments which preceded it. In education at least, the evidence that is offered in support of this interpretation is drawn almost exclusively from an English experience and there appears to be little interest in learning from the policy histories of other countries in Britain, even where these contain much that is relevant to thinking about the relationship between educational organization, opportunity, achievement and social class.

The Green Paper *Schools Building on Success* (DfEE 2001) begins with an overview of the first thirty years of the post-war period. For Eric Hobsbawm, as we have seen, this was the golden age that after 1976 was swept away. The document takes a different view: the golden age from its perspective was a period in which the governments of Attlee and Wilson – like the Tory regimes sandwiched in between – presided over a largely 'unskilled' working population which had possessed 'jobs for life' in local industries (2001: 4). An undynamic economy produced a school system in its own image. In the supposedly static society of 1944–76 there was no strong demand for certification and there was a 'general acceptance that only a minority would reach the age of 16 with formal skills and qualifications' (2001: 4). Comprehensive reform had not done enough to challenge this acceptance and by setting 'social' as opposed to 'economic' goals – emphasizing egalitarianism at the expense of standards – it had contributed to stasis. Overreacting to the failings of the 11+ exam, and dominated by the 'ideology of unstreamed teaching' (Blair 1996: 175), it had failed to differentiate among students and to 'link different provision to individual attitudes and abilities' (2001: 5). One of the results was mass illiteracy; another, relatively slow rates of economic growth.

Attached to this evaluation of the overall system, there were more particular criticisms, which touched especially on teachers. Previous Labour governments – at least until Callaghan's Ruskin speech – had assumed that teachers would provide ground-level implementation of reform. New Labour rejected this position: teachers were not a source of change but a barrier to it – 'forces of conservatism' in Blair's words (R. Smithers 1999). The welfare state had created teachers in their hundreds of thousands, managed them only lightly, allowed them to develop cultures both radical and inertial, and set them to work in a system of low-level mass schooling. Schooling increased its share of the national resources; teachers were seen as the main initiators of curricular change; government kept its distance from the workings of the system, sponsoring but not directing educational expansion and reform, and relying on teachers and local authorities, not central intervention, to secure school-level change. New Labour summarized this pattern of behaviour as 'support without pressure', a system in which government-tolerated low expectations of students on the part of some teachers coexisted with a world-view held by others in which 'schools made no difference and were essentially agents of social control' (Barber 1996; 1998a).

A different and more appreciative story was told about Conservatism. Its faults were a lack of concern for social cohesion and an underestimation of the potential of active government. But, for Blair, it still accomplished much necessary destructive work. The reforms of the 1980s destroyed the old education system and 'dismantled collective power' – Blair referred appreciatively to this process as 'picking out weeds' (Blair 1996: 216). New Labour's first major legislation – the 1998 School Standards and Frameworks Act – accordingly took as its starting point the inviolability of much Conservative law-making. It retained testing, league tables, the national curriculum and local management of schools. Beyond these specific legacies, there were more general inheritances. When New Labour made its critique of what was alleged to be the 'one size fits all' philosophy of comprehensive education (DfEE 2001: 15), and when it spoke in praise of differentiation, selection, streaming and setting by ability, it echoed Conservative voices. It was the Conservative White Paper of 1992 which had castigated what it took to be the founding belief of comprehensive education that 'children are all basically the same' (Chitty 2001: 23). 'Differentation' was a special concern of Keith Joseph. 'Specialization', so central to post-1997 policy, had a long history in the right's attempts to devise a system which was selective, yet not based on rigid and unpopular tripartite divisions. It figured in Tory rethinkings of the 1950s (see p. 48) and resurfaced in 1992 when the Education Secretary John Patten described it as the principle on which schooling would in the future be based (Chitty 2001: 23). New Labour's attempts to remake or remanage the teaching force likewise had Conservative antecedents, as did the appreciation it acquired of the capacities of the private sector.

But Conservatism, in this account, had one major failing. It did not 'plant new seeds' (Blair 1996: 217). Its affection for English heritage and traditionalist versions of national identity created long-term problems for curricular change – 'culture' in the Conservative sense was not the best lens through which to understand the contemporary world (Blair 1996). It relied too much on the market to promote leadership and school effectiveness. It overlooked the importance of social cohesion. It could not find ways of intervening effectively in classroom-level processes. New Labour insisted that it had by contrast met these challenges and synthesized the right's programme of diversity with the left's aspirations to social justice. It followed that 'the old arguments that have bedevilled education in this country should be put behind us' (Labour Party 1997: 7).

New Labour's policies for schools, then, need to be situated in several contexts – of government policy as a whole, of global policy discourse, of divergent models of policy within Britain, and of New Labour's reading of the past whose errors it aims to correct. The sections that follow draw from these contextualizations. They aim to discuss the themes and effects of policy in more detail, attempting in the process to suggest how the system that New Labour is creating in England differs from that of previous periods, post-1944 and post-1979. My interest here is in three broad themes, which the following sections treat in an interwoven rather than separated way. The first has to do with the issues of agency on which earlier chapters have frequently touched: who has the power and the capacity to shape the work of schooling, and how do policy and wider social and political changes alter the distribution of such capacity? The second, related theme concerns the kinds of culture that are created in schools, and the kinds of relationship that exist between the school and cultural movements and situations outside it. The third concerns the projects of 'selective universalism' and social inclusion that are central features of New Labour social and educational policy. Then, in the last section of this chapter, consideration turns to the more general ambitions and tensions of the system that is being created.

Re-agenting

This section discusses the 're-agenting' of schooling, and the new discursive themes and cultural practices to which it is giving rise. Rikowski (2001: 2) argues that New Labour's 'biggest idea' is probably the knowledge economy. He quotes the Department of Trade and Industry's observation that in the global economy, 'capital is mobile [and] technology spreads quickly.' British business has to compete by exploiting capabilities – knowledge, skills and creativity – which competitors find hard to imitate (Department of Trade and Industry 1998, cited in Rikowski 2001). The education system needs to produce such capabilities – hence a focus on international competitiveness, and on performance in relation to 'hard' criteria of test and exam results, rather than the mixed and less precise objectives of earlier periods (and of other parts of Britain).

Around its project of transformation, New Labour seeks to create new kinds of educational alliance, although 'alliance' is perhaps too politicized a term for the new networks by which education is governed and through which change is organized. There is no place in this new system for the forces associated with earlier periods of reform, nor do the relationships through which it is constructed make much allowance for the negotiation of different pre-existing or potentially conflicting interests: the often tense and certainly unequal 'partnership' between unions, local authorities and national government that influenced educational change between 1944 and 1979 has not been restored. Instead, 'partnership' has acquired a new meaning, which relates primarily to the operational accomplishment of strategies devised by a single, powerful agency – national government (K. Jones and Bird 2000). In this sense the field of education policy has been reworked, so that the development of policy through an explicitly political process of encounter between different social interests has become less important than its elaboration through networks of agencies, local and national, whose origins and points of reference lie in the priorities of national government. Indeed, New Labour – with some assistance from its Conservative predecessors – has itself brought into being some of the main forces with which it now seeks to build 'partnerships'.

First among the partners are those operationally powerful but not strongly autonomous agencies, which through mechanisms of target-setting, resource allocation, programme specification, training, audit and inspection penetrate deeply into the everyday procedures of educational institutions and the life-world of those who work and study in them. Taylor and her colleagues noted the emergence in the 1990s of an OECD-led consensus around the idea of a 'performance-orientated' public sector, with a focus on 'results, efficiency and effectiveness', and with a bias towards a strengthening of the 'strategic capacities of the centre' at the expense of local units, which possess operational autonomy but only within firm national guidelines' (Taylor et al. 1997: 81). Following this model, New Labour has retained the agencies of Conservative centralization and added others of its own making: Ofsted, the Teacher Training Agency, the Standards and Effectiveness Unit at the Department for Education and Skills (DfES) and the Qualifications and

Curriculum Authority (QCA) are complemented by major conjunctural initiatives – the DfES-funded 'Excellence in Cities' and Literacy and Numeracy Strategies – which are nationally directed and locally pervasive.

Via such bodies and through the work of new units of the DfES such as that dealing with Standards and Effectiveness (A. Smithers 2001), New Labour has installed a regulatory system – set out in the Schools Standards and Frameworks Act – that is aimed to ensure high average levels of attainment, enabled by national curricula and measured by national tests, within a pattern of schooling marked by increasing diversity among the institutions that provide it. Government sets national targets for student performance. LEAs submit to the DfES Education Development Plans, part of which state how these targets will be locally delivered. Schools are required to produce target-related plans, and are measured against performance and assessment reports which compare their output with that of schools with a similar mix of pupils. Teachers, through a salary system which relates pay to performance, are 'performance managed' in the relation to these objectives (Forrester 2002).

In this climate the tendencies towards managerialism noted in the previous chapter have been strengthened, as has the link between the micro-world of classroom interactions and macro-level objectives of standards and achievement. Schools have perforce developed management regimes that can achieve the targets required of them by government and its regulatory agencies. These regimes have produced some immediate successes: primary school leavers achieve ever higher standards of literacy and numeracy, as measured by the national testing system; GCSE results continue to improve (DfEE 2001: 13). In the same process, schools have been defined more strongly than at any other time in the period of this book as places where management authority, rather than collegial culture, establishes the ethos and purpose of the school. Before 1988, the pattern of educational initiative had been at least partly shaped by teachers – hence its diversity, its occasional radicalism, its counter-tendencies towards inertia. After 1988 a variety of forces – the national curriculum, Ofsted, a league-table-based system of accountability – had removed from teachers much of this capacity. From 1997, these latter developments were complemented by a systematic enhancement of the capacities of school managers, whose brief was conceived by government as to effect at school level a break with the past. Barber and Phillips, two advisers to government, illustrate this feature of the new culture of schooling very clearly in their advice to 'leaders':

> Beliefs do not necessarily change behaviour. More usually...behaviours shape beliefs. Only when people have experienced a change do they revise their beliefs accordingly....Sometimes it is necessary to mandate the change, implement it well, consciously challenge the prevailing culture and have the courage to sustain it until beliefs shift....The driving force at this critical juncture is leadership....It is the vocation of leaders to take people where they have never been before and to show them a new world from which they do not want to return. (Barber and Phillips 2000: 9–11)

Teachers are thus ambivalently placed in the process of change. They are operationally central but strategically marginal; they have become accustomed to government-generated innovation and have acquired, through their participation in the drive to raise standards, new kinds of skill. Yet in terms of the management and direction of the school they are subordinate. Their involvement in change proceeds not along the classic avenues of teacher professionalism – representative pressure or classroom autonomy – but rather through a variety of organizations, projects and procedures which are designed to secure by means of directive and incentive their incorporation within a government framework of priorities. The National College for School Leadership is intended to create a cadre of heads and deputies capable of raising standards of performance and of promoting the new kinds of co-operation, the new practices of teaching and learning, that can make this possible. The General Teaching Council has been designed by government to 'represent' the interests of teachers, and simultaneously to act as a transmission belt for the policies of government. At the same time, a nationally directed programme of 'Continuing Professional Development' is meant to ensure that the in-service education of teachers corresponds to national priorities, while performance-related pay provides another connection between the work of classrooms and the central concerns of government; and a set of government and government-instigated initiatives – 'Best Practice Research Scholarships', 'Teacher of the Year' ceremonies – create new forms of recognition.

In all this a cultural shift has occurred. Earlier chapters of this book have described periods in which 'culture' was not so much a management project as an uncertain space where the formal curriculum and procedures of the school encountered and to varying extents negotiated with the cultures of students; the work of teachers from this point of view had an essentially cultural character, and to a significant – albeit minority – extent drew from the knowledge and identities created by social movements. In the processes exemplified by Barber and Phillips, cultural practice of this type is not present; it has been replaced by a project that draws from an international set of norms for school improvement that will provide the new, focused organizational culture of the school that the leadership cadre is meant, according to management theory, to create: the main function of leaders, in some versions of school improvement, being to remake cultures (Stoll and Fink 1996).

Business

Alongside new forms of regulation and management, a further strand that runs through these dense networks of change is constituted by private 'edubusiness'. In contrast to much of the post-1944 period, in which private-sector involvement in education was in the main limited to the 'independent' sector, it is now extensively entwined with state schooling itself. Before 1997, public/private-sector partnerships had already become a feature of the institutional landscape, as 'mixed economies' of welfare were created (Butcher 1995). The 1999 White Paper *Modernizing Government* approved this growing tendency 'in which distinctions between services delivered by the public and private sectors are breaking down ... opening the way to ideas, partnerships and opportunities for devising and delivering what the public wants' (Cabinet Office 1999: 5). New Labour thus took up and amplified Conservative 'partnership' initiatives with the private sector, focusing in the first instance on 'raising standards in disadvantaged areas'. Education Action Zones, launched in England in 1998, were intended as 'a new crusade uniting businesses, schools, local authorities and parents to modernize education in areas of social deprivation' (DfEE 1998c). Transnational companies – Shell, for instance, and various ICT firms – were recruited, with some difficulty and to no great effect (Ofsted 2001), to support a cautious programme of locally based innovation, within DfEE guidelines.

From 2000, this aspect of 'partnership' was less in evidence. Parts of the private sector had an interest in the development of e-learning, and the construction industry benefited from the Private Finance Initiative, which subsidized it to build schools and lease them back to local authorities (Whitfield 1999). But, these issues apart, big business showed little inclination to become directly involved in state education and later initiatives relied more on the participation of the small but growing edubusiness sector than on reluctant transnationals. Private educational companies were given contracts to run failing English LEAs, and New Labour sought business sponsorship for 'City Academies', in which the private sector would play a central managerial role. The government Green Paper and White Paper of 2001 envisaged more extended private involvement: companies would be encouraged to take over failing – or even successful – schools (DfEE 2001; DfES 2001). Local authorities, once a major political force in reform, were advised by the Green Paper to seek a future for themselves in 'promoting a more open market in services for schools' and to 'trial new ways' of establishing public–private partnerships (DfEE 2001: 90).

Underlying Labour's new strategy was an admiration for the capacities of business. The rhetoric of change employed by previous Labour governments had always been careful to lay the blame for economic problems on 'both sides of industry'. Restrictive practices among the workforce and conservatism in the boardroom were in this account the two dispiriting sides of the same British coin. Post-1997 rhetoric – at least in respect of the qualities of the boardroom – was different. Private-sector leaders were valued as sources of expertise. Much more generally, circulating through the international policy community was a deepening appreciation of the dynamism of business. 'Fast capitalism' and the 'knowledge economy' were understood as private creations; and educationalists had begun to celebrate the modern workplace in terms which stressed its educational character and potential:

> Commitment, responsibility and motivation are won by developing a workplace culture in which the members of an organization identify with its vision, mission and corporate values. The old vertical chains of command are replaced by the horizontal relations of teamwork. A division of labour into its minute, deskilled components is replaced by 'multi-skilled' well-rounded workers who are flexible enough to be able to do complex and integrated work.... Traditional structures of command and control are being replaced by relationships of pedagogy: mentoring, training and the learning organization. (New London Group 1996: 66)

Creativity

From this recognition of the capacities created by the workplace it is just a short step to another striking phenomenon of the later 1990s – the celebration of 'creativity' as an *essential* element of business. In discursive terms, this entailed a re-presentation of the relation between the school and work. In chapter 1, we saw how policy documents in England and Scotland expressed concerns about the effects of industry and industrialism on learning and on communities. Chapters 2 and

3 depicted at points the influence of progressive and radical educators who believed either that the purposes of schooling should not intersect with business priorities, or more strongly that they should be fundamentally opposed to them. Conservatism, as we have seen, defined itself against progressive education, and regarded 'creativity' as a term which disguised educators' lack of commitment to raising standards and to passing on established values. In the 1990s, by contrast, there was a rising chorus of voices insisting that 'creativity' and 'business' were not opposites but friends. The 'creativity' of learners was once again recognized, but this time not from the viewpoint of a romantic or militant culture-critique but from that of contemporary capital, appreciative of what 'creativity' could add to the value of the workforce in a competitive (and largely post-industrial) economy. 'This government knows that culture and creativity matter,' wrote Blair in 2001:

> They matter because they can enrich all our lives, and everyone deserves the opportunity to develop their own creative talents and to benefit from those of others. They matter because our rich and diverse culture helps bring us together. They also matter because creative talent will be crucial to our individual and national economic success in the economy of the future. (Blair 2001: 3)

Interest in 'creativity' among educationalists suddenly boomed (Buckingham and Jones 2001). Whereas in the 1980s and early 1990s Conservative traditionalism linked the cultural work of schools to the perpetuation of English heritage, under New Labour a cluster of reports appeared, all aiming to justify art, music, or the creativity of teachers in the name of business need. *All Our Futures* – the report of a government advisory committee which was the most developed of these – argued that there is 'an incessant need for businesses to develop new products and services and to adapt management styles and systems of operation to keep pace with rapidly changing market conditions'. As a result, the 'growing demand in businesses worldwide is for forms of education and training that develop "human resources" and in particular the powers of communication, innovation and creativity.' Knowledge-based and cultural industries, it went on, had increased in size and significance, providing 'opportunity for the creative abilities of young people'. Creativity was fundamental now not only to the arts but to 'the sciences ... politics, business and in all areas of everyday life' (DfEE/DCMS 1999: 19–27).

Though in formal terms the report was not accepted, these were assertions that New Labour accepted and began to integrate into its educational projects (DfES 2001). In doing so, it achieved perhaps its most profound accommodation with business. The discourse of business/creativity synthesized and transvalued elements from the past, rehabilitating 'creativity' under the sign of capital, so that earlier themes of progressive education began to recirculate, translated into a new, post-1997 language. Creativity was valued, not as something rescued from the grim routines of industrial capitalism, but as a set of qualities now intrinsic to the knowledge economy's further development.

Differentiation

If questions of management and the role of business provide some of the defining elements of New Labour policy for schools, it is further distinguished by the combination of a secondary education system that is highly differentiated, alongside a social policy in which inclusion is strongly emphasized. As Croxford suggests and educational historians have long concluded, what distinguishes the English secondary system from those of Wales, Scotland, Ireland and most countries in continental Europe is an institutionalized diversity of provision, around which differences in status, material resources and educational outcomes have solidified (Johnson 1989; A. Green 1990). Under previous Labour governments this system was challenged, partly by government sponsorship of comprehensive reform, partly by tendencies of a more dispersed and local kind that sought further and more egalitarian change. New Labour has by contrast designed a new institutional pattern, and a new symbolic order of schooling in which 'ability', 'aptitude' and 'differentiation' are central principles, and Conservative legacies a powerful influence.

On taking office, New Labour broke from some aspects of Conservatism. The Assisted Places Scheme, which provided one of many state subsidies to private education, was ended, and the 1998 Act also abolished the grant-maintained status enjoyed by 17 per cent of English secondary schools. But in most respects the diversity of the Conservative years was allowed to remain. In place of the Conservative distinction between grant-maintained and local authority schools, Labour introduced a new terminology – 'foundation' and 'community' – which preserved a status differential that created in the view of one researcher 'significant opportunities to perpetuate traditional patterns of segregation' (Whitty 2001b: 14). The 2001 Green Paper indicated a willingness to preserve another feature of English diversity. The established church, at one time seen as constituting a problem for educational reform, was offered a stronger place in the state system: the Green Paper signalled a change in funding arrangements so as to prompt the stronger involvement of the Anglican community and of other 'faith groups' in setting up secondary schools. Alongside them, Labour envisaged 'beacon' and 'specialist' schools. Beacon schools were selected from an OFSTED list of top-performing institutions and awarded extra funds for sharing with others the methods that had brought them success. The specialist school, as we have seen, was a Conservative invention: specialist schools received higher levels of state funding and could select 10 per cent of their students on the basis of aptitude for whatever specialism they provided. The 1997 government expanded the initiative. The 2001 Green Paper took it further, envisaging that 50 per cent of secondary schools would become specialist, receiving more funds, and marked out in status terms from the remainder. It also encouraged the foundation of 'City Academies', privately run institutions, part-funded by government. Within each school in this highly variegated pattern, New Labour wished there to be a further pattern of differentiation: 'express sets', fast-tracking of 'gifted' individuals, new types of testing for the exceptionally talented, earlier entry for some to GCSE and A-level examinations, 'setting' as a general principle of school organization.

For many observers, including those who admired the government's achievement in raising the level of success in national tests, these policies perpetuated a 'monstrously...unfair secondary education system' (A. Smithers 2001). It is certainly reasonable to assume that they will accentuate the pattern identified by Gewirtz et al. (1995) – in which greater complexity and diversity in local 'markets' of schooling increases the advantages available to social groups which have the cultural and material resources to gain access to higher-status schools. Young, for instance, suggests that in London there has already been a 'strategic withdrawal' of middle-class families from socially mixed state education; with parents taking measures to avoid schooling in boroughs where the majority of pupils are from 'socially excluded' families (Young 1999, cited in Whitty 2001a). Such accentuation, which has not abated since 1997, would, of course, reverse both the intentions of earlier Labour administrations and the effects noted by Croxford and other researchers, in which the degree of 'mixing' of students from different social groups has a positive effect on the attainment of students from working-class backgrounds.

Inclusion

The differentiating logic of this system is counter-balanced by New Labour's emphasis on inclusion. The term includes programmes of differing kinds. As Dyson and Slee point out, throughout the 1990s there has been an increasing attention, among professionals and policy communities, to the 'rights of the child'. This concept was endorsed in general terms by the United Nations Declaration of 1990, and elaborated more specifically by the UNESCO Salamanca Statement of 1994, to relate to the inclusion of students – such as those deemed to have special needs – whose education has been damaged by their separation from mainstream schooling. Inclusion in this case is motivated on grounds of equal treatment and children's rights and is plainly a well-established and government-sanctioned project, however inhibited it may be by lack of resources and by market pressures which place a premium on schools admitting the academically able. The same is true of other projects, such as the 'Widening Participation' programme, directed at increasing the numbers of 'disadvantaged' students in higher education. Likewise the government has focused far more strongly on the achievement of ethnic minority students than its predecessor: following an Ofsted report that had shown the continuing low achievement of many Bangladeshi, Pakistani and Afro-Caribbean students, the 2001 Green Paper was notably more alert to 'race' than Labour's first such publication, the 1997 *Excellence in Schools*. (DfEE 1997; OFSTED 1999; DfEE 2001).

The Question of 'Responsibility'

In other respects, though, inclusion is premised on different principles. Anthony Giddens, the writer who has done most to explain the coherence of New Labour politics, and to draw together their economic and social threads, writes that 'exclusion is not about gradations of inequality, but about mechanisms that act to detach groups of people from the social mainstream' (Giddens 1998: 104). This detachment is understood in part as a result of social and economic damage inflicted by forces outside the control of individuals. But for New Labour, if not so much for Giddens, repairing the damage is something for which individuals, even – or especially – damaged individuals, must take responsibility. The route to social cohesion is seen to pass both through the territory of more extensive state provision, and also through the ability of excluded groups to reintegrate themselves. Inclusion policies are intended to produce capacities for integration, and also where necessary to enforce 'responsibilization' upon those who have not internalized it (Gewirtz 1998; Rose 1990). David (2002) has pointed out the importance of the School

Standards and Framework Act in this respect. It legislated for 'a whole range of whole-school relations through statutory home–school agreements and homework policies, including study support and homework centres, literacy and numeracy strategies ... and various forms of parenting education'.

Such activities, combining extra provision and a pressure for responsibilization (home–school agreements), are strong features of both the government's major programmes for urban education – the Education Action Zones and Excellence in Cities initiatives. They are complemented by a range of other measures that cover truancy, individual support ('learning mentors') for disadvantaged students, a new careers service intended to increase the number of school-leavers employed or in further education or training, and by Learning Support Units designed to keep on site students who would otherwise have been suspended or expelled. Specifically, as David (2002) and Bullen et al. (2000) have noted, there is a particular focus on reducing teenage pregnancy, which, despite its relatively low rate of occurrence, is read as an indicator of the low educational expectations and potential welfare dependency of teenage mothers.

The overall effect is to connect the school to other social agencies in the work of responsibilizing students who are not successful in the performance culture of the school. Gewirtz (2001) goes so far as to detect a 'massive programme of resourcing and re-education which has as its ultimate aim the eradication of cultural difference by transforming working-class parents into middle-class parents', complete with an interest in making consumer choices about schools, monitoring their work and supporting their children's learning (2001: 366). She underlines therefore the strong cultural element in policy discourse, exemplified in David Blunkett's view that 'we need parents who are prepared to take responsibility for supporting their children's education and we need a culture which values education and demands the best' (cited in Gewirtz 2001: 365). But like other writers she finds in Labour policy a central problem. Although it frequently addresses questions of 'culture' it does so in a way which almost entirely neglects what educators of a previous period found central. Recapitulating earlier debates, Whitty writes that, in the 1970s, explanations of the failure of working-class children in education went beyond ideas of cultural and material deficit to consider that 'failure was a relational outcome of middle-class power to define what counts as knowledge and achievement' (Whitty 2001a: 287). By contrast, New Labour operates with what Whitty calls an unquestioning attitude to educational processes: while it has stressed that schools matter in terms of access and achievement, 'it has almost entirely accepted and even reinforced conventional notions of what counts as education' (2001a: 288). It adopts also a view of 'culture' as something made from above: just as leaders remake the culture of the school around authorized meanings and values, so New Labour politicians desire to remake the cultures of communities. A teacher quoted in chapter 2 suggested that 'there exists not merely this sort of elite culture ... but some different kind of culture which it is necessary to seek out by going into other people's experience'; but this 'different culture', and its implications for teaching and learning, remains outside the framework of current policy. Maud Blair and her colleagues, writing about race, draw out the consequences of this position: a policy which is content with the existing procedures of the school – and 'fetishes league tables and exam results' – is inclined to detect responsibility not in the official culture of the school, but in the cultural practice of certain groups of students. These students, as a result of 'low academic and behavioural expectations' on the part of their teachers, are then especially likely to be placed in low-status groups and face harsh disciplinary regimes (M. Blair et al. 1999: 9); Gillborn and Youdell (2000) suggest that such a pattern of failure is regularly produced by schools which focus on 'results' in examination terms, rather than a broader and more open agenda of needs.

What Comes After?

This final chapter has tried both to show the ambitions and the tensions of New Labour policy, and to sketch its relationship to what came before it. About what comes after, we can only make guesses, informed by our understanding of the past and alert to the difficulties of the present. But some things seem clear enough. In terms of purpose, New Labour has the most coherent education programme of any government since 1944: preparing for the knowledge economy and securing social inclusion are objectives that are plainly stated, and systematically operationalized:

> The national curriculum sets the standards.... All schools set targets and measure their performance.... They can easily access best practice information.... They have increasing opportunities for professional development.... They are held to account through inspection and published performance tables. (DfEE 2001: 8)

This is what could be called a driven system, whose functioning is subordinated to limited and overriding objectives, and whose actors are exposed to the intense demands of testing, inspection and performance management. It is a divided system, which nevertheless makes universal promises. It is a public system which is edging ever closer to full partnership with profit-orientated forces. Insistent on the necessity of social inclusion on responsibilized terms, it is less tolerant of cultural difference than some of the systems that have preceded it. Also, as one would expect from such a normative artefact, it is less rich in aspects of its ecology: diversified institutionally, it promotes sameness in pedagogy and curriculum. Finally, it is not one system but four, and it is exposed as much to the centrifugal pressures of national difference as it is to the preferences of the global policy community and the Westminster government. From these features, and from the history that this book has tried to reconstruct, one can predict the likely occurrence of certain conflicts, even if their outcome remains obscure.

First, New Labour may be expecting too much from schooling – or, at least, from schooling as presently constituted. At the core of its policy is the belief that there can be 'success against the odds', a contention that has encouraged New Labour to think that the methods employed by effective schools offer an adequate response not only to questions of raising standards but to those of inequality (Thrupp 2000). Others are more doubtful. Mortimore and Whitty, summarizing recent findings, state that 'there remains a strong negative correlation between most measures of social disadvantage and school achievement' (1997: 4): the 'social' sets limits to the 'educational', and – as we have seen – the changes in the distribution of wealth that New Labour has been able to effect are not large. Moreover, raising standards will not in itself resolve the problems of inequality which have preoccupied educationalists for most parts of the post-1944 period – relative inequalities can increase, between students of different social groups, even while overall standards rise (Hatcher 1998: 268). Department for Education and Employment publications discount this argument, and claim that it is in the most disadvantaged areas that standards are most quickly rising (DfEE 2001: 13 11). But the persistence of this trend, its connection to employment outcomes and its relation to class inequalities remain debatable. New Labour has set aside social arguments about educational success and failure on the grounds that they provide only excuses for poor schooling. 'We are determined', Michael Barber told a House of Commons select committee, 'to expect high standards and have high expectations of every pupil regardless of their background and circumstances.' By discounting the latter factors, government 'had taken all excuses off the table' (Barber 1999). Blair,

likewise, attacked 'the culture of excuses', which 'tolerates low ambition, rejects excellence and treats poverty as an excuse for failure'
(cited in R. Smithers 1999). But these perspectives may well give rise
to misdirected pressures, demanding too much of schools, and planning too little for wider sorts of social change.

Second, policy is vulnerable to claims that it cannot resolve an
inbuilt conflict between private interest and social need: this is the
gist of the campaigns against privatization in several English cities
(Regan 2001; Wood 2001). Third, its performance-centred regime
will provoke continual conflict with teachers. Labour's policy of
imposing pressure to meet targets set by government means that
conflicts over workload become both everyday issues and ones that
immediately connect to controversies over policy, while teachers'
input into fundamental – 'strategic' in Reay's terms – decisions
about the content and purposes of education has been minimized.
This demanding pattern of centralization is – Ozga suggests – 'at the
heart of the problem of teacher morale, motivation and recruitment'
(1998: 9). Teaching's recruitment crisis did not diminish after 1997;
and there remained a simmering discontent over issues of workload
and performance management. Fourth, there is a connected problem,
perhaps harder to detect than teacher responses. Occupational change
has expanded the number of careers for which formal qualifications
are a condition of entry. This shift, alongside the pressures of central
government and school managements, has created a school regime
centred on performance and certification, and organized around
testing programmes that since 1988 have grown to include almost
every year-group of schooling, from under-fives to 18-year-olds. As
with the 11+ in the 1950s, the reliability of the testing is frequently
questioned. Continual testing makes very great demands on the intellectual and emotional energies of students. Chapter 4 referred to the
annual rituals in which students celebrate exam success; here we can
note the darker side of competition, as when in 1999 the columnist
Ros Coward wrote of witnessing

> scenes at the entrance exam for one so-called comprehensive school –
> a flagship for the borough of Wandsworth. One child was sobbing and
> shaking as she went into the room, another wet himself during the
> exams. More dramatic was the child who ran out of the hall in tears,
> chasing his mother down the road. Mother and child then stood in the
> street sobbing and screaming at each other. 'It's your future,' she
> shouted. 'If you don't go back in, I'll have nothing more to do with
> you.' 'I'm not going back in there,' he yelled and ran off, leaving his
> distressed mother to scour the streets by car.... Under the banner of
> improved educational standards, maltreatment is ignored. It's not sur-

prising these 10–year-olds buckle under the pressure. Most of the children at this school were on their fourth or fifth exam of the season – normal for young Londoners of that age. Many 'desirable' schools are grant-maintained and conduct their own exams. There's no guarantee of local places and no way of expressing preferences, so children enter all the exams. (Coward 1999: 22)

Whether these experiences will have political as well as psychological effects remains an open question. At present, parents and students comply with pressure. Students take tests, with rising levels of success. Parents enter a marketplace in which hardware and software, curriculum guides and books of test papers form a booming education sector (Buckingham and Scanlon 2002). From one angle, this looks like endorsement of the government's vision. From another, it contains stresses that may find expression in protest; many parents in the 1950s sought to 'buy' individual success in the 11+, but this did not prevent growing levels of resentment at the social costs of the selective system. Moreover, the highly pressured regime of schooling post-1997 is at odds with other elements that make up the discursive space of childhood. The UN Convention on the Rights of the Child speaks of 'the full, harmonious development of the personality' and of the atmosphere of 'love and understanding' that should surround childhood. (United Nations 1991). The Convention gives voice to a strong contemporary belief in childhood as a protected space, and of children's rights as ones which include, but also exceed, material well-being. From this perspective, the educational reforms of the post-1988 period are permanently in question, and, given the pace and extent of the changes New Labour envisages, it seems reasonable to expect a tension between the direction in which policy attempts to lead 'the child', and other, increasingly well-established positions.

Fifth, there are problems along the road to social inclusion, most evidently those associated with race. After the riots and social unrest in several northern English towns in the summer of 2001, several reports commissioned by government and local authorities wrote of the divide between white working-class and 'Asian' working-class communities, a divide created less by institutional racism than by 'self-segregation'. A report commissioned by the Home Secretary, David Blunkett, suggested that the divide might be narrowed if migrants made a cultural turn towards Britishness, swearing an oath of allegiance and expressing their 'primary loyalty' to Britain; the proposal, echoing Blunkett's own belief that there were 'norms of acceptability' to which migrant communities should submit, highlighted enduring tensions (Travis 2001a; 2001b). The effects of global conflicts, religious difference and poverty had polarized urban life in many parts of England. A government response couched in terms of civic responsibility, allegiance, loyalty and normative behaviour set an agenda for schools that expressed in a very strong form the cultural programme criticized by Gewirtz and others, above. Whether such a programme is capable of addressing deep social, cultural and political conflicts must be debatable.

Finally, in a book which has frequently sought to draw out the peculiarities of England, amid the several versions of schooling that circulate in Britain, it is appropriate to think over the political situation in which these peculiarities are presently enmeshed. Since devolution, the education systems of England, Northern Ireland, Scotland and Wales have in important respects diverged. Divergence has very often taken the form of policy communities outside England expressing a preference for models of schooling that seem less diverse, more equitable and less punitive towards the teaching force than the English template. There has been growing awareness of these differences, which are being used – by teaching unions, for instance – to demonstrate that alternatives exist to current policy. New Labour's programme, thus, is vulnerable to 'policy learning' – post-1997, the lessons of policy in any one of the 'home international' countries are more likely to be assimilated and passed on to others, and a radical initiative in one place can more swiftly become a reference point for agitation in others. New Labour is confident that it has closed the book on the past, and put serious policy conflict behind it. It is too soon to be certain about that.

References

Abrams, M. (1959) *The Teenage Consumer*. London: London Press Exchange.

Adamson, D. (1999) Poverty and social exclusion in Wales today. In D. Dunkerley and A. Thompson, *Wales Today*. Cardiff: University of Wales Press.

Ainley, P. (1994) *Degrees of Difference: higher education in the nineties*. London: Lawrence & Wishart.

Ainley, P. (1998) Towards a learning or a certified society? Contradictions in the New Labour modernisation of lifelong learning. *Journal of Education Policy*, 13, 4, 559–74.

Ainley, P. (1999) *Learning Policy: towards the certified society*. London: Macmillan.

Aitchison, J., and Carter, H. (1999) The Welsh language today. In D. Dunkerley and A. Thompson, *Wales Today*. Cardiff: University of Wales Press.

Akenside, D. H. (1973) *Education and Enmity: the control of schooling in Northern Ireland*. Newton Abbott: David and Charles.

Albemarle Report (1960) Report of the departmental committee on the Youth Service in England and Wales. In Maclure (1979).

Aldcroft, D. (1992) *Education, Training and Economic Performance 1944–90*. Manchester: Manchester University Press.

Alexiadou, N., Lawn, M., and Ozga, J. (2001) Educational governance and social integration/exclusion: the cases of Scotland and England. In S. Lindblad and T. Popkewitz, *Educational Governance and Social Integration and Exclusion*. Uppsala: Uppsala University.

Amis, K. (1981) Postscript to 'Lone Voices'. In *What Became of Jane Austen and other questions?* Harmondsworth: Penguin.

Angus, L. (1993) The sociology of school effectiveness. *British Journal of Sociology of Education*, 14, 4, 333–45.

Arnot, M. (1991) Equality and democracy: a decade of struggle over education. *British Journal of Sociology of Education*, 12, 4, 447–66.

Arnot, M., David, M., and Weiner, G. (1996) *Educational Reform and Gender Equality in Schools*. Manchester: Equal Opportunities Commission.

Arnot, M., David, M., and Weiner, G. (1999) *Closing the Gender Gap: post-war education and social change*. Cambridge: Polity.

Arshad, S., and Dinez, F. A. (1999) Race equality in Scottish education. In Bryce and Humes (1999).

Atkinson, N. (1969) *Irish Education: a history of educational institutions*. Dublin: Allen Figgis.

Audit Commission (1996) *Trading Places: the supply and allocation of school places*. London: Audit Commission.

Ball, S. (1994) *Educational Reform: a critical and post-structural approach*. Buckingham: Open University Press.

Bantock, G. H. (1947) The cultural implications of planning and popularisation. *Scrutiny*, 14, 3, 171–84.

Barber, M. (1996) *The Learning Game*. London: Gollancz.

Barber, M. (1998a) The dark side of the moon: imagining an end to failure in urban education. In L. Stoll and K. Myers (eds), *No Quick Fixes: perspectives on schools in difficulty*. London: Falmer Press.

Barber, M. (1998b) Creating a world-class education service. Speech delivered to North of England Education Conference, Bradford, January.

Barber, M. (1999) Evidence to House of Commons Select Committee on Education and Employment, 14 July.

Barber, M., and Dann, R. (eds) (1996) *Raising Educational Standards in the Inner Cities*. London: Cassell.

Barber, M., and Phillips, V. (2000) Fusion: how to unleash irreversible change (Lessons for the Future of System-Wide School Reform). Paper to DfEE Conference on Education Action Zones, March.

Barker, M. (1984) *A Haunt of Fears: the strange history of the British horror comics campaign*. London: Pluto Press.

Barker, R. (1972) *Education and Politics 1900–51: a study of the Labour Party*. Oxford: Oxford University Press.

Barnett, C. (1986) *The Audit of War: the illusion and reality of Britain as a great nation*. London: Macmillan.

Benn, C., and Chitty, C. (1996) *Thirty Years On: is comprehensive education alive and well or struggling to survive?* Harmondsworth: Penguin.

Benn, C., and Simon, B. (1972) *Half-way There: report on the British comprehensive school reform*. 2nd edn. Harmondsworth: Penguin.

Bennett, N. (1976) *Teaching Styles and Pupil Progress*. London: Open Books.

Bentley, T., and Selzer, K. (1999) *The Creative Age*. London: Demos.

Bernstein, B. (1971) *Class Codes and Control*, Vol. 1: *Theoretical Studies towards a Sociology of Language*. London: Routledge & Kegan Paul.

Bernstein, B., and Davies, B. (1969) Some sociological comments on Plowden. In R. S. Peters (ed.), *Perspectives on Plowden*. London: Routledge & Kegan Paul.

Bew, P., Gibbon, P., and Patterson, H. (1995) *Northern Ireland 1921–1994: political forces and social classes*. London: Serif.

Blackburn, F. (1954) *George Tomlinson*. London: Heinemann.

Blair, M., Gillborn, D., Kemp, S., and MacDonald, J. (1999) Institutional racism, education and the Stephen Lawrence inquiry. *Education and Social Justice*, 1, 3, 6–15.

Blair, T. (1995) The power of the message. *New Statesman*, 29 September, 19–22.

Blair, T. (1996) *New Britain: my vision of a young country*. London: Fourth Estate.

Blair, T. (1997a) Quoted in *The Guardian*, 30 May.

Blair, T. (1997b) Speech at Stockwell Park School, Lambeth, 2 June.

Blair, T. (1997c) Speech at Aylesbury Estate, Southwark, 8 December.

Blair, T. (2001) Foreword to Department of Culture, Media and Sport, *Culture and Creativity: the next ten years*. London: The Stationery Office.

Blishen, E. (1955) *Roaring Boys*. London: Thames & Hudson.

Blunkett, D. (2001) *Education into Employability: the role of the DfEE in the economy*. Speech to the Institute of Economic Affairs. www.dfee. gov.uk / dfee_speeches /

Boyle, E. (1963) Foreword. *Half our Future: a report of the Central Advisory Committee for England*. Newsom Report. London: HMSO.

Boyle, E., and Crosland, A., in conversation with Kogan, M. (1971) *The Politics of Education*. Harmondsworth: Penguin.

Bradbury, J. (1998) The devolution debate in Wales during the Major governments: the politics of a developing union state? In Elcock and Keating (1998).

Brent LEA (1986) *Race Equality in Schools*. London: Brent LEA.

Broadfoot, P. (2001) Empowerment or performativity? Assessment policy in the late twentieth century. In Phillips and Furlong (2001).

Brown, G. (1997) Interview with Larry Elliott. *The Guardian*, 27 September.

Brown, R. K. (1990) A flexible future in Europe: changing patterns of employment in the UK. *British Journal of Sociology* 41, 3, 301–28.

Bryce, T., and Humes, W. (1999) *Scottish Education*. Edinburgh: Edinburgh University Press.

Buckingham, D., and Jones, K. (2001) New Labour's cultural turn: some tensions in contemporary educational and cultural policy. *Journal of Education Policy*, 16, 1, 1–14.

Buckingham, D., Davies, H., Jones, K., and Kelley, P. (1999) *Children's Television in Britain: history, politics, discourse*. London: British Film Institute.

Buckingham, D., and Scanlon, M. (2002) *Education, Entertainment and Learning in the Home*. Buckingham: Open University Press.

Bullen, E., Kenway, J., and Hey, V. (2000) New Labour, social exclusion and risk management: the case of 'gymslip mums'. *British Education Research Journal*, 26, 4, 441–56.

Bullock Report (1975) *A Language for Life*. London: HMSO.

Burgess, A. (1983) A foreword to the revised edition. *The Wanting Seed*. London: Hamlyn.

Butcher, T. (1995) *Delivering Welfare: the governance of the social services in the 1990s*. Buckingham: Open University Press.

Butler, R. A. (1961) Popular culture and personal responsibility. Speech to National Union of Teachers Conference. Verbatim account. London: NUT.

Butler, R. A. (1971) *The Art of the Possible: the memoirs of Lord Butler*. London: Hamish Hamilton.

Cabinet Office (1999) *Modernising Government*. London: The Stationery Office.

Caldwell, B., and Spinks, J. (1988) *The Self-Managing School*. Lewes: Falmer Press.

Callaghan, J. (1987) *Time and Chance*. London: Collins.

Cameron Report (1969) *Disturbances in Northern Ireland: report of the commission appointed by the government of Northern Ireland*. Cmnd 532. Belfast: HMSO.

Campbell, J. (2001) The colonisation of the primary curriculum. In Phillips and Furlong (2001).

Carter, A. (1988) Truly, it felt like Year One. In S.Maitland (ed.), *Very Heaven: looking back at the sixties*. London: Virago.

Carter, M. (1962) *Home, School and Work: a study of the education and employment of young people in Britain*. Oxford: Pergamon Press.

Carter, T., with Coussins, J. (1986) *Shattering Illusions: West Indians in British Politics*. London: Lawrence & Wishart.

Castells, M. (1998) *The Information Age: economy, society and culture, Vol. 3: End of Millennium*. Oxford: Blackwell.

Central Advisory Committee – England (1947) *School and Life*. London: HMSO.

Central Advisory Council for Education (England) (1954) *Early Leaving*. Extracted in Maclure (1979).

Centre for Contemporary Cultural Studies (1981) *Unpopular Education: Schooling and social democracy since 1944*. London: Hutchinson.

Chessum, L. (1997) 'Sit down – you haven't reached that stage yet': African-Caribbean children in Leicester schools 1960–1974. *History of Education*, 26, 4, 409–29.

Chitty, C. (1989) *Towards a New Education Act: the victory of the new right?* Lewes: Falmer Press.

Chitty, C. (2001) Selection by specialisation. In C. Chitty and B. Simon, *Promoting Comprehensive Education in the 21st Century*. Stoke-on-Trent: Trentham Books.

Clancy, P., Drudy, S., Lynch, K., and O'Dowd, L. (1995) *Irish Society: sociological perspectives*. Dublin: Institute of Public Administration.

Clark, M. (1997) Education in Scotland: setting the scene In M. Clark and P. Munn (eds), *Education in Scotland: policy and practice from pre-school to secondary*. London: Routledge.

Clarke, J., and Newman, J. (1997) *The Managerial State*. London: Sage.

Clarke, J., Gewirtz, S., and McLaughlin, E. (2000) Reinventing the welfare state. In J. Clarke, S. Gewirtz, and E. McLaughlin (eds) *New Managerialism, New Welfare?* London: Sage.

Coard, B. (1971) *How the West Indian Child is made Educationally Subnormal in the British School System*. London: New Beacon Books.

Cohen, P. (1984) Against the new vocationalism. In I. Bates, J. Clarke, P. Cohen, D. Finn, R. Moore and P. Willis, *Schooling for the Dole?* London: Macmillan.

Cohen, P. (1997) *Rethinking the Youth Question: education, labour and cultural studies*. London: Macmillan.

Cormack, R., and Osborne, R. (1995) Education in Northern Ireland: the struggle for equality. In P. Clancy, S. Drudy, K. Lynch and L. O'Dowd, *Irish Society: sociological perspectives*. Dublin: Institute of Public Administration.

Corner House Bookshop and School Without Walls (1978) *Lunatic Ideas, or, a lesson in what school is all about, or, to be more precise, an analysis of the way the newspapers dealt with the subjects of education, young people and schools during the summer of 1977*. London: Corner House Bookshop and School Without Walls.

Cowan Report (1976) *Reorganisation of Secondary Education in Northern Ireland – a Consultative Document*. Department of Education for Northern Ireland (DENI). Belfast: HMSO.

Coward, R. (1999) Suffering in Year Six. *Guardian*, 19 January.

Cowling, M. (1987) The sources of the New Right: irony, geniality and malice. *Encounter*, 73, 4, 1–13.

Cox, Brian (1992) *The Great Betrayal: memoirs of a life in education*. London: Chapman.

Cox, C. B., and Dyson, A. E. (1969) *Fight for Education: a Black Paper*. London: Critical Quarterly.

Craig, F. W. S. (1982) *Conservative and Labour Party Conference Decisions 1945–81*. Chichester: Parliamentary Research Services.

Crook, D., Power, S., and Whitty, G. (1999) *The Grammar School Question: a review of research on comprehensive and selective education*. London: Institute of Education.

Crosland, A. (1956) *The Future of Socialism*. London: Jonathan Cape.

Crowther Report (1959) *Report of the Central Advisory Council for Education (England): 15 to 18*, Volume 1. London: HMSO.

Croxford, L. (1999) *League Tables: who needs them?* Centre for Educational Sociology Briefing No. 14. Edinburgh: Centre for Educational Sociology.

Croxford, L. (2000) *Inequality in Attainment at Age 16: a 'home international' comparison*. Centre for Educational Sociology Briefing No. 19. Edinburgh: Centre for Educational Sociology.

Cunningham, P. (1988) *Curriculum Change in the Primary School since 1945: dissemination of the progressive ideal*. Lewes: Falmer Press.

Curriculum Council for Wales (1991) *Community Understanding: a framework for the development of a cross-curricular theme in Wales*. Cardiff: CCW.

Dale, R., and Robertson, S. (2002) The varying effects of regional organisations as subjects of globalisation of education. *Comparative Education Review*, 46, 1, 10–36.

Daniels, H. (1990) The modified curriculum: help with the same or something completely different. In P. Evans and V. Varma (eds), *Special Education: past, present and future*. Lewes: Falmer Press.

Daniels, H. V. (1947) *Activity in the Primary School*. Oxford: Blackwell.

Darling, J. (1999) Scottish primary education: philosophy and practice. In T. Bryce and W. Humes (eds), *Scottish Education*. Edinburgh: Edinburgh University Press.

David, M. (1980) *The State, the Family and Education*. London: Routledge & Kegan Paul.

David, M. (2002) Teenage parenthood is bad for parents and children: a feminist critique of family, education and social welfare policies and practices. In M. Bloch and T. Popkewitz, *Restructuring the Governing Patterns of the Child, Education and the Welfare State*. London and New York: Palgrave.

Davies, N. (1998) *Dark Heart*. London: Vintage Books.

Davies, N. (2000) Blunkett's magic tricks and the £19 billion for education that doesn't exist. *Guardian*, 7 March.

Dean, D. (1991) Education for moral improvement, domesticity and social cohesion: the Labour government 1945–51. *Oxford Review of Education*, 13, 3, 269–86.

Dean, D. W. (1992) The Churchill government and education policy 1951–55. *History of Education*, 21, 1, 15–36.

Deem, R. (1978) *Women and Schooling*. London: Routledge & Kegan Paul.

Dent, H. C. (1954) *Growth in English Education: 1946–52*. London: Routledge & Kegan Paul.

Department of Education and Science (1971) *The Education of Immigrants*. London: HMSO.

Department of Education and Science (1972) *Education: a framework for expansion*. London: HMSO.

Department of Education and Science (1977a) *Education in Schools: a consultative document*. Cmnd 6869. London: HMSO.

Department of Education and Science (1977b) *A New Partnership for our Schools: the Taylor Report*. London: HMSO.

Department of Education and Science (1978) *Primary Education in England: a survey by Her Majesty's Inspectorate of Schools*. London: DES.

Department of Education and Science (1987) Consultation Document on the National Curriculum. Mimeograph. July.

Department of Education and Science (1991) *The Parents' Charter*. London: DES.

Department of Trade and Industry (1998) *Our Competitive Future: building the knowledge economy*. London: The Stationery Office.

Desai, R. (1994) Second-hand dealers in ideas: think-tanks and Thatcherite hegemony. *New Left Review*, 203, 27–64.

Devlin, B. (1969) *The Price of my Soul*. Harmondsworth: Penguin.

DfEE (Department for Education and Employment) (1997) *Excellence in Schools*. London: The Stationery Office.

DfEE (1998a) *The Learning Age: a renaissance for a new Britain*. Green Paper. London: The Stationery Office.

DfEE (1998b) *Teachers: meeting the challenge of change*. London: The Stationery Office.

DfEE (1998c) £75 million boosts radical action zones to raise standards. Press release 318/98.

DfEE (2001) *Schools Building on Success: raising standards, promoting diversity, achieving results*. London: The Stationery Office.

DfEE/DCMS (1999) *All Our Futures: creativity, culture and education*. Report of the National Advisory Committee on Creative and Cultural Education. London: The Stationery Office.

DfES (Department for Education and Skills) (2001) *Schools Achieving Success*. London: The Stationery Office.

Dixon, J. (1961) Contribution, Popular Culture and Personal Responsibility. Verbatim account. Speech to National Union of Teachers Conference. London: NUT.

Dixon, J. (1975) *Growth through English Set in the Perspective of the Seventies*. Oxford: Oxford University Press.

Dixon, J. (1991) *A Schooling in English: critical episodes in the struggle to shape literacy and cultural studies*. Buckingham: Open University Press.

Dunkerley, D., and Thompson, A. (eds) (1999) *Wales Today*. Cardiff: University of Wales Press.

Dunn, S. (2000) Northern Ireland. In D. Phillips (ed.), *The Education Systems of the United Kingdom*. Oxford: Symposium Books.

Dunning Report (1977) *Assessment for All*. Edinburgh: HMSO.

Durkheim, E. (1961) *Moral Education* (1925). New York: Free Press.

Dyson A., and Slee, R. (2001) Special needs education from Warnock to Salamanca: the triumph of liberalism? In Phillips and Furlong (2001).

Echols, J., McPherson, A., and Willms, J. (1990) Parental choice in Scotland. *Journal of Education Policy*, 5, 3, 207–22.

Edgar, D. (1986) The free and the good. In R. Levitas (ed.), *The Ideology of the New Right*. Cambridge: Polity.

Elcock, H., and Keating, M. (1998) *Remarking the Union: devolution and British politics in the 1990s*. London: Frank Cass.

Eliot, T. S. (1949) *Notes Towards the Definition of Culture*. London: Faber & Faber.

Ellis, T., McWhirter, J., McColgan, D., and Haddow, B. (1976) *William Tyndale: the teachers' story*. London: Writers and Readers.

Ellison, N. (1996) Consensus here, consensus there . . . but not consensus everywhere: the Labour Party, equality and social policy in the 1950s. In Jones and Kandiah (1996).

Epstein, D., Elwood, J., Hey, V., and Maw, J. (eds) (1998) *Failing Boys? Issues in gender and achievement*. Buckingham: Open University Press.

Epstein, D., and Johnson, R. (1998) *Schooling Sexualities*. Buckingham: Open University Press.

European Commission (1996) *Accomplishing Europe through Education and Training: study group on education and training report*. The Reiffers Report. Brussels: European Commission.

European Commission (1999) *Constructing New Programmes in Education*. Brussels: European Commission.

Evans, P., and Varma, V. (eds) (1990) *Special Education: past, present and future*. Lewes: Falmer Press.

Fairley, J., and Paterson, L. (1995) Scottish education and the new managerialism. *Scottish Educational Review*, 27,1, 13–36.

Fallon, M. (1991) Speech to the National Association of Headteachers Primary Conference, York, November. Quoted in *Education*, 8 November.

Farren, S. (1992) A lost opportunity: education and community in Northern Ireland. *History of Education*, 21, 1, 71–82.

Fenwick, I. G. K. (1976) *The Comprehensive School 1944–1970*. London: Methuen.

Fergusson, R. (1994) Managerialism in education. In J. Clarke, A. Cochrane and E. McLaughlin (eds), *Managing Social Policy*. Sage: London.

Fitchett, C. (1975) Comprehensive or coexistence in Edinburgh? *This Magazine is about Education*, 1 (September), 13–14.

Fitz, J., Halpin, D., and Power, S. (1997) Between a rock and a hard place: diversity, institutional identity and grant-maintained schools. *Oxford Review of Education*, 23, 1, 17–30.

Floud, J. E., Halsey, A. H., and Martin, F. M. (1956) *Social Class and Educational Opportunity*. London: Heinemann.

Forrester, G. (2002) Performance-related pay for teachers: an examination of its underlying objectives and its application in practice. *Public Management Review*, 4, 1, 617–25.

Gallagher, A. M., and Smith, A. (2000) *The Effects of the Selective System of Secondary Education in Northern Ireland: main report*. Belfast: Department of Education.

Galton, M., Simon, B., and Croll, P. (1980) *Inside the Primary Classroom*. London: Routledge & Kegan Paul.

Gamble, A. (1974) *The Conservative Nation*. London: Routledge & Kegan Paul.

Gamble, A. (1981) *Britain in Decline*. London: Macmillan.

Gamble, A. (1988) *The Free Economy and the Strong State*. London: Macmillan.

Gewirtz, S. (1998) Post-welfarist schooling: a social justice audit. *Education and Social Justice*, 1, 1, 52–64.

Gewirtz, S. (2001) Cloning the Blairs: New Labour's programme for the resocialisation of working-class parents. *Journal of Education Policy*, 16, 4, 365–78.

Gewirtz, S., Ball, S., and Bowe, R. (1995) *Markets, Choice and Equity in Education*. Buckingham: Open University Press.

Giddens, A. (1998) *The Third Way: the renewal of social democracy*. Cambridge: Polity.

Giles, G. C. T. (1946) *The New School Tie*. London: Pilot Press.

Gillborn, D., and Youdell, M. (2000) *Rationing Education: policy, practice, reform and equity*. Buckingham: Open University Press.

Gilroy, B. (1976) *Black Teacher*. London: Cassell.

Gittins Report (1967) *Primary Education in Wales: a report of the Central Advisory Committee (Wales)*. London: HMSO.

Glennerster, H. (1995) *British Social Policy since 1945*. Oxford: Blackwell.

Glennerster, H. (1998) Education: reaping the harvest? In I I. Glennerster and J. Hills (eds), *The State of Welfare: the economics of social spending*. Oxford: Oxford University Press.

Glennerster, H. (2001a) Social policy. In A. Seldon (ed.), *The Blair Effect: the Blair Government 1997–2001*. London: Little Brown.

Glennerster, H. (2001b) Quoted in H. Stewart, C. Denny and W. Woodward, Labour cut education spending to 40-year low. *Guardian*, 4 September, 1.

Glennerster, H., Power, A., and Travers, T. (1991) 1991: a new era for social policy. *Journal of Social Policy*, 20, 389–414.

Gorard, S. (1998) Schooled to fail? Revisiting the Welsh school-effect. *Journal of Education Policy*, 13, 1, 115–24.

Grace, G. (1978) *Teachers, Ideology and Control*. London: Routledge & Kegan Paul.

Grace, G. (1987) Teachers and the state in Britain: a changing relation. In M. Lawn and G. Grace (eds), *Teachers: the culture and politics of work*. Lewes: Falmer Press.

Gratton, J., and Jackson, M. (1976) *William Tyndale: collapse of a school or a system?* London: Allen & Unwin.

Gray, J., McPherson, A. F., and Raafe, D. (1983) *Reconstructions of Secondary Education: theory, myth and practice since the war*. London: Routledge & Kegan Paul.

Green, A. (1990) *Education and State Formation*. London: Macmillan.

Green, P. (1985) Multi-ethnic teaching and the pupils' self-concepts. In Swann Report (1985), 46–53.

Greenslade, R. (1976) *Goodbye to the Working Class*. London: Marion Boyars.

Grosvenor, I. (1997) *Assimilating Identities: racism and educational policy in post-1945 Britain*. London: Lawrence & Wishart.

Hall, S. (1988) *The Hard Road to Renewal*. London: Verso.

Hall, S., and Whannel, P. (1964) *The Popular Arts*. London: Hutchinson.

Hall, S., Critcher, C., Jefferson, T., Clarke, J., and Roberts, B. (1978) *Policing the Crisis: mugging, the state and law and order*. London: Macmillan.

Halpin, D. (1997) Fragmenting into different types of school: diversifying into the past. In R. Pring and G. Walford (eds), *Affirming the Comprehensive Ideal*. Lewes: Falmer Press.

Halsey, A. H. (1965) Education and equality. *New Society*, 17 June, 13–15.

Halsey, A. H. (ed.) (1972) *Educational Priority: EPA problems and priorities*, Vol. 1. London: HMSO.

Halsey, A. H. (1988) Education. In *Trends in British Society since 1900 – a guide to the changing social structure of Britain*. London: Macmillan.

Halsey, A. H. (1996) *No Discouragement: an autobiography*. London: Macmillan.

Halsey, A. H., Heath, A., and Ridge, J. M. (1980) *Origins and Destinations: family, class and education in modern Britain*. Oxford: Oxford University Press.

Halsey, A. H., Lauder, H., Brown, P., and Wells, A. S. (1997) Introduction. *Education: Culture, Economy, Society*. Oxford: Oxford University Press.

Hansard (1946a) *The Parliamentary Debates*. HC (series 5), vol. 420, cols 2196–7, 22 March.

Hansard (1946b) *The Parliamentary Debates*. HC (series 5), vol. 420, col. 2232, 22 March.

Hansard (1946c) *The Parliamentary Debates*. HC (series 5), vol. 420, col. 2233, 22 March.

Hansard (1950) *The Parliamentary Debates*. HC (series 5), vol. 490, cols 1871–2, 17 July.

Hargreaves, D. (1967) *Social Relations in a Secondary School*. London: Routledge & Kegan Paul.

Harvie, C. (1993) *No Gods and Precious Few Heroes: Scotland since 1914*. Rev. edn. Edinburgh: Edinburgh University Press.

Harvie, C. (1999) *Travelling Scot: essays on the history, politics and future of the Scots*. Glendarnel, Argyll: Argyll Publishing.

Haslam, D. (1999) *Manchester, England: the story of the pop cult city*. London: Fourth Estate.

Hatcher, R. (1998) Social justice and the politics of school effectiveness and improvement. *Race Ethnicity and Education*, 1, 2, 267–89.

Hatcher, R. (2001a) *The Business of Education: how business agendas drive Labour's policies for schools*. London: Socialist Education Association.

Hatcher, R. (2001b) Getting down to business: schooling in the globalised economy. *Education and Social Justice*, 3, 2, 45–59.

Heath, A. (1989) Class in the classroom. In B. Cosin, M. Flude and M. Hales (eds), *School, Work and Equality*. London: Hodder & Stoughton.

Held, D., McGrew, A., Goldblatt, D., and Perraton, J. (1999) *Global Transformations: politics, economics and culture*. Cambridge: Polity.

Hewitt, R. (1989) The New Oracy: another critical glance. Paper to the conference of the British Association of Applied Linguistics.

Hickman, M. J. (1995) *Religion, Class and Identity: the state, the Catholic Church and the education of the Irish in Britain*. Aldershot: Avebury Press.

Hills, L. (1990) The Senga syndrome: reflections on 21 years in Scottish education. In F. Paterson and J. Fewell (eds), *Girls in their Prime*. Edinburgh: Academic Press.

Himmelweit, H. T. (1954) *Social Status and Secondary Education since the 1944 Act: some data for London.* In D. V. Glass (ed.), *Social Mobility in Britain.* London: Routledge & Kegan Paul.

Hirst, P., and Thompson, G. (1996) *Globalization in Question: the international economy and the possibilities of governance.* Cambridge: Polity.

Hobsbawm, E. (1994) *Age of Extremes: the short twentieth century 1914–1991.* London: Michael Joseph.

Hoggart, R. (1958) *The Uses of Literacy.* Harmondsworth: Penguin.

Holland, P. et al (1976) *Lunatic Ideas.* London: Corner House.

Holly, D. (ed.) (1974) *Education or Domination? A critical look at educational problems today.* London: Arrow Books.

Humes, W. (1995) the influence of Michael Forsyth in Scottish education. *Scottish Affairs,* 11 (Spring), 112–30.

Hutton, W. (1995) *The State We're In.* London: Jonathan Cape.

Inner London Education Authority (1983a) *Improving Secondary Schools.* (The Hargreaves Report.) London: ILEA.

Inner London Education Authority (1983b) *Race, Class and Gender.* London: ILEA.

Jackson, B., and Marsden, D. (1962) *Education and the Working Class.* London: Routledge & Kegan Paul.

James, C. (1968) *Young Lives at Stake.* London: Collins.

Jenkins, R. (1959) *The Labour Case.* Harmondsworth: Penguin.

Jephcott, A. P. (1942) *Girls Growing Up.* London: Faber & Faber.

Johnson, R. (1989) Thatcherism and English education: breaking the mould or confirming the pattern? *History of Education,* 18, 2, 91–121.

Johnson, R. (1991) A new road to serfdom? A critical history of the Education Reform Act. In Cultural Studies, Birmingham, *Education Limited: schooling and training and the new right since 1979.* London: Hutchinson.

Johnson, R. W. (1997) Enoch Powell by Robert Shepherd. *London Review of Books,* 19, 2, 8–9.

Johnson, R., and Epstein, D. (2000) Sectional interests: sexuality, social justice and moral traditionalism. *Education and Social Justice,* 2, 2, 27–37.

Jones, B., and Lewis, I. (1995) A Curriculum Cymreig. *Welsh Journal of Education,* 4, 2, 22–35.

Jones, G. E. (1990) *Which Nation's Schools? Direction and devolution in Welsh education in the twentieth century.* Cardiff: University of Wales Press.

Jones, G. E. (1992) Education in Wales. a different 'Great Debate'. In M. Williams, R. Daugherty and F. Banks (eds), *Continuing the Education Debate.* London: Cassell.

Jones, G. E. (1997) *The Education of a Nation.* Cardiff: University of Wales Press.

Jones, H. (1996) A bloodless counter-revolution: the Conservative Party and the defence of inequality 1945–1951. In Jones and Kandiah (1996).

Jones, H., and Kandiah, M. (1996) *The Myth of Consensus: new views on British history 1945–1964.* London: Macmillan.

Jones, K. (1983) *Beyond Progressive Education*. London: Macmillan.

Jones, K. (1989) *Right Turn: the conservative revolution in education*. London: Hutchinson Radius.

Jones, K. (1992) The Cox Report: working for hegemony. In K. Jones (ed.), *English and the National Curriculum: Cox's revolution*. London: Kogan Page.

Jones, K. (1994a) Cultural problems of Conservatism. *Changing English*, 1, 2, 1–14.

Jones, K. (1994b) A new kind of cultural politics: the teachers' boycott of testing. *Changing English*, 2, 1, 88–114.

Jones, K. (1996) Cultural politics and education in the 1990s. In R. Hatcher and K. Jones (eds), *Education after the Conservatives: the response to the new agenda of reform*. Stoke-on-Trent: Trentham Books.

Jones, K., and Bird, K. (2000) 'Partnership' as strategy: public–private relation in education action zones. *British Educational Research Journal*, 26, 4, 491–506.

Jones, R., Morris, D., Roberts-Young, D., Popkins, G. and Young, E. (2002) Keeping up appearances: Welsh language provision in higher education. *Planet: The Welsh Internationalist*, 154, 7–15.

Kearney, H. (1989) *The British Isles: a history of four nations*. Cambridge: Cambridge University Press.

Kelly, A. (1981) *The Missing Half: girls and science education*. Manchester: Manchester University Press

Kenway, J. (ed.) (1994) *Economizing Education: Post-Fordist directions*. Geelong: Deakin University Press.

Kerckhoff, A., Fogelman, K., Crook, D., and Reeder, D. (1996) *Going Comprehensive in England and Wales: a study of uneven change*. London: Woburn Press.

Knight, C. (1990) *The Making of Tory Education Policy in Post-war Britain 1950–1986*. Lewes: Falmer Press.

Kovacs, K. (1998) Combating failure at school: an international perspective. In L. Stoll and K. Myers (eds) (1998) *No Quick Fixes: perspectives on schools in difficulty*. London: Falmer Press.

Labour Party (1964) *Let's Go With Labour for the New Britain: the Labour Party's manifesto for the 1964 general election*. London: Labour Party.

Labour Party (1974) *Britain Will Win With Labour: Labour Party manifesto, October 1974*. London: Labour Party.

Labour Party (1997) *New Labour: because Britain deserves better*. London: Labour Party.

Lacey, C. (1970) *Hightown Grammar: the school as a social system*. Manchester: Manchester University Press.

Laïdi, Z. (1998) *A World Without Meaning: the crisis of meaning in international relations*. London: Routledge.

LATE (London Association for the Teaching of English) (n.d. [1982]) *Race, Society and School: Education in a Multicultural Society*. London: LATE.

Law, R. (1950) *Return from Utopia*. London: Faber & Faber.

Lawn, M. (1996) *Modern Times? Work, professionalism and citizenship in teaching*. Lewes: Falmer Press.

Lawn, M. (2001) Borderless education: imagining a European education space in a time of brands and networks. *Discourse: studies in the cultural politics of education* 22, 2, 173–184.

Lawn, M. (2002) The 'usefulness' of learning: the struggle over governance, meaning and the European Education Space. Unpublished Paper.

Learner, S. (2001) Call for end to 11+ in Ulster. *Times Educational Supplement*, 26 October.

Levacic, R. (1999) New Labour education policy in the UK: the Third Way. IARTV Seminar Series No. 82. Jolimont, Victoria.

Levitas, R. (1998) *The 'Inclusive' Society: social exclusion and New Labour*. Houndmills: Macmillan.

Leys, C., and Panitch, L. (1997) *The End of Parliamentary Socialism: from New Left to New Labour*. London: Verso.

Little, A., and Westergaard, J. (1964) The trend of social class differentials in educational opportunity in England and Wales. *British Journal of Sociology*, 15, 301–16.

Lloyd, J. M. (1983) Tom Johnston's parliament on education: the birth of the Sixth Advisory Council on Education in Scotland 1942–3. *Scottish Educational Review*, 16, 2, 104–15.

Lovering, J. (1996) New myths of the Welsh economy. *Planet: the Welsh internationalist*, 116.

Lovering, J. (2000) Hoping for a honeypot: the bid for Objective One funding. *Planet: the Welsh internationalist*, 139, 6–16.

Lowe, Rodney (1993) *The Welfare State in Britain since 1945*. London: Macmillan.

Lowe, Roy (1997) *Schooling and Social Change 1964–1990*. London: Routledge.

Mac an Ghaill, M. (1988) *Young, Gifted and Black*. Buckingham: Open University Press.

Maclure, S. (ed.) (1979) *Educational Documents: England and Wales 1816 to the present day*. 4th edn. London: Methuen.

McCrone, D. (1996) We're a' Jock Tamson's bairns: social class in twentieth-century Scotland. In T. M. Devine and R. J. Finlay (eds), *Scotland in the Twentieth Century*. Edinburgh: Edinburgh University Press.

McCulloch, G. (1998) *Failing the Ordinary Child: the theory and practice of working-class secondary education*. Buckingham: Open University Press.

McKenzie, R. F. (1970) *State School*. Harmondsworth: Penguin.

McKeown, P. (2001) Rethinking choice: the reorganisation of secondary education in Northern Ireland. Unpublished paper, for Keele University Conference, Travelling Policy / Local Spaces, June.

McKeown, P., and Byrne, G. (1999) In search of equity? Lessons from secondary schooling in Northern Ireland. *Education and Social Justice*, 2, 1, 2–12.

McKibbin, R. (1998) *Classes and Cultures: England 1918–1951*. Oxford: Oxford University Press.

MacKinnon, D., Statham, J., and Hales, M. (1996) *Education in the UK: facts and figures*. Rev. edn. London: Hodder & Stoughton.

McLean, I. (2001) The national question. In Seldon (2001).

McPherson, A., and Raab, C. (1988) *Governing Education: a sociology of education since 1945*. Edinburgh: Edinburgh University Press.

McPherson, A., and Willms, J. (1987) *Equalisation and Improvement: the effect of comprehensive reorganisation in Scotland*. Edinburgh: Centre for Educational Sociology, University of Edinburgh.

McRobbie, A. (1994) Folk devils fight back. *New Left Review*, 203, 107–16.

Major, J. (1993) *Conservatism in the 1990s: our common purpose*. Speech to Carlton Club. London: Conservative Central Office, London.

Marshall, G., Rose, D., Newby, H., and Vogler, C. (1988) *Social Class in Modern Britain*. London: Routledge.

Marshall, T. H. (1963) Citizenship and social class. In *Sociology at the Crossroads and Other Essays*. London: Heinemann.

Maude, A., and Lewis, R. (1952) *Professional People*. London: Phoenix House.

Mays, J. B. (1962) *Education and the Urban Child*. Liverpool: Liverpool University Press.

Ministry of Education (1947) *The New Secondary Education*. London: HMSO.

Ministry of Education (1958) *Britain's Future and Technical Education*. London: HMSO.

Moon, B. (1991) *A Guide to the National Curriculum*. Oxford: Oxford University Press.

Morgan, K., and Mungham, G. (2000) *Redesigning Democracy: the making of the Welsh Assembly*. Bridgend: Seren.

Morgan, K. O. (1981) *Rebirth of a Nation: a history of modern Wales*. Oxford: Oxford University Press.

Morgan, R. (2000) World ambition in the e-commerce age. *The Western Mail* (*Engineering Wales* Supplement), 14 April, 1.

Morris, B. (1967) The school: how do we see it functioning (past, present and future)? In Schools Council, *The New Curriculum*. London: HMSO.

Morris, M. (1953) *Your Children's Future*. London: Lawrence & Wishart.

Mortimore, J., and Blackstone, T. (1982) *Disadvantage and Education*. London: Heinemann.

Mortimore, P., and Whitty, G. (1997) *Can School Improvement Overcome the Effects of Disadvantage?*. London: University of London Institute of Education.

Mulhern, F. (1998) *The Present Lasts a Long Time*. Cork: Cork University Press.

Munn, P. (1997) Devolved management of schools. In M. Clark and P. Munn (eds), *Education in Scotland: policy and practice from pre-school to secondary*. London: Routledge.

Munn, P. (2001) Schooling and Social inclusion in Scotland. Unpublished paper for Keele University Conference, Travelling Policy/Local Spaces, June.

Munn Report (1977) *The Structure of the Curriculum*. Edinburgh: HMSO.

Murdock, G. (1974) The politics of culture. In D. Holly (ed.), *Education or Domination? A critical look at educational problems today*. London: Arrow Books.

Murray, D. (1985) *Worlds Apart: segregated schools in Northern Ireland*. Belfast: Appletree Press.

Nairn, T. (1977) *The Break-up of Britain*. London: New Left Books.

National Assembly for Wales (2001) *The Learning Country* www.wales. gov.uk

New London Group (1996) A pedagogy of multi-literacies: designing social futures. *Harvard Educational Review*, 66, 1, 60–92.

Newbolt Report (1921) *The Teaching of English in England*. London: HMSO.

Newsom Report (1963) *Half our Future*. London: HMSO.

Norman, E. R. (1977) The threat to religion. In C. B. Cox and R. Boyson, *Black Paper 1977*. London: Temple Smith.

Norwood Report (1943) *Report of the Committee of the Secondary Schools Examination Council on Curriculum and Examinations in Secondary Schools*. London: HMSO.

O'Connor, F. (1993) *In Search of a State: Catholics in Northern Ireland*. Belfast: Blackstaff Press.

O'Dowd, L. (1995) Development or dependency? State, economy and society in Northern Ireland. In Clancy et al. (1995).

O'Leary, B. (1998) The nature of the British–Irish agreement. In *New Left Review*, 233, 66–96.

Ofsted (Office for Standards in Education) (1999) *Raising the Attainment of Minority Ethnic Pupils*. London: Ofsted.

Ofsted (2001) *Education Action Zones: commentary on the first six zone inspections*. London: Ofsted.

Oppenheim, C., and Lister, R. (1997) The growth of poverty and inequality. In Walker and Walker (1997).

Organization for Economic Co-operation and Development (1974) *Education Development Strategy in England and Wales*. Paris: OECD.

Ouston, J. (1999) Keynote Address *BEMAS Annual Conference*, September.

Owen, G. (2001) 'Industry'. In Seldon (2001).

Ozga, J. (1998) The teaching profession: two scenarios. In P. Hunter (ed.), *Developing education: fifteen years on*. London: Paul Chapman.

Ozga, J. (1999) Two nations? Education and social inclusion–exclusion in Scotland and England. *Education and Social Justice*, 1, 3, 44–51.

Ozga, J., and Gewirtz, S. (1994) Sex, lies and audiotape: interviewing the education policy elite. In D. Halpin and B. Troyna (eds), *Researching Education Policy: ethical and methodological issues*. Lewes: Falmer Press.

Palmer, F. (1986) *Anti-Racism: an assault on education and value*. London: Sherwood Press.

Papadopoulos, G. (1994) *Education 1960–1990: the OECD perspective*. Paris: OECD.

Paterson, L. (1996) Liberation or control? What are the Scottish traditions of the twentieth century? In T. Devine (ed.), *Scotland in the Twentieth Century*. Edinburgh: Edinburgh University Press.

Paterson, L. (1998) Scottish Home Rule: radical break or pragmatic adjustment? In Elcock and Keating (1998).

Patten, J. (1993) Speech to Conservative Party Conference, 7 October 1992. Cited in P. Fraser, Chaucer with chips: right-wing discourse about popular culture. *The English and Media Magazine*, 28 (Summer), 16–19.

Phillips, R., and Daugherty, R. (2001) Educational devolution and nation building in Wales: a different 'Great Debate'. In Phillips and Furlong, (2001).

Phillips, R., and Furlong, J. (eds) (2001) *Education, Reform and the State: twenty-five years of policy and practice*. London: Routledge.

Pickard, W. (2000) The history of Scottish education, 1980 to the present day. In W. Humes and T. Bryce, *Scottish Education*. Edinburgh: Edinburgh University Press.

Pierson, C. (1998) *Beyond the Welfare State: the new political economy of welfare*. Cambridge: Polity.

Pietrasik, R. (1987) The teachers' action 1984–6. In M. Lawn and G. Grace (eds), *Teachers: the culture and politics of work*. Lewes: Falmer Press.

Plato (1955) *The Republic* (*c.* 380 B C), ed. D. Lee. Harmondsworth: Penguin.

Plowden Report (1967) *Children and their Primary Schools*, Volume 1. London: HMSO.

Plummer, G. (2000) *Failing Working-Class Girls*. Stoke-on-Trent: Trentham Books.

Public Schools Commission (1967) *Second Report*, Vol. I, ii: *Scotland* London: HMSO.

Pyke, N. (1998) Ofsted figures support failing schools poverty link. *Times Educational Supplement*, 14 August.

Quinton, A. (1978) *The Politics of Imperfection: the religious and secular traditions of conservative thought in England from Hooker to Oakeshott*. London: Faber & Faber.

Raban, J. (1989) *God, Man and Mrs Thatcher*. London: Chatto & Windus.

Rae, J. (1981) *The Public School Revolution: Britain's independent schools 1964–1979*. London: Faber & Faber.

Raffe, D., Brannen, K., Croxford, L., and Martin, C. (1999) Comparing England, Scotland, Wales and Northern Ireland: the case for 'home internationals' in comparative research. *Comparative Education*, 35, 1, 9–25.

Raffe, D., Howieson, C., and Tinklin, T. (2001) *What Happened to the Consensus on Higher Still?* CES Briefing No. 21. Edinburgh: Centre for Educational Sociology.

Rampton Report (1981) *West Indian Children in our Schools*. London: HMSO.

Reay, D. (1998) Micro-politics in the 1990s: staff relationships in secondary schooling. *Journal of Education Policy*, 13, 2, 179–96.

Reed, L. R. (1995) Reconceptualizing equal opportunities in the 1990s: a study of radical teacher culture in transition. In M. Griffiths and B. Troyna (eds), *Anti-Racism, Culture and Social Justice in Education*. Stoke-on-Trent: Trentham Books.

Rees, G., and Delamont, S. (1999) Education in Wales. In D. Dunkerley and A. Thompson, *Wales Today*. Cardiff: University of Wales Press.

Rees, G., and Rees, T. (1980) Educational inequality in Wales: some problems and paradoxes. In G. Rees and T. Rees (eds), *Poverty and Social Inequality in Wales*. London: Croom Helm.

Regan, B. (2001) *Not for Sale: the case against privatisation in education*. London: Socialist Teachers Alliance.

Reid, I. (1989) *Social Class Differences in Education*. Glasgow: Fontana.

Reid, I. (1998) *Class in Britain*. Cambridge: Polity.

Reynolds, D. (1990) The great Welsh education debate 1980–1990. *History of Education*, 19, 3, 251–60.

Reynolds, D. (1997) *Times Educational Supplement*, 21 March.

Reynolds, D., and Sullivan M., with Murgatroyd, S. (1987) *The Comprehensive Experiment: a study of the selective and non-selective systems of school organisation*. Lewes: Falmer Press.

Richards, C. (1992) Teaching popular culture. In K. Jones (ed.), *English and the National Curriculum: Cox's revolution?* London: Kogan Page.

Riddell, S., Adler, M., Farmakopoulou, N., and Mordaunt, E. (2000) Special needs and competing policy frameworks in England and Scotland. *Journal of Education Policy*, 15, 6, 621–35.

Rikowski, G. (2001) Six points on education for human capital, employers' needs and business in New Labour's Green Paper. Paper prepared for a meeting on 'Promoting Comprehensive Education in the 21st Century', London.

Robbins Report (1963) *Higher Education: report of the Committee on Higher Education*. Cmnd 2165. London: HMSO.

Robertson, S., and Lauder, H. (2001) Restructuring the education / social class relation: a class choice? In Phillips and Furlong (2001).

Rolston, B. (1998) What's wrong with multi-culturalism? Liberalism and the Irish conflict. In D. Miller (ed.), *Rethinking Northern Ireland: culture, ideology and colonialism*. London: Longman.

Rose, N. (1990) *Governing the Soul: the shaping of the private self*. Cambridge: Cambridge University Press.

Ross, D. (1986) *An Unlikely Anger: Scottish teachers in action*. Edinburgh: Mainstream Publishing.

Ross, H. (1999) The Scottish Consultative Council on the Curriculum. In Bryce and Humes (1999).

Rowbotham, S. (2000) *Promise of a Dream*. London: Penguin.

Rowntree Foundation (1995) *Inquiry into Income and Wealth*. York: Joseph Rowntree Foundation.

Rubinstein, D., and Simon, B. (1973) *The Evolution of the Comprehensive School 1926–1972*. London: Routledge & Kegan Paul.

Sammons, P., Hillman, J., and Mortimore, P. (1995) *Key Characteristics of Effective Schools: a review of school effectiveness research*. London: Ofsted.

Samuel, R. (1989) Then and now: a revaluation of the New Left. In R. Archer, D. Bubeck, H. Glock, L. Jacobs, S. Moglen, A. Stenhouse and D. Weinstock (eds), *Out of Apathy: voices of the New Left 30 years on*. London: Verso.

Sanderson, M. (1999) *Education and Economic Decline in Britain, 1870 to the 1990s*. Cambridge: Cambridge University Press.

Saunders, H., and Marsh, J. (1980) Sex discrimination in schools. *Schooling and Culture*, 7 (Spring), 4–10.

Schools Council (1965) *English: a programme for research and development in English teaching*. London: HMSO.

Schwarz, B. (1991) The tide of history: the reconstruction of Conservatism 1945–51. In N. Tiratsoo (ed.), *The Attlee Years*. London: Pinter Publishers.

Scottish Education Department (1947) *Secondary Education: a report of the Advisory Committee on Education in Scotland*. Cmnd 7005. Edinburgh: HMSO.

Scottish Education Department (1965) *Primary Education in Scotland*. Edinburgh: HMSO.

Scottish Executive (1999) *Improving our Schools: consultation on the improvement in Scottish Education bill*. www.scotland.gov.uk / education. Edinburgh: Scottish Executive.

Scottish Executive (2001) *National Priorities in School Education*. www.scotland.gov.uk / education.

Scottish Office Education Department (1991) *Curriculum and Assessment in Scotland – National Guidelines: English Language 5–14*. Edinburgh: SOED.

Scottish Office Education and Industry Department (1998) *Setting Targets – Raising Standards in Schools*. Edinburgh: The Stationery Office.

Scruton, R. (1984) *The Meaning of Conservatism*, 2nd edn. London: Macmillan.

Searle, C. (1987) Your daily dose: racism and the *Sun*. *Race and Class*, 29, 1, 55–71.

Secretary of State for Education and Science (1976) *School Education in England: problems and initiatives*. London: DES.

Seifert, R. (1987) *Teacher Militancy: a history of teacher strikes 1896–1987*. Lewes: Falmer Press.

Seldon, A. (ed.) (2001) *The Blair Effect: the Blair government 1997–2001*. London: Little Brown.

Sexton, S. (1977) Evolution by choice. In C. B. Cox and R. Boyson, *Black Paper 1977*. London: Temple Smith.

Shepherd, R. (1996) *Enoch Powell: a biography*. London: Hutchinson.

Shuttleworth, I. (1995) The relationship between social deprivation, as measured by free schools eligibility, and educational attainment at GCSE in Northern Ireland: a preliminary investigation. *British Education Research Journal*, 21, 4, 487–504.

Silver, H. (ed.) (1973) *Equal Opportunity in Education*. London: Methuen.

Simon, B. (1953) *Intelligence Testing and the Comprehensive School*. London: Lawrence & Wishart.

Simon, B. (1974) *Education and the Labour Movement 1870–1920*. London: Lawrence & Wishart.

Simon, B. (1988) *Bending the Rules, the Baker 'Reform' of Education*. London: Lawrence & Wishart.

Simon, B. (1991) *Education and the Social Order: 1940–1990*. London: Lawrence & Wishart.

Simon, B. (1992) The politics of comprehensive reorganisation. *History of Education*, 21, 1, 355–62.

Sinclair, J., Ironside, M. and Seifert, R. (1996) Classroom struggle? Market-oriented education reforms and their impact on the teacher labour process. *Work, Employment and Society*, 10, 4, 641–62.

Slee, R., and Weiner, G. (1998) Introduction: school effectiveness for whom? In R. Slee and G. Weiner with S. Tomlinson (eds), *School Effectiveness for Whom? Challenges to the School Effectiveness and School Improvement Movements*. London: Falmer Press.

Smith, G., Smith, T., and Wright, G. (1997) Poverty and schooling: choice, diversity of division. In A. Walker and C. Walker (eds), *Britain Divided: the growth of social exclusion in the 1980s and 1990s*. London: Child Poverty Action Group.

Smithers, A. (2001) Education policy. In Seldon (2001).

Smithers, R. (1999) Unions angered by Blair attack on teachers. *Guardian*, 22 October, 7.

Snicker, J. (1998) Strategies of autonomist agents in Wales. In Elcock and Keating (1998).

Spens Report (1938) *Report of the Consultative Committee of the Board of Education with Special Reference to Grammar Schools and Technical High Schools*. London: HMSO.

Stenhouse, L. (1967) *Culture and Education*. London: Thomas Nelson.

Stoll, L., and Fink, D. (1996) *Changing Our Schools: linking school effectiveness and school improvement*. Buckingham: Open University Press.

Swann Report (1985) *Education for All: the report of the committee of inquiry into the education of children from ethnic minority groups*. Cmnd 9453. London: HMSO.

Tawney, R. H. (1973a) Secondary education for all (1922). In H. Silver (ed.), *Equal Opportunity in Education*. London: Methuen.

Tawney, R. H. (1973b) Equality (1931). In H. Silver (ed.), *Equal Opportunity in Education* London: Methuen.

Taylor, S., Rizvi, F., Lingard, B., and Arnold, M. (1997) *Educational Policy and the Politics of Change*. London: Routledge.

Taylor, W. (1963) *The Secondary Modern School*. London: Faber.

Thatcher, M. (1993) *The Downing Street Years*. London: HarperCollins.

Thom, D. (1986) The 1944 Education Act: the art of the possible? In H. Smith (ed.), *War and Social Change: British Society in the Second World War*. Manchester: Manchester University Press.

Thompson, N. (1996) *Political Economy and the Labour Party*. London: UCL Press.

Thornton, S. (2001) Northern Ireland scraps divisive league tables. *Times Educational Supplement*, 12 January.

Thrupp, M. (2000) Compensating for class: are school improvement researchers being realistic? *Education and Social Justice*, 2, 2, 2–11.

Tooley, J. (1999) *Reclaiming Education*. London: Cassell.

Toynbee, P., and Walker, D. (2001) *Did Things Get Better? An audit of Labour's successes and failures*. London: Penguin.

Tracey, M., and Morrison, D. (1979) *Whitehouse*. London: Macmillan.

Travis, A. (2001a) Blunkett in race row over culture tests. *Guardian*, 10 December.

Travis, A. (2001b) Race riot reports urge immigrant loyalty. *Guardian*, 12 December.

Troyna, B. (1987) *Racial Inequality and Education*. London: Tavistock.

Troyna, B. (1992) Can you see the join? An historical analysis of multicultural and anti-racist policies. In D. Gill, B. Mayor and M. Blair (eds), *Racism and Education: Strategies and Structures*. London: Sage.

Troyna, B. (1993) *Racism and Education: research perspectives*. Buckingham: Open University Press.

Troyna, B. (1993) Private Finance Initiative: the commodification and privatization of education. *Education and Social Justice*, 1, 1, 213.

Turner, E., Riddell, S., and Brown, S. (1995) *Gender Equality in Scottish Schools: the impact of recent educational reform*. Manchester: Equal Opportunities Commission.

United Nations (1991) *Convention on the Rights of the Child 1989*. New York: United Nations.

Vernon, P. E. (1957) *Secondary School Selection*. London: Methuen.

Wagg, S. (1996) 'Don't try to understand them': politics, childhood and the new education market. In J. Pilcher and S. Wagg (eds), *Thatcher's Children: politics, childhood and society in the 1980s and 1990s*. London: Falmer Press.

Walker, A., and Walker, C. (eds) (1997) *Britain Divided: the growth of social exclusion in the 1980s and 1990s*. London: Child Poverty Action Group.

Walkerdine, V. (1984) Developmental psychology and the child-centred pedagogy: the insertion of Piaget in early education. In J. Henriques, W. Holloway, C. Urwin, C. Venn and V. Walkerdine, *Changing the Subject: psychology, social regulation and subjectivity*. London: Methuen.

Warnock Report (1978) *Report of the Committee of Enquiry into the Education of Handicapped Children and Young People*. Cmnd 7212. London: HMSO.

Waugh, E. (1942) *Put Out More Flags*. London: Chapman & Hall.

Wedell, K. (1990) Children with special educational needs: past, present and future. In Evans and Varma (1990).

Weiner, G. (1997) Educational reform, gender and class in Britain: epistemological and methodological questions. Paper for the European Conference on Educational Research, Frankfurt.

White Paper (1943) *Educational Reconstruction*. Cmnd 6458. London: HMSO.

White Paper (1956) *Technical Education*. Cmnd 9703. London: HMSO.

White Paper (1979) *The Government's Expenditure Plans 1980–81*. Cmnd 7746. London: HMSO.

Whitfield, D. (1999) Private Finance Initiative: the commodification and privatization of education. *Education and Social Justice*, 1, 1, 2–13.

Whitty, G. (1985) *Sociology and School Knowledge: curriculum theory, research and politics*. London: Methuen.

Whitty, G. (2001a) Education, social class and exclusion. In *Journal of Education Policy*, 16, 4, 287–95.

Whitty, G. (2001b) Has comprehensive education a future under New labour? In C. Chitty and B. Simon (eds), *Promoting Comprehensive Education in the 21st Century*. Stoke-on-Trent: Trentham Books.

Whitty, G., Edwards, T., and Gewirtz, S. (1993) *Specialisation and Choice in Urban Education: the City Technology College experiment*. London: Routledge.

Whitty, G., Power, S., and Halpin, D. (1998) *Devolution and Choice in Education: the school, the state and the market*. Buckingham: Open University Press.

Wiener, M. (1981) *English Culture and the Decline of the Industrial Spirit 1850–1980*. Cambridge: Cambridge University Press.

Wilby, P. (1997) Tribalism in British education. *New Left Review*, 222, 139–46.

Wilkinson, E. (1947) Foreword. *The New Secondary Education*. London: HMSO.

Willetts, D. (1992) *Modern Conservatism*. Harmondsworth: Penguin.

Williams, G. A. (1985) *When Was Wales?* Harmondsworth: Penguin.

Williams, R. (1961) *The Long Revolution*. London: Chatto & Windus.

Williams, R. (ed.) (1968) *May Day Manifesto*. 2nd edn. Harmondsworth: Penguin.

Willis, P. (1977) *Learning to Labour: how working-class kids get working-class jobs*. Farnborough: Saxon House.

Wilson, H. (1964) *The New Britain: Labour's plan – selected speeches*. Harmondsworth: Penguin.

Wolpe, A. -M. (1977) *Some Sexist Processes in Education*. London: Women's Research and Resources Centre.

Wood, R. (2001) Political interference: campaigning for a democratic and accountable education service in Leeds. *Education and Social Justice*, 3, 2, 8–11.

Woodward, W. (2001) Great Wales. *Guardian*, 2 October.

Worpole, K. (1974) The school and the community. In Holly (1974).

Wright, N. (1989) *Free School: the White Lion experience.* Leicester: Libertarian Education.

Young, M. (1958) *The Rise of the Meritocracy 1870–2033: an essay on education and equality.* London: Thames & Hudson.

Young, M. F. D (ed.) (1971) *Knowledge and Control.* London: Macmillan.

Young, M. F. D. (1999) Some reflections on the concepts of social exclusion and social inclusion: beyond the third way. In A. Hayton (ed.), *Tackling Disaffection and Social Exclusion.* London: Kogan Page.

Index